W9-CFF-969

Exploring New Ethics
for Survival

Also by Garrett Hardin

Nature and Man's Fate
Biology: Its Principles and Implications
Birth Control

Edited by Garrett Hardin

Population, Evolution, and Birth Control
Science, Conflict, and Society
39 Steps to Biology

GARRETT HARDIN

Exploring New Ethics
for Survival

The Voyage of the Spaceship *Beagle*

NEW YORK | The Viking Press

Copyright © 1968, 1972 by Garrett Hardin

All rights reserved

First published in 1972 by The Viking Press, Inc.
625 Madison Avenue, New York, N.Y. 10022

Published simultaneously in Canada by
The Macmillan Company of Canada Limited

SBN 670–30268–6

Library of Congress catalog card number: 78–186737

Printed in U.S.A.

ACKNOWLEDGMENTS

W. H. Freeman and Company: From *Population, Resources, Environment* by
Paul Ehrlich.

Harper & Row, Publishers: From *The Meaning of the Twentieth Century* by
Kenneth Boulding.

William L. Langer: From "Europe's Initial Population Explosion" by William
L. Langer. Originally appeared in *American Historical Review* 69: 1–17, 1963.

The Trustees of the late Sir David Low's Estate: For the "Colonel Blimp" car-
toon by Sir David Low.

The University of Chicago Press: For the figure from *Ecological Animal Geography* by Richard Hesse, translated by W. C. Allee and Karl P. Schmidt.

To Ray Cowles

Preface

As we withdraw our attention from the moon and focus it once more on problems in our back yard we inevitably discover that the nearer problems are the more difficult. The real difficulties, as Shakespeare's Cassius said, lie not in the stars but in ourselves. Our minds are trapped by unexamined assumptions and subconscious resistances. There are nettles we fear to grasp. We hope for easy solutions.

For too long have we supposed that technology would solve the "population problem." It won't. I first became fully aware of this hard truth when I wrote my essay "The Tragedy of the Commons," which can be found in the Appendix of this book. Never have I found anything so difficult to work into shape. I wrote at least seven significantly different versions before resting content with this one, which was published in 1968. It was obvious that the internal resistance to what I found myself saying was terrific. As a scientist I wanted to find a scientific solution; but reason inexorably led me to conclude that the population problem could not possibly be solved without repudiating certain ethical beliefs and altering some of the political and economic arrangements of contemporary society. As I became used to living with the unaccustomed conclusions, a restructuring of my psyche took place and I found I could accept them. I appreciated as never before the wisdom of Hegel's aphorism, "Freedom is the recognition of necessity." In the end I felt free again, but in a different way.

My essay has had a curious reception: much notice, but only

guarded comment. It has, to date, been reprinted in some two dozen anthologies in the fields of biology, ecology, political science, sociology, law, and economics. I am sure people are aware of it; but few grapple directly with the issues raised therein. I sometimes feel as if I were living in the eye of a hurricane, waiting . . .

Following the publication of this essay I was invited to speak in many places. The encounters have been educational experiences for me. They have made me realize that my original statement is too compact for the general reader. It presumes, for instance, a view of "responsibility" that is far from being the common one. As I set about securing the logical bases of my argument I was led, like Tristram Shandy, to go farther and farther back both in time and in logic to make the structure of the argument clear. This book is the result.

In a world confronted by troubles that seem so different from those known in the past, two duties (as I see it) fall on the serious writer. First, he should try to relate the new problems to those successfully solved in the past. To demonstrate such genetic relationships is to diminish the probability of panic. Secondly, the writer should arm his reader with the conviction that solutions can be found, even to the most recalcitrant problems. Both duties I try to fulfill here, though what I say only partially fills the need because the complete specification of the answers will require the work of many men.

There are, to quote the cliché, "no easy answers"—by which is meant, we cannot solve our deepest problems without making changes in our way of life that genuinely deserve the name "revolutionary." Whatever may be said against our civilization (and it is not a little), one of its glories is that an ever larger proportion of the populace is willing, even anxious, to find the truth even when it is unpleasant upon the first sighting. People recognize that longstanding social problems call for surprising, and even shocking, solutions. If the answers were easy, and easily acceptable, we would have found them long ago.

We have been conscious of the population problem for almost two hundred years now, and during all that time we have, of course, found no easy answers, though a great deal of effort has been devoted to this quest. The "shape" of the problem has changed as knowledge and technology have increased. With the flowering of concern for environmental quality and the growth of theory in ecology the time is now ripe, I think, for a concerted attack on the population-environment-quality complex. I think it is almost time to grasp the nettle of population control, which we sometime must, if we are to survive with dignity. I hope that my efforts will help evoke the courage, and wisdom, needed for this revolutionary step.

GARRETT HARDIN

Santa Barbara
November 1971

Contents

Preface   ix

PART ONE

1. From the Spaceship *Beagle:* Embarkation   3
2. Cheating on a Spaceship   16
3. Guk—Cycle or Sequester?   22
4. When Dilution Fails   29
5. What the Hedgehog Knows   38
6. Evil: State or Process?   49
7. Guilty Until Proven Innocent   57
8. Word Magic   66
9. Sweet-Singing Economists   71
10. How Did We Get Here? Where Are We Going?   77

PART TWO

11. On Board the *Beagle:* The Dawn of Responsibility   91
12. A Piece of the Action   101
13. The Third Political System   109
14. Commons, Cryptic and Overt   119
15. Reconciling Freedom with Coercion   128
16. The *Quis Custodiet* Problem   133

17. To Kill Progress That Responsibility May Live   141
18. Progress: The Next Coming   150

PART THREE

19. On Board the *Beagle:* Freedom's Harvest   155
20. End of an Orgy   168
21. Parenthood: Right or Privilege?   177
22. Three Phases of Population Control   190
23. Beyond Lysistrata?   205
24. Beyond Fatalism   212
25. The Return of the *Beagle*   216

Appendices

A. Notes and References   241
B. "The Tragedy of the Commons" (the original essay)   250

Index   265

Part One

CHAPTER 1

From the Spaceship *Beagle:*
Embarkation

Morning. It must be morning, Jerry Wood thought, because it *was* getting lighter. He pulled the blanket higher over his face, trying to blot out the necessity of getting up. But it didn't work. Grudgingly, he opened his eyes a slit, looking for the sun on the horizon. He saw it, and suddenly he remembered it wasn't the real sun but a contraption worked by projectors and rheostats. He wasn't on Earth; he was on a spaceship, the good ship *Beagle.*

He started, now wide awake. Stretched out before him, a hundred feet below, was a rolling plain, green with grass and spotted with trees, reaching to the horizon nearly two kilometers distant, where it met the transparent plastic bubble overhead, "that inverted Bowl we call the Sky, whereunder crawling" the celestial mariners were to live and die—for who knew how long before they reached their destination? Wood himself, a newspaper reporter on Earth continuing his profession here, was (with a dozen others) encased in a jagged structure that looked like a small and somber mountain to the plainsmen below but was really a cleverly contrived mass of one-way glass, perfectly transparent to those inside, but quite opaque to those on the outside. The outsiders were to fulfill the primary mission of the spaceship. Those inside were to observe and report back to Earth. If absolutely necessary for the survival of the mission they could intervene in the affairs of the plainsmen. Such intervention was, however, to be avoided if at all possible. The plainsmen were to know nothing of their observers, who had been put on board the spaceship first, in absolute secrecy. The entire plain was thoroughly bugged with microphones and miniaturized television eyes. Every-

3

thing done or said outside the mountain observatory was piped to the observers inside the mountain. The mountain itself, solidly built and virtually impregnable, was liberally posted with signs warning the plainsmen not to touch it lest they disturb the sensitive automated control mechanisms inside. As a further precaution, it was thoroughly electrified externally; the shock it delivered was just short of lethal.

All this was known to people back on Earth, who received periodic reports from Wood. But observing and reporting the activities of the voyagers in space were the secondary goal of the mission; the primary goal, Earthlings were told, was to reach and colonize another world, somewhere out in the galaxy.

So they were told. But it was not true.

The primary mission was the activity itself—and spending the astronomical sums it cost.

The venture had its origin in an unsolved puzzle known as the "Pyramid Problem." It had often been remarked that no large capitalistic nation in modern times had ever achieved a balanced economy without resorting to some kind of institutionalized waste. Perhaps it was always so. Was this not the explanation of the wasteful building of pyramids in ancient Egypt? And in medieval Europe, did not the erecting of cathedrals serve the same function, namely keeping society on an even keel? In modern times it could be argued that fantastically expensive technological war served as a social balance wheel, preventing something even worse than external wars, namely civil wars.

According to the Marxists, only capitalism stands in need of the balance wheel of waste. Capitalist economists denied the assertion categorically—but they were hard put to defend their position. Certainly for a half-century the United States had not achieved peaceful, nonwasteful stability. In the Depression of the thirties massive public-works programs had been instituted to mitigate the sufferings of the unemployed, with only equivocal success. Not until industrial preparations for World War II began in earnest did the American economy return to a state of health. Then there was the Korean war. Then the Southeast Asian war. Then . . .

The trouble with the Pyramid thesis was that it was neither proved nor disproved. It was like the Four Color Problem in topology: plausible and not disproved—but it might not be true either.

Can capitalism survive without its metaphorical pyramids? As the

Asian war ground to a halt the President's economic advisers were told to come up with an answer. The result was a Scotch verdict— not proven. Since, however, the nation was faced with the eminently practical problem of survival, the economists went beyond the bare statement of the indubitably true and described some possible courses of action, in a Top Secret document. The heart of the document was this:

From this point onward we will assume that the Marxist position is true. We do not for a moment think that it is, but we hold that actions based on this assumption deserve the name of "conservative" in the very best sense. If the Marxist position proves not to be true, no permanent harm will have been done by momentarily assuming that it is.

Assuming, then, the correctness of Marxist analysis, the following are the principal lines of action open to the nation.

1. Abandon free enterprise, replacing it with a planned totalitarian state.

2. De-industrialize production, so as to remove economies of scale, increase inefficiency, and produce full employment.

3. Permit, or even encourage, political corruption with the formation of a nationwide Tammany-type organization, thus supporting the population in a different way.

4. Disestablish the welfare state and let simple natural selection eliminate the unemployed and their families by starvation.

5. Liquidate the unemployed by positive action.

6. Lower the population size to the point where economies of scale in manufacture do not prevent full employment. (In passing we note that options 4 and 5, to be successful, must in fact achieve the goal of option 6.)

7. Embark on a course of perpetual pyramid-building, to speak metaphorically.

Needless to say, we regard option 7 as the least undesirable of the lot, and recommend that the Administration immediately set about implementing it.

The question is: What sort of pyramid shall we build first?

The obvious answer was "Space," the most expensive pyramid known to man. For Space *is* expensive. Don de Sylva noted that the entire budget of the National Science Foundation in 1969 ($400 million) was just barely more than the cost of a *single* aborted moonshot in 1970, the Apollo 13—$384 million—surely (as de Sylva put it) "the most expensive legal abortion in history."

But such professional carpings had little influence on the decision-makers, most of whom believed (or professed to believe) that President Kennedy had been right back in 1962 when he said we must go to the moon because (like Mount Everest) "it is there."

This, however, might be criticized as an irrational reason, and so the President's advisers set out to manufacture a rational one for the new enterprise. Fortunately, by this time Science had for so long been the kept creature of government that truth could be bought like barbecue buns. The president of the Walla Walla Institute of Technology was told what was needed and given $500 million for a "feasibility study." In three weeks the institute scientists found that a space spectacular was indeed feasible. Thereupon they were awarded a $60-billion performance grant; and they performed.

In less than six months the orbital-electronic-cybernetic seismologists of WWIT produced absolutely convincing evidence that there was a high probability that the earth would go completely off its rocker in less than fifty years, and that it was therefore necessary to start *immediately* on a program to save the precious germ plasm of *Homo sapiens* by exporting some of it to distant and safer planets. The WWIT conclusions and program were kept under security wraps until the President was ready to announce a practical response to this threat, the program called CRASH—Cybernetic Rocket Accelerator Service, Haste! The coinage wasn't very good, but acronyms are better than arguments. CRASH lifted the spirits of the war-deprived people to new heights. The construction of the spaceship began immediately, and reports of its progress dominated the media from that time on.

"Well, here we are," said Jerry to himself, looking out at the plainsmen moving below, "on our way to Alpha Centauri to look for planets." Four and three-tenths light years away; 25 million million miles; 480 years' travel time, according to their computer-generated timetable. And if Alpha Centauri had no planets—or if all of them were too hot or too cold, too heavy or too light, or blanketed with ammonia or cyanide—then they would have to set sail again. ("Set sail"? Technology plays havoc with language. "Set rockets"? Here was an interesting problem for the journalist.)

Anyway, they would have to blast off on another tack, looking for a more suitable, and more distant, solar system. After Alpha Centauri there was Epsilon Indi to investigate; then Sigma Draconis, Beta Hydri, and HR 753 A. HR 753 A was 22 light years away. A long trip. Would success forever recede from them? Were they to become a celestial *Flying Dutchman?* No matter. However far the *Beagle* might wander, it was Wood's duty to note carefully everything that happened and to laser a generous account of it back to Earth to let those left behind know what the space wanderers were doing.

They *must* know, because they must not be permitted to think about their own misery. They must never start to ask questions.

Standing at the edge of his bedroom, leaning against the ceiling-to-floor glass of the one-way mirror, Wood looked at the scene below. It was a smaller world than the one he had left, but it was not too different. It was newer, shinier, and neater; but basically it resembled the better parts of the United States. The resemblance was no accident. It was "like home" because it had been made that way for profound political reasons. The reasons traced back to the early seventies, to the time of the short-lived "ecology kick."

There had been something like a panic in those days, when ecologists discovered the environment and the world discovered ecologists. "DDT is poisoning the world," they said, "killing everything: peregrine falcons yesterday, pelicans today, and politicians tomorrow. Soon it will poison diatoms in the ocean and we will all die of oxygen starvation. Industrial sludge has killed Lake Erie, mercury from paper mills has turned our fish into a lethal luxury, automobile smog is suffocating us in the cities, and the greenhouse effect of carbon dioxide in the air will roast us all in our beds (unless the curtain effect of airplane jet trails freezes us to death first)."

A little bit of this kinda stuff goes a long way. In ancient times absolute monarchs disemboweled messengers for less. Today we are not much different. But now the absolute monarch is "the Pee-pull." During the 1970s the Pee-pull finally got sick and tired of the apocalyptic rantings of Paul Ehrlich, and one fine night after he had given a rabble-rousing speech at the Marblehead Junior College he was tarred and feathered by the Youth for American Freedom, loaded into a cart borrowed from the town museum, and pulled to the edge of town, where he was thrown ignominiously into the Fort Mudge Memorial Dump. A great sigh of relief arose from the Pee-pull, whose patience had been taxed beyond endurance. Patriots can take only so much.

By this time Americans had discovered the price of ecology. In the beginning they had hoped that ecological reform could be carried out on a "business as usual" basis. Pick up a beer can here, sweep up the sidewalks there, and scold your neighbor—that was a pattern of good behavior they understood. . . . Oh, yes: and go to church on Sunday.

But the more the ecologists talked, the more apparent it became that only the most widespread reforms could put the world on a sound ecological footing. At this point, everyone dug in his heels. Ecology was attacked from the Right as a Communist conspiracy dedicated to the destruction of the American way of life. Ecologists, it was said, wanted to make industries pay for the use of the water and air which it is everyone's natural right to use. Ecologists sought to destroy the American family because it produced too many children. Ecologists intended to subject every new product to a lengthy testing procedure before certifying it for public use, thus making further technological progress impossible. In a word, these blessed ecologists wanted to remove all joy and spontaneity from life.

Spokesmen for the Left said that the whole ecology kick was just a cop-out. Ecologists were more interested in saving a redwood tree than they were in saving the life of a little black child in the inner city. Ecologists were more interested in finding a nesting place for the downy woodpecker than they were in building apartments for exploited minorities. Ecologists cared more for the natural rights of wild animals than for the civil rights of their fellow men. Plainly, the Leftists said, ecology was just a capitalist conspiracy to perpetuate the enslavement of the exploited.

Unintentionally, ecology brought peace to America. The radical Right and the radical Left, finding they had a common enemy, joined forces to eliminate that enemy. The tarring and feathering of Paul Ehrlich at Marblehead touched off the Ecology Pogrom. Barry Commoner was hung from the stainless steel Gateway Arch in St. Louis, where his body was left until the buzzards (two especially imported from South America for the occasion) picked his bones clean. Gordon Orians was pushed out of a helicopter onto a field of sharpened bamboo stumps, while his sidekick Ed Pfeiffer had a gallon of herbicide poured down his throat. Ed died in exquisite agony, to the ineffable ecstasy of all Right-thinking people. LaMont Cole was drawn and quartered by a delegation of the American Society of Agricultural Entomologists, led by their honorary president, Philip Handler; while John Milton (the naturalist, not the poet) was tied to the ground in the ungulate cage at the zoo and trampled to death by wildebeests. Ray Cowles, who saw peril in rocks, death in babbling brooks and population in everything, was simply shot. Ralph

Nader, Victor Yannacone, Buzz Holling, John Cantlon, and Ed Deevey disappeared without a trace. Garrett Hardin, the notorious abortionist, was castrated with a dull aluminum spoon.

The pogrom was short, bloody, and sweet. When it was over, a feeling of well-being, the like of which had not been sensed since Salem, swept across the country. "What's wrong with US?" crowds would ask; and answer with a thunderous "NOTHING!—we're all right, Jack!" An American, it was decided, could do no wrong. As economists had been pointing out for years, if the advice of ecologists had been followed from 1776 onward, development in the United States would have been so stifled that the nation would never have become more than a tiny cluster of villages on the Eastern Seaboard. If you want progress, they said, you've got to pay the price.

The Pee-pull decided they were willing to pay the price, and closed their ears henceforth to ecological audits. Freed of the incubus of the doom-merchants, the American economy took off like a rocket. The GNP soared to $15,000 billion in less than a decade. In the next election the Presidency was won on a firm anti-ecology plank, by G. Morticia Peewee, the first undertaker to rise to that high office. She was the richest woman in the United States. Her chain of more than sixty thousand funeral homes, the Progress-Memorial Slumber Parlors, had a cash flow exceeding that of General Motors. She was the best-known (and most called-upon) servant of the public in America. She won by a landslide on the campaign slogan:

THE FINAL SOLUTION TO ECOLOGY: BURY IT!

So when the time came to outfit the spaceship there was no uncertainty about most of the details. The inhabitants of the great spaceship were not merely the bearers of human life to distant parts of the galaxy: they were also the emissaries of the American way of life to the entire universe. Everything about the spaceship had to be as American as apple pie.

One point only gave trouble for a few weeks: the naming of the ship. President Peewee, being a Democrat, proposed to name it the *Kennedy,* but this evoked an immediate uproar from the Republican-controlled Senate, which favored the name *Hoover.* There was nothing in the Constitution about the right to name spaceships, but Republican Senators maintained that anything having to do with sending emissaries out into space surely fell under the heading of foreign affairs—how more foreign could you get?—and that therefore the President could not act without the "advice and consent" of the Senate. Stalemate.

The stalemate was broken as the result of a casual conversation that took place in the rose garden of the White House. One of the few old, nonpolitical friends the President still made time for in her busy schedule was her college roommate, Hepburn Daye. A more unlikely pair would be difficult to imagine. Their professional paths had diverged completely since college: while Peewee went on to become the woman of affairs (subhead, business), Daye had developed into a great scholar. She was the world's number one authority on the life and times of Charles Darwin.

The contrast in the physical appearance of the two old friends was equally great, as they stood talking to each other in the garden: Hepburn lean, angular, vibrant with life; the President, hair cropped as close as Gertrude Stein's, standing like a massive plinth of obsidian, whining out her troubles.

"Hep, I don't know what I'm going to do about this name business. My instinct tells me it should be a President, but I don't see how the Senate and I can ever agree."

"What you need, Pee, is a nonpartisan President."

"That's a contradiction in terms if there ever was one."

"No it isn't. How about George Washington? He's not identified with either party. Spaceship *Washington* would sound nice. And neutral. Wouldn't it?"

The President's face lit up. She thought a while. Then her face darkened.

"It won't do, Hep. It just won't do. Too neutral. Who can imagine Washington, really? A wooden face on a wooden nickel. A nobody, a nonperson. No warmth. No personality. Won't do."

She closed her mouth firmly. A minute or more elapsed before the silence was broken by Hepburn, her eyes sparkling mischievously as she said, "I've got it! Name the ship after a dog. Everybody loves dogs. Who could object?"

"You're right," said the President, "absolutely right! Those bloody Republicans would look like damned fools if they dared to object. You're right. So the next question is, what dog?"

"Well . . . How about a beagle? Spaceship *Beagle*? How does that grab you?"

Hepburn waited expectantly for the reaction.

"Oh, Hep, you remembered! Poor little Snoopycums, run over the very day I took office. Tragic, tragic!" Tears flowed down the granitic face. "That would be so lovely. Oh, Heppy, I can always rely on you for a bright idea."

Hepburn's face fell. "That wasn't exactly what I had in mind," she said, her voice trailing off; but Peewee didn't hear her. The President's mind was following another trail.

"The Republicans wouldn't put up with naming it spaceship *Snoopycums*. But they can't possibly object to spaceship *Beagle* . . . Spaceship *Beagle*. That's it."

And so it was.

Jerry Wood and his companions never knew how their ship happened to be called the *Beagle,* but it didn't bother them. Good as any name. As a matter of fact, though they usually referred to the whole ship by its official title (especially in dispatches back home), they soon found themselves speaking of the people they were observing as the Republic of the Status Quo, and of the landscape below them as the Plain of Quo. Which made the inhabitants Quotions.

Wood was ruminating about the Quotions and their world as he looked down upon them through the transparent wall. It was sure one helluva big spaceship, he thought. Three kilometers in diameter —that meant it had an area of about three and a half square miles, to put it in terms of the old system, which still felt natural to him. Assembled in Space, from components blasted off over many months, the ship was a marvel of what was once called "applied science." (By this time there was no other kind, so it was just called Science, with a capital S; and worshiped.) Because all the controls of the *Beagle* were completely automated there was no need for a large number of people on it—just enough to carry a decent sample of human germ plasm (American) to the waiting universe. The initial population was slightly less than a thousand. Everything possible had been done to make the Quotions feel at home. Apartment buildings, utilities, soil, bushes, even trees had been blasted into the holding ellipse in Space and assembled into a little world. The inhabited side of the disk always faced away from the sun, and an artificial sun traversed the plastic sky once a day. Artificial gravity made walking natural.

All this Jerry Wood recounted at length in his lasered dispatches back to Earth. ("Migawd, nothing really happens here," he muttered to himself. Nothing *would* happen on the *Beagle* for 480 years, so it was necessary to tell and retell the history and all the trivia of the project, to keep Earthlings from thinking about Earth.)

How *homey* the *Beagle* is, Wood told them: *How American.* "Each family lives in their own little apartment, cooking their meals in the usual way, spending a great deal of time watching television programs. The internal TV station has enough miniaturized tapes to last three years without repeats."

The TV programs were dominated by the dearly beloved advertisements. This was quite right, because the ads, for three decades, had been technically the most perfect part of the TV programs. (A program that cost $50,000 to produce was dominated by advertisements that cost up to $5 million.) The most noticeable contrast with life on Earth was the total lack of automobiles. There had been considerable grumbling about this; in the first week half a dozen citizens had to be treated for exhaustion because they had walked a full circuit of the spacecraft in a single day. But, like the good American soldiers that they were, the people soon toughened up and stopped complaining.

"Just like home," the dispatches said. Wood knew even before he set foot on the ship that his dispatches would have to say this to be believed, no matter what really happened. *Truth is what you expect* —this had long been the beacon light of responsible journalism.

But after a few weeks Wood wondered if the spacecraft was not a bit too much like home, and his dispatches delicately hinted as much. The odor of frying bacon that was so delicious on the morning air of the first day smelled a little rancid by the fifth. Old onion smells were less than delightful, and cabbage was almost unbearable. (Of course, these odors didn't come from the real McCoy, but from "genuine synthetic essences" that had been brought along to make eating interesting.)

Then someone opened a tin of Limburger cheese.

Somebody else complained, but he was promptly shouted down. "This is America," he was told, "and America means freedom. If you don't like the smell, go back where you came from."

One thoughtful but addlebrained woman—no contradiction in terms, she was doing the best she could with what she had—turned on her electric fan to blow the odor away.

The real trouble began several months later. With true Yankee ingenuity one of the Quotions built a small factory to make plastic galaxies to sell to his neighbors. When he had exhausted the demand on the Plain of Quo he continued to turn them out, stockpiling them against the day when the ship should touch down on one of Centauri's planets, where the Quotions would undoubtedly discover Intelligent Beings, that is to say, Customers. Neatly lettered over the door of his factory was this sign:

> THE BUSINESS OF AMERICA
> IS BUSINESS. —CALVIN COOLIDGE
> THIS IS AMERICA, SO SHUT UP!

The plastics factory belched forth an execrable amount of smoke. Eventually it was too much for the owner himself, Fred J. C. Hartley IV, who stopped production for a while to build a smokestack. Having flunked out of engineering school, Hartley knew the rule-of-thumb for the height of smokestacks: two and a half times the height of the nearest building. The neighboring apartment building (two hundred feet away) was two hundred and forty feet high, but Hartley's factory, to which the smokestack was attached, was only fourteen feet in height, so he made the smokestack thirty-five feet high. When he began production again the plume of luxuriant black smoke rose fifty feet and then fanned out horizontally, enveloping the seventh to twelfth floors of the apartment building.

There were complaints.

Hartley promptly retorted: "Two point five times fourteen equals thirty-five, so this factory meets the most rigorous engineering specifications. Cut out your bellyachin'."

All this the observers inside the mountain heard and saw, thanks to electronic bugs. When a delegation of apartment-dwellers appealed to Hartley as a good citizen to cease and desist he ridiculed them.

"What kind of Americans are you anyway? Don't you recognize the sacredness of private property? Don't I own the property my factory sits on? Ownership means rights. I have the right to do what I want on it. Rights are indivisible. Freedom is indivisible. You talk as if you owned the air. What are you anyway—Communists?"

There was no answering that. The delegates shamefacedly left.

Three weeks later the observers inside the mountain noted another factory, on the opposite side of the apartment building, taking form.

Many months passed. Jerry Wood, who had thought he would never have anything interesting to report back to Earth, was ecstatic. He drafted an expansive Lasergram:

Free enterprise has really taken hold. One out of five of the adult males now has his own little factory, making some sort of souvenir or gewgaw. Raw material is limited, but they steal from each other, the inventory of one enterpriser becoming the raw material of the next. For a short while there was a movement to establish an effective security system to prevent this sort of thing, but when someone pointed out that this would bring manufacturing to a halt, the idea was abandoned.

"It was Consumption that made America great, not Conservation; and Consumption will make the *Beagle* great." Words to this effect have been said over and over.

The daylight hours have been radically altered by all this creative activity. The "sun" is no longer visible, except as a dull glow in the clouds of multicolored smoke. Night has been changed even more. In the beginning the stars shone far more brightly here than on earth because of the much thinner layer of atmosphere. Now they are invisible. Factories run both day and night, in order not to waste precious time. (One cynic asked, "What are you going to do with the time you save?" He was promptly trampled to death.) Our night must be seen to be appreciated. Periodic flare-ups from opened furnaces fitfully illuminate the billowing clouds of smoke that surge across the landscape. The nearest earthly equivalent I can think of can be seen in the Gemäldegalerie in Vienna. It is the background of *The Last Judgment* by my distinguished ancestor, Hieronymus Bosch. Take a look at it: you'll see what it's like here. The foreground of Bosch's painting is not to be found on the *Beagle*—at least not yet.

All this industrial activity has affected the passengers of our spaceship. "Side-effects," people say. Everybody is coughing. Eyes water. Some of the elderly are bedridden. The Staff Scientist has pointed out that the side-effects are but one more exemplification of the beneficial "multiplier effect" of capitalistic economics. The single doctor, who was virtually unemployed for the first few months of our voyage, now has more patients than he can handle. Lately, he's taken to coughing himself. Our three nurses are complaining of lack of sleep, so they too are being benefited.

We have only one chronic complainer on board. He sounds like an ecologist from the 1970s. There are mutterings about him.

Two weeks later Wood's Lasergram returned to this subject:

Our ecologist was killed. After he passed on, it was established that he was indeed an ecologist: a membership card of the Ecological Society of America was found sewed into the lining of his coat. [This subversive society has been underground in the United States since 1976, when it was put on the Attorney General's list of Un-American Organizations.] Before the miscreant was finally disposed of, he was castrated with a dull aluminum spoon—or "garretted," as the *Beagle Sentinel* put it. Approbation of the outcome was universal (among the survivors).

The doctor and the three nurses have also died. Natural deaths.

CHAPTER 2

Cheating on a Spaceship

The earth is a spaceship. We should have known this for the past two thousand years, and in a sense we have—in a coldly intellectual sense, as a mere fact of physics, the human implications of which almost completely eluded us. Before we can make "decisions for survival" wisely we must see these implications clearly. We must feel in our bones the inescapable truth that we live on a spaceship. From now on no major political decision can safely be made without taking into consideration this basic fact.

Such a revolutionary change in the thinking of the great masses of people—nearly four billion of them—will not come easily or soon; but the process has been started. The biggest shift took place when our astronauts took photos of the earth from a distance and brought them back for all to see. There it was, our earth—a little bluish ball, draped in a swirl of white clouds. A very little thing in an immensity of space. Limited; confined. A spaceship.

Curious, how purpose and product often conflict in human endeavors. A man sets out on a tour abroad, his purpose being (say) to see Europe in order to understand it. In the end a new vision of his own back yard may be the principal product of his costly trip.

What happens when a man visits Venice for the first time? The purpose of his visit is, no doubt, to see the canals of which he has heard so much. He sees them; and they look (and smell) much as he expected them to. But in addition, if he is at all alert, he experiences something else, something for which the guidebooks utterly failed to prepare him: he experiences the deliciousness of life in a city without automobiles. In Venice you *walk*. (Canals, gondolas, and motorboats are only minor parts of Venetian life.) In a short time you can get almost anywhere. People abound, but they do not irritate you the way motorized behemoths do. Because no provision has to be made for space-consuming automobiles, the streets are narrow but adequate. As a result the city is compact, cozy. And quiet. Strolling in the Piazza San Marco with a thousand people has more in common with walking in a hushed redwood forest than it does with fighting one's way around cacophonous Times Square. The soft shuffle of human feet and the woody flapping of pigeons' wings make an auditory fretwork to the space-filling silence.

Venice shows what a city could be, but almost nowhere is. An understanding of what could be is almost as rare among today's city-planners as it is among wilderness-lovers. The latter, thinking only of cities like New York and anti-cities like Los Angeles, condemn all city life and thus repudiate one of the delights of living; urban planners, fettered to false models, work to insure that the worst fears of the wilderness-lovers will be realized.

On a larger scale, there has been a similar contrast between purpose and product in the American "Space" program. We spent something like $30 billion to get to the moon, 239,000 miles away. It was a magnificent technical achievement. But in the end, the principal product of the Space program may prove to be a deepened understanding of our situation here on earth. We may come at last to feel *in our bones* that the earth is truly finite, and not very big at that; and that we must learn to use it without destroying it.

Shortly before his death in 1965, Adlai Stevenson expressed the mood of the world-to-come with characteristic felicity:

We travel together, passengers on a little spaceship, dependent on its vulnerable reserves of air and soil; all committed for our safety to its security and peace; preserved from annihilation only by the care, the work and, I will say, the love we give our fragile craft.

To the person who *knows* he is living on a spaceship the sight of a smokestack is intolerable. Implicitly, every smokestack shouts aloud, for all to hear: "We have noxious fumes to get rid of, so we're going to throw them away."

But there is no "away" to throw things to.
Not on a spaceship.
And that's where we're living.
Why did it take us so long to discover this elementary truth? There are several reasons, not the least of which is that we didn't want to see the truth. We didn't want to see it because the worst of the filth was produced by industry. Industry produced wealth. And we wanted the wealth.

"Muck is money," they say in Manchester, certainly one of the filthier fruits of the industrial revolution. Muck is money—and who is so foolish as to attack money?

Blindness, as Freud has taught us, is more often the consequence of a positive act than the result of mere defect. It is not that we *are* blind—*we choose blindness*, for good reasons.

Not all of us, of course. Poets, for instance, to their acute discomfort, are afflicted with vision. Almost alone in the first decade of the nineteenth century William Blake inveighed against "those dark Satanic mills" that were ruining "England's green and pleasant land." Though impotent in his time, Blake and his vision of a New Jerusalem may yet shape our future; if so, it will be because (as Shelley said) "Poets are the unacknowledged legislators of the world." By the time we succeed in cleaning up our environment (assuming that we do) we will have survived something like two centuries of increasing pollution of air and water.

Why didn't pollution do us in earlier? Three processes worked in our favor: displacement, dilution, and recycling.

Displacement. Prevailing winds insure that some areas get more smoke than others. Knowing this, those who are rich and powerful locate their homes and offices where pollution is least, to the windward of their factories and on imposing hills, leaving powerless peasants to live wherever they can. The classic arrangement, reading from upwind to downwind, is this:

FACTORY OWNERS (*upwind*)—FACTORIES—
FACTORY WORKERS (*downwind*)

Those who suffer most from pollution, the workers and the unemployed, have least access to the decision-making processes. If they do succeed in making their voices heard, they will be asked: "How would you like to have your job taken away from you by some bureaucrat? Do you want bureaucrats to run your life?"

After all, "Muck is money."

TRANSLATION: "Muck for you is money for me."

Dilution. The taller the chimney, the more the *guk* is diluted by air before it comes back to earth again. "The solution to pollution is dilution." At low enough levels it may be, for a while.

Recycling. Many pollutants can be converted by natural processes into harmless or even useful substances. Deadly carbon monoxide is turned to carbon dioxide, which is harmless in low concentrations. Sulfuric acid is changed to sulfates, lethal cyanides become harmless carbon and nitrogen compounds, and so on. If toxicity is a function of chemical configuration, natural recycling processes may produce a harmless compound.

My grandfather used to say, "Running water purifies itself every ten miles." In his day, perhaps it did. There were few enough people so that the sewage dropped into a stream was soon made inoffensive by natural processes. But not now. Each cycling process has its own inherent limit, and our burgeoning population long ago overstressed most of the unassisted natural cycles.

Displacement, dilution, and recycling may in the past have been adequate to keep the world reasonably pure, but they are not now. Why not?

Displacement fails because of population increase. When more people are scattered over the same area, when factories are to be found everywhere, displacement fails to solve even the rich man's problem, because he who lives upwind of one factory finds himself downwind from another. The rich are now joining the poor in the murky soup. ("Welcome to the club!")

Dilution fails because of population increase. There's only a finite amount of atmosphere: 5.2×10^{18} kilograms, to be exact. Double the number of factories and you double the concentration of pollutants. Or, to keep the over-all concentration the same, each individual factory must be twice as effective in reducing the pollutants in its emissions. This costs money. As we try harder and harder to purify the air, pollution-control costs escalate faster than population, faster than productivity. It is no wonder that the owners and managers of factories fight desperately to keep the public from instituting healthy pollution standards. Managers want "realistic" standards—in quotes.

"Prosperity" increases pollution. If we define prosperity in the usual materialistic way to mean more autos, more air-conditioners, more jet travel, et cetera, then even if the population were to stay constant in size, pollution (and the costs of controlling it) would increase step by step with prosperity. Possibly we should not define prosperity in so materialistic a way; but we do. As defined, it generates pollution.

If we don't want the pollution, we must give up some of our prosperity to reduce pollution, or to pay for needed pollution-control equipment.

A smokestack is not a piece of pollution-control equipment. Neither is an exhaust pipe, nor the outfall from an untreated sewage-collection system.

Displacement is not control—not on a spaceship.

It is cheating.

Prophecy is hazardous, but let me risk a small one. I foresee a Museum of Antiquities, say a hundred years from now. Inside there will be thousands of old and often puzzling objects, including corset stays, bed-warmers, hurricane lamps, hourglasses, Persian wells, muzzle-loaders, torture racks, Iron Maidens, and chastity belts. Outside, in a courtyard, visitors will encounter a carefully reassembled tapered tube of bricks, seventy-five feet high. Out of the top of this there will come a plume of steam, to which a harmless, decomposable black dye has been added to make it look like industrial smoke. Busloads of schoolchildren will be brought from great distances to view this incredible object. On its base there will be a large bronze plaque:

SMOKESTACK

QUAINT DEVICE USED BY OUR PRE-ECOLOGIC ANCES-
TORS, IN THE SUPERSTITIOUS BELIEF THAT THERE
WAS AN "AWAY" TO THROW THINGS TO. LAST USED
IN 1987. THIS WELL-PRESERVED SPECIMEN IS ONE OF
ONLY THREE EXTANT IN WORLD. GIFT OF THE POL-
LUTION COLLECTORS CLUB OF NEW JERUSALEM.

DO NOT TOUCH.

CHAPTER 3

Guk–Cycle or Sequester?

Who first realized that the earth was a spaceship? Nobody. Nobody was first. Great visions grow slowly in the minds of men, as unconscious hypotheses at first, only later to be converted into explicit statements from which practical consequences can be deduced.

The first step toward the spaceship view of the world was taken by the Pythagoreans of ancient Greece when they insisted (contrary to common sense) that the world is round. If the world is flat (as it appears to be) and if the horizon recedes forever (as it does), no matter how long I walk toward it there is no limit to my possible wanderings. I am justified in believing that there is always *more* of everything . . . out there—toward the unreachable horizon. More forests. More farmland. More freedom.

This view has moral consequences, and they are mostly bad. Like believing in Santa Claus, or fairies, or genies. If there is always the possibility of my being bailed out of trouble by some supernatural beings or processes (egotistically supposed to be working in my interest) I am unlikely ever to do my bookkeeping conscientiously. I always have a "fudge factor" to fall back on.

The Pythagoreans junked the idea of an unbounded flat area, replacing it with a sphere. Psychologically this amounted to an act of closure. A world that is round is psychologically limited. In the fifth century B.C. the Pythagoreans made the world round and finite, and from then on rigorous principles of accounting were applicable. No fudge factor. No mysterious disappearances of matter, and no creation of it either. No Santa Claus. Just rigorous accounting.

So much was implicit in the Pythagorean view, but it was not made explicit for more than two thousand years. It was not until the nineteenth century that the Conservation of Matter and the Conservation of Energy were explicitly asserted.

A little later the new conservative view was seriously challenged when radioactivity was discovered. Momentarily it looked as though the idea of conservation would have to go by the board. Then Einstein, in his celebrated equation $E = mc^2$, showed that matter and energy were interconvertible in a precise mathematical way, and the concept of conservation was once again enthroned. (As a purely practical matter many day-to-day decisions require nothing more precise than the pre-Einstein formulations. But we must always use some sort of conservation laws—they keep us honest.)

In common speech we praise the "open mind"; yet it is noteworthy that the survival, and most of the progress, of science is dependent upon having a mind that is, in a sense, closed—closed to the possibility of genies, Santa Claus, and a *deus ex machina*. Einstein's equation was hailed because it validated and re-established the discipline of closed-system thinking.

In the operation of any factory there are two accounting problems:

a. Accounting for money. Income, expenses, profit and loss—that sort of thing.

b. Accounting for matter. What is the raw material, what are the salable products, and *what are the so-called by-products and wastes?* Wastes also are products, even if they are not salable.

Money-accounting was accepted as a discipline by the businessmen of Babylon at least as early as 2300 B.C., and was put on a firm basis with the invention of double-entry bookkeeping by the Italians in the thirteenth century A.D.

The necessity of matter-accounting has still not been accepted by the business community. Ponder over this news report of January 1971 (slightly shortened, but omitting nothing essential).

> Attorney General John N. Mitchell announced yesterday that the General Motors Corp. has agreed to stop polluting the Hudson River with chromium and other poisonous metals.

Mitchell said GM agreed to a consent judgment filed in the U.S. District Court for the Southern district of New York.

Under terms of the judgment, GM will eliminate immediately all discharges of caustics and of toxic metals, such as chromium, from its Tarrytown, N.Y., plant.

. . . The consent judgment specifies that GM will pump out tanks within the plant and haul away in railroad tank cars any effluents containing deadly metals and caustics.

The noxious material is to be hauled "away"—away where? GM will "eliminate" materials—how? By suspending the Conservation Laws? There is no real accounting for matter here; it is as though the scientific developments of the nineteenth and twentieth centuries had never occurred. By legal fiat (apparently), matter is to be made to disappear.

Matter is never so obliging. Every poisonous atom that is hauled "away" in tank cars will turn up somewhere, and we had better find out:

Where?

In what form?

And with what consequences?

How curious it is that hardheaded businessmen who wouldn't dream of taking a step without the support of a completely rigorous system of money-accounting should bitterly fight the ecologists' proposal to institute an equally rigorous system of matter-accounting! Twentieth-century money-accounting exists side by side with pre-Babylonian matter-accounting. Curious, but understandable. God help the accountant who fails to make the books—the money books, that is—balance down to the last penny. But as for the matter books . . . well, the factory just doesn't keep any. You aren't supposed to ask what happens to the gukky matter produced by an "efficient" factory. "Out of sight, out of mind"—*and please wait a moment till I put this guk out of sight.*

What are we to do with the guk we don't want? In a greatly underpopulated world it might not hurt if we were to throw it any old place. Dilution by large empty spaces might be enough to keep the concentration below the irritation point for a long time to come.

Sooner or later, however, with continued accumulation of wastes and continued growth of population, we become irritated by the concentration of randomly dispersed trash. We decide to sequester it—in junkyards, "sanitary landfills," and the like. Some nice-Nellies among us may propose that we plant rose hedges around our junkyards. This may not get rid of the guk, but the reduction in man-guk contacts makes us feel better. (It keeps us from knowing that we have a problem, always a delightful form of ignorance.)

Ultimately, the nice-Nellie approach is not enough. The piles of guk grow bigger, population increases, and open spaces vanish. The world is finite. Something more fundamental than rose-covered junkyards is called for.

The many kinds of guk require almost as many kinds of treatment. These can be divided into two large classes—cycling and sequestering—depending on whether the problem is one of "molecular pollution" or "elemental pollution."

Molecular pollution. Carbon monoxide (CO) is a poisonous molecule. The elements of which it is composed (carbon and oxygen) are not inherently poisonous; other combinations of them are scarcely dangerous at all (e.g., carbon dioxide, CO_2), and some are even humanly useful (e.g., the sugar molecule glucose, $C_6H_{12}O_6$). Molecular pollution can be controlled by converting dangerous molecules to nondangerous ones. (When we say that a molecule is "destroyed" we mean that a particular configuration of atoms is disrupted. Atoms themselves are not destroyed. The chemist is unable to destroy [or create] atoms, but he can destroy and create configurations. In fact, doing so is his profession.)

Carbon monoxide takes part in many reactions in nature and the laboratory. Part of the cycling of carbon is shown below:

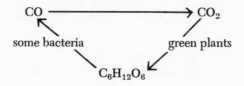

In a very general way, molecular pollutants are part of cycles of the following sort:

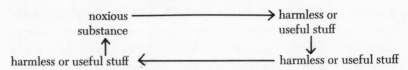

Faced with a surplus of something noxious, we have the practical problem of nudging it along the cycle faster. Carbon monoxide, produced by imperfect oxidation in an automobile engine, will naturally change slowly into carbon dioxide in the outside world. The engineer's job is to encourage the $CO \rightarrow CO_2$ reaction to take place inside the automobile engine, before the gases are released into the general environment.

Elemental pollution. Mercury is a good example of an elemental poison. All compounds of mercury are poisonous. Some mercury compounds are extremely insoluble in water and consequently pose no immediate danger to man and other animals. But insoluble compounds can be converted to soluble ones, given suitable circumstances. Hence all mercury compounds are potentially lethal.

The hazard arises from the fact that mercury coagulates proteins and inactivates enzymes. Without active enzymes there is no life. Moreover, in the higher animals, mercury damages nervous tissue, thus producing behavioral abnormalities. The conversion of fur into felt for hats used to be accomplished with mercury compounds. Felters were not shielded from the mercury they were using. The resulting nervous disease gave rise to the expression "mad as a hatter."

We've known of the toxicity of mercury for a long time, but you would hardly guess it from the way we behave. An elemental poison simply cannot be gotten rid of by running it around the cycle faster. We have to sequester it—put it under lock and key, as it were. And let it out only under rigid supervision.

We often use some pretty unreliable locks in corralling our mercury. Some of the German submarines in the Second World War used metallic mercury as ballast. One of these, with nearly two hundred tons of mercury, was sunk in the Gulf of Mexico near New Orleans in 1942. Twenty-nine years later it turned up off the coast of Florida, where it had drifted, a straight-line distance of four hundred miles. As long as such a vessel remains intact, the mercury is no hazard, but steel submarines cannot forever withstand the corrosive effect of seawater. What will happen when the mercury is released

into the ocean someday? And how fast will it happen? No one
knows; but two hundred tons of mercury suddenly desequestered is
not a pleasant thought.

As salvage, the cache is tempting—it's worth more than a million
and a half dollars at present prices. A nice package; but it is part of a
package deal that includes TNT, torpedoes, and other explosives of
unknown reliability after three decades of aging.

The mercury in the U-boat poses a spectacular problem, but an
atypical one. Day-by-day peacetime operations confront us with far
greater threats than do the military ones. Every year men dig about
nine thousand tons of mercury out of the earth and scatter it around
the world. It has many important uses in agriculture and industry;
some of the uses may even be "essential" (though that remains to be
proved). As a fungicide mercury is used to preserve seeds until ger-
mination, and to prevent moldiness in the slurries from which paper
is made. These are one-time uses. The used mercury goes into the
runoffs from fields, and into the streams flowing past the paper mills.
In water it is sooner or later converted into soluble methyl mercury
compounds, which are picked up by algae which are eaten by water
fleas which are eaten by little fish which are eaten by big fish—which
are eaten by man.

And if a big fish dies without being eaten by a man, its body is
decomposed by bacteria and the mercury is put back into the cycle
again.

So man has a second chance to be poisoned.

And a third . . . and a fourth.

In fact, an infinite number of chances, so long as the mercury is
circulating freely in the environment.

The answer to the mercury-pollution problem is, of course, to sequester. The mercury was sequestered originally in ores in the
ground. The trouble began when we desequestered it. We began
mining mercury in antiquity, but the use of this element—and the
dispersion of it in our environment—has sharply increased in recent
times. We know this by virtue of some Swedish studies of the distribution of mercury in bird feathers. "Study skins" of birds in mu-
seums are dated according to the time of their collection. Feathers
from birds collected in Europe between 1840 and 1940 show no significant differences in the concentration of mercury in them, which is

low. But between 1940 and 1966 the mercury content increased ten- to twentyfold, indicating a corresponding change in the environment of the birds. And of man as well.

Obviously what is now called for is a disciplined accounting for every gram of mercury put into circulation, and strenuous efforts to prevent its escaping from control. It is dangerous to broadcast this perpetual poison, as we do with mercury-treated seeds. Industries should be compelled to keep books on mercury.

And what about the mercury that is already cycling in nature—how can we recapture that? Recently it has been found dangerously concentrated in swordfish, so instead of eating these fish, we might mine them for mercury! In a freely competitive market such mercury would be prohibitively expensive. But that's not the point. Either we must mine the fish or we must give up eating many kinds of fish until some as yet undemonstrated processes of natural sequestration remove the mercury from the cycles in nature and deposit it in some safe place, perhaps in the depths of the ocean.

But there may be no safe place in nature.

Unwittingly, we have made our world a more dangerous one by desequestering mercury and releasing it into cycles that sometimes intersect with man's activities. Now we must separate these cycles and resequester the mercury. How long that will take, and what will be the cost, we do not know. But this much is perfectly clear: just as we now legally require business concerns to use precise methods of total money-accounting, so also must we legally require them to use precise methods of matter-accounting.

It's time for business to move beyond Babylon.

CHAPTER 4

When Dilution Fails

The solution to pollution is dilution. This is the unspoken motto of industrial society: unspoken, perhaps, because putting the belief into words would have called attention to it, would have invited testing it and ultimately refuting it. It was the "econuts"—the self-appointed spokesmen of the ecological point of view—who first put this hidden belief into words. They verbalized it in order to refute it. (You can't attack an invisible enemy.)

Of all the mistakes made in life, the most enlightening are those made by intelligent men. Discovering how a good man can go wrong inevitably uncovers hidden assumptions that hold most of us in thrall. Such a mistake was made by the very great organic chemist Sir Robert Robinson, O.M., F.R.S., Nobel Laureate (1947), when the jeremiads of the econuts finally became too much for him, provoking him to write a letter to the editor which the London *Times* published on February 4, 1971:

> Sir, Neither our "Prophets of Doom," nor the legislators who are so easily frightened by them, are particularly fond of arithmetic and I would like to draw attention to the approximate figures relating to a recent warning by Professor Jean Picard.
> The eminent Professor's researches and exploits in the Jules Verne tradition are so well known and admired that particular weight must be attached to his judgment. His claim, as reported by the B.B.C., is that, at the present rate of pollution of the oceans by lead compounds derived from leaded petrol, the growth of

29

plankton in the upper layers of the oceans will be inhibited and this, in turn, will reduce the oxygen content of the atmosphere, possibly to a dangerously low level. If, however, we look at the simple arithmetic of the situation, and take cognizance also of the toxicity of lead, it can be seen that the risk is biologically negligible. . . .

What does it mean, to "look at the simple arithmetic of the situation"? It means the following, according to Sir Robert. On the conservative assumption that the average depth of the ocean is 2.5 miles, there must be some 325,750 cubic miles of water in the ocean. The annual production of the lead compounds we call "ethyl," which we add to gasoline (or petrol, as the British have it), is 800,000 metric tons, of which 40 percent by weight is lead. If we add all of a year's production to the ocean, we find that it produces a concentration of lead in water of 2.36×10^{-10}. Alternatively, this may be expressed as:

$$0.000000000236$$
or: $\qquad 0.0000000236$ percent
or: $\qquad$ one part lead in 4,240,000,000 parts of water*

Although lead is a serious cumulative poison, this concentration is so small that we are quite justified in regarding it, says Sir Robert, as "biologically negligible." *If* his argument is correct . . .

But it isn't, as Dr. J. David George of the Natural History branch of the British Museum pointed out in the *Times* a week later. The "simple arithmetic of the situation" is all but irrelevant, as biologists have known for decades. The reasons are several.

Using "simple arithmetic" presupposes complete mixing of the components, a natural enough assumption for a practicing chemist to make. In the ordinary chemical investigation the first thing you do is see to it that the reactants are homogeneously mixed. You stir. Thoroughly. Nonhomogeneity is an abomination. The unconscious occupational bias of five decades of laboratory chemistry led Robertson

---

* Actually, Sir Robert gave the answer as 1 part in 425×10^{10}, making an error of a thousandfold. Misplacing a decimal point in a published paper is a recurrent nightmare of scientists, but we need not linger over this one because (as we shall see) the arithmetic error, great as it is, is trifling compared with the conceptual error in the chemist's argument.

quite naturally to use "simple arithmetic" with its hidden assumption of complete mixing.

But no great Chemist in the Sky stirs the ocean into one homogeneous soup. Lead enters the ocean in two ways: as fallout from the air, and as dissolved, suspended, and organism-bound matter in river water. River water is lighter than ocean water and tends to spread out on the surface; and fallout reaches the surface first. Lead tends to remain at the surface—and it is here that *all* of the photosynthesis takes place. Below about 250 feet there is too little light for photosynthesis. We need to know how much lead there is in the first 250 feet of the ocean. How much there is in the remaining 13,000 feet doesn't matter much. The "window" through which lead enters is where the action takes place. The dynamic geometry of the earth-system is quite different from that of a Waring Blendor in the chemical lab.

But that isn't all. "Simple arithmetic" fails for another reason that a chemist might not suspect: biological concentration, or "biological magnification," as it is sometimes called. This phenomenon, long known to biologists, was forcibly called to everyone's attention seventeen years before Sir Robert wrote his letter; but probably very few of the world's three and a half billion inhabitants have yet got the message. In this regard, Sir Robert is in good, or at any rate multitudinous company.

Some 300 million cubic miles of ocean water should be enough of a dilution factor for any poison. But it doesn't quite work out that way, as we learned in 1954. On March 1 of that year the first thermonuclear bomb was exploded at Bikini, in the Pacific Ocean. The physicists who planned the explosion knew that radioactive atoms would be released into the sea, but they counted on the great volume of the ocean to dilute the lethal material far beyond the point of any real danger to man.

A reasonable assumption; but it was wrong. In a few months, fish turning up at docks in Japan were found to be dangerously radioactive. But the ocean water out of which they were taken was not significantly radioactive. What had happened?

Biological magnification was the explanation. A substance present in almost undetectably low concentration in water may be concentrated by the metabolic processes of living cells until it is hundreds or thousands of times more concentrated in the organism than it is in the medium surrounding it. Biological magnification is especially important when the atoms being concentrated are radioactive. Some of the known concentration factors are displayed in Table 1. The figures are only approximations, as is implied by the nice round numbers given. It is obvious that as fast as man tries to solve his radioactive-pollution problems by dilution, metabolism unsolves them by concentration. This fact raises serious doubts about the ultimate safety of a burgeoning atomic-power program with its ever-increasing quantities of radioactive effluents and spent fuel elements calling for safe disposal—*for thousands of years.*

TABLE 1

Estimated Concentration Factors in Aquatic Organisms

RADIOACTIVE ATOM	SITE	PHYTO-PLANKTON	FILA-MENTOUS ALGAE	INSECT LARVAE	FISH
Na-24 (sodium)	Columbia River	500×	500×	100×	100×
Cu-64 (copper)	Columbia River	2,000×	500×	500×	50×
Rare earths	Columbia River	1,000×	500×	200×	100×
Fe-59 (iron)	Columbia River	200,000×	100,000×	100,000×	10,000×
P-32 (potassium)	Columbia River	200,000×	100,000×	100,000×	100,000×
P-32 (potassium)	White Oak Lake	15,000×	850,000×	100,000×	30–70,000×
Sr-90—Y-90 (strontium, yttrium)	White Oak Lake	75,000×	500,000×	100,000×	20–30,000×

SOURCE: M. Eisenbud, *Environmental Radioactivity.* N.Y.: McGraw-Hill, 1963.

As a practical matter it is convenient to divide biological concentration into two categories: idiosyncratic concentration and food-chain concentration. Let's see what is meant by these terms.

Some species of sea-squirts—tunicates—concentrate vanadium in their bodies. Vanadium is almost undetectable in sea water. The sea-squirts concentrate it to nearly 500,000 times the amount found in the water. Other kinds of tunicates concentrate niobium, also a rare metal, in their tissues. A protozoan, *Tetrahymena,* concentrates cobalt. Some jellyfish accumulate titanium.

There are no general rules for predicting idiosyncratic concentration. Species simply differ. And there are millions of different species.

Even inside a single individual there are idiosyncratic differences among the tissues. Mammalian thyroid tissue removes most of the iodine from the bloodstream, while other tissues ignore it. This is why radioactive iodine (iodine-131) from atomic bomb tests may cause cancerous growth of the thyroid without affecting other tissues. In a similar way bone tissue accumulates calcium atoms (which are needed to make bone) and strontium atoms, which are chemically much like calcium. When the strontium atoms are the radioactive species Sr-90, the normal metabolic accumulation of them in the bones stores up trouble in the future for the individual.

The second category of biological magnification, food-chain concentration, is exemplified by DDT. In recent years many species of birds have been brought close to extinction by this insecticide, which, when sufficiently concentrated in the female bird, interferes with the formation of the protective calcareous shell of the egg, thus preventing reproduction. DDT is extremely insoluble in water. How, then, does it become concentrated in birds?

The data in Table 2 give us a clue. Note that the concentration of DDT in the plankton, i.e., the microscopic water plants and animals

TABLE 2

Biological Magnification

DDT content of water and various organisms in a restricted area of Long Island

SAMPLE	DDT RESIDUES, PARTS PER MILLION
Water	0.00005
Plankton, mostly zooplankton	0.040
Shrimp	0.16
Chain pickerel	1.33
Various terns, herons, and gulls	3.15 to 18.5
Double-crested cormorant (immature)	26.14
Ring-billed gull (immature)	75.5

Selected data from G. M. Woodwell, C. F. Wurster, and P. A. Isaacson, *Science:* **156**:821–24, 1967.

(principally the latter), is 800 times as great as it is in water. The DDT in shrimp is 4 times that in the plankton. Pickerel have 8 times as much DDT as shrimp. Various gulls have from 3 to 14 times as much as the fish. One bird specimen in this study had 57 times as much DDT as the fish—and 1.5 million times as much as the water!

How is this biological magnification brought about? The explanation is connected with that ecologists call the "food chain," which tells us who eats whom. The complete story is very complex, but the principles involved can be best seen by simplifying the truth into a single chain of organisms feeding on one another:

Algae ——→ protozoa ——→ waterfleas ——→ smallfish ——→ tuna

In the chain above, algae (principally diatoms in the sea) are called "primary producers," because they capture the energy of sunlight and turn it into chemical energy (food). Protozoa merely convert the organic riches already produced by the algae into other organic compounds. Various small crustaceans of the sort called waterfleas convert protozoa-compounds to waterflea-compounds, and so on. There are five *trophic levels* ("feeding levels") indicated in the scheme just given. Only the first trophic level produces food energy from nonfood energy (sunlight). All the others merely repackage the food energy.

. . . repackage it—*with a big loss.* About 90 percent, to speak generally.

Rule of the Ecological Tithe: *The total energy content at each trophic level is only about one-tenth that of the level below it.* One practical implication of this is fairly widely known: a larger population of human beings is supportable on a vegetarian diet than on a carnivorous diet or a mixed one. If our goal is to support the largest possible population of mankind on earth—though why we should have such a goal is never explained—then our advice is simple: Don't eat the chicken, eat the chickenfeed. Don't eat the pig, eat the garbage. Don't eat tuna, eat the algae of the ocean: the algae that ultimately feed the tuna have 10,000 times as much food value in them as the tuna. (Gathering the algae and making them palatable is something else again.)

Now let's see how the food chain causes a magnification of unwanted pollutants as we ascend to higher trophic levels (Figure 1).

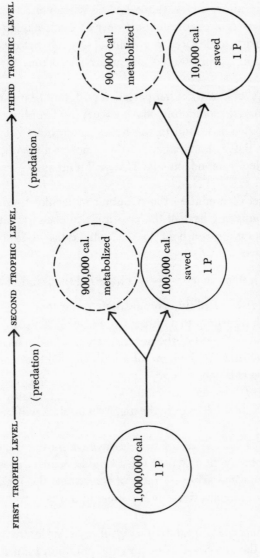

FIRST TROPHIC LEVEL ⟶ SECOND TROPHIC LEVEL ⟶ THIRD TROPHIC LEVEL

(predation)

(predation)

1,000,000 cal.
1 P

900,000 cal.
metabolized

100,000 cal.
saved
1 P

90,000 cal.
metabolized

10,000 cal.
saved
1 P

FIGURE 1. Showing how nonmetabolizable pollutants (P) bound to living tissue are concentrated in the food chain

Suppose the organisms at the first trophic level have a total food value of 1,000,000 calories. As a predator engulfs this mass of organisms it burns up the calories in its metabolic furnace and thus manages to continue to move, think, and do whatever else it does. About 900,000 calories of chemical energy are so used, leaving little beyond carbon dioxide and water as a residue. Organic materials with a caloric value of about 100,000 are incorporated into the flesh of the predator.

Now let's look at what happens to a pollutant that is not metabolically destroyed: something like mercury or strontium-90 or DDT. Something that is bound to the living tissue but is of no use to it. Something that is metabolized little or not at all; something that is excreted slowly or not at all. This pollutant is represented in the figure by "1 P."

In the act of predation the pollutant molecules become detached from the vanishing flesh of the prey and attached to that of the predator—substantially without loss. So the ratio of flesh-to-pollutant changes thus:

a million to one ———→ a hundred thousand to one

That is, there is a tenfold magnification in the concentration of pollutant at each transition to a higher trophic level. This is why, now that mercury is a pollutant of the ocean, there is a health hazard in eating tuna and swordfish, which are at a high trophic level, and not much of one in the eating of shrimp.

Someday (if we do not mend our ways), even the shrimp will become inedible. Ultimately the algae themselves will be toxic.

Life can never be free of risk; always we must balance the probable costs of an action against the probable benefits. If we can agree to designate some arbitrary ratio of the two as the limit of the "acceptable," to reach a decision we must find a way to measure costs and benefits.

Unfortunately for pollution control it is easier to measure the benefits of the activity that creates the pollution than it is to determine the costs of the pollution itself. The defenders of DDT (for example) can say: "If we forgo the use of all synthetic insecticides, agricultural productivity will go down 15 percent," and their estimate, though not spectacularly accurate, is good enough.

But what are the costs of this, and of all other environmental pollutants? Food chains are only imperfectly known; the extent of biological magnification is imperfectly known; long-term, subclinical effects on human beings need more study; and we do not know the probability that the whole system of nature will ultimately be disrupted and human existence imperiled. But it is greater than zero. The data for benefits are "hard," those for costs "soft." Methodologically, one tends always to give a heavier weighting to hard data than to soft.

But since the survival of man hangs in the balance, perhaps we'd better think twice.

CHAPTER 5

What the Hedgehog Knows

Among the fragments left us by the Greek poet Archilochus there is a line, dark in meaning, that says:

The fox knows many things; the hedgehog knows one big thing.

Isaiah Berlin, who resurrected this enigmatic utterance, uses it to good effect to divide the great literary figures into two classes. (He is fully aware of the dangers of pressing any dichotomy too far, but he finds this one useful nonetheless.)

There exists [he says] a great chasm between those, on the one side, who relate everything to a single central vision, one system less or more coherent or articulate, in terms of which they understand, think and feel—a single, universal, organizing principle in terms of which alone all that they are and say has significance—and, on the other side, those who pursue many ends, often unrelated . . .

Among the latter—the foxes—he places Aristotle, Montaigne, Molière, Goethe, Balzac, and Joyce. The hedgehogs include Plato, Lucretius, Pascal, Nietzsche, and Proust.

Ecologists, in my opinion, are hedgehogs. The one big thing they *say* is this:

We can never do merely one thing.

This simple sentence imperfectly mirrors the one big thing ecologists *know*—the idea of a system. So large an idea is best defined ostensively, i.e., by pointing to examples.

The ostensive work of defining a system can begin with a not entirely sober example, first cited by Charles Darwin:

> The number of humble-bees in any district depends in a great measure upon the number of field-mice which destroy their combs and nests; and Col. Newman who has long attended to the habits of humble-bees, believes that "more than two-thirds of them are thus destroyed all over England." Now the number of mice is largely dependent, as everyone knows, on the number of cats; and Col. Newman says, "Near villages and small towns I have found the nests of humble-bees more numerous than elsewhere, which I attribute to the number of cats that destroy the mice." Hence it is quite credible that the presence of a feline animal in large numbers in a district might determine, through the intervention first of mice and then of bees, the frequency of certain flowers in that district!

Darwin published this story in the *Origin of Species,* in 1859. Others, amused, embroidered on it. It was pointed out, on the one hand, that cats are kept (as is well known) by old maids; and, on the other, that red clover (which requires humble-bees as pollinators) is used to make the hay that nourishes the horses of the cavalry, on which the defense of the British Empire depends. Putting all this into a causal chain, we see:

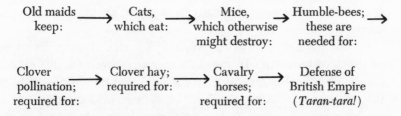

Old maids → Cats, → Mice, → Humble-bees; →
keep: which eat: which otherwise these are
might destroy: needed for:

Clover → Clover hay; → Cavalry → Defense of
pollination; required for: horses; British Empire
required for: required for: (*Taran-tara!*)

Thus, "it logically follows" that the perpetuation of the British Empire is dependent on a bountiful supply of old maids!

Far-fetched? A bit; but counsel for the defense can offer this fact in evidence: old maids are much less common in England now than they were when Colonel Newman and Darwin started this train of thought. And what has happened to Britain's possessions in India? In

East Africa? And what about the Suez Canal? If correlation is causation . . .

Now for a completely serious example. Everyone has heard of the Aswan Dam in Egypt. Actually, a succession of dams has been constructed on the Nile at Aswan during the twentieth century, of which the "High Aswan," built with Russian help, is only the latest. The builders meant to do only one thing—dam the water—and that for two purposes: to generate electricity and to provide a regular flow of water for irrigation of the lower Nile basin. Ecology tells us that we cannot do merely one thing; neither can we do merely two things. What have been the consequences of the Aswan dams?

First, the plain has been deprived of the annual fertilization by flooding that served it so well for five thousand years. Where else in the world can you point to farmland that is as fertile after five millennia of cultivation as it was in the beginning? (Much of the farmland in the southeastern United States was ruined in half a generation.) Now the Egyptians will have to add artificial fertilizer to the former floodplains of the Nile—which will cost money.

Second, controlled irrigation without periodic flushing salinates the soil, bit by bit. There are methods for correcting this, but they too cost money. This problem has not yet been faced by Egypt.

Third, the sardine catch in the eastern Mediterranean has diminished from 18,000 tons a year to 400 tons, a 97 percent loss, because the sea is now deprived of floodborne nutrients. No one has reimbursed the fishermen (who are mostly not Egyptians) for their losses.

Fourth, the rich delta of the Nile is being eroded away by storms on the Mediterranean. In the past, a nearly "steady state" existed between the deposition of silt by the river and the erosion of it by the sea, with a slight positive balance in favor of deposition, which gradually extended the farmlands of Egypt. With deposition brought to a virtual halt, the balance is now negative and Egypt is losing land.

Fifth, schistosomiasis (a fearsomely debilitating disease) has greatly increased in the Nile valley. The disease organism depends on snails, which depend on a steady supply of water, which constant irrigation furnishes but annual flooding does not. Of course, medical control of the disease is possible—but that too costs money.

Is this all? By no means. The first (and perhaps only a temporary) effect of the Aswan Dam has been to bring into being a larger population of Egyptians, of whom a greater proportion than before are chronically ill. What will be the political effects of this demographic fact? This is a most difficult question—but would anyone doubt that there will be many political consequences, for a long time to come, of trying to do "just one thing," such as building dams on the Nile? The effects of any sizable intervention in an "ecosystem" are like ripples spreading out on a pond from a dropped pebble; they go on and on.

Ironically, in the end, the whole wretched game will return to the starting point. All dam-ponds are transient: in the scale of historical time they are soon filled by siltation behind the dam, and then they are useless. Theoretically, a dam-pond could be dredged clean, but engineers, inclined though they are to assume they can do anything, never suggest this. Evidently the cost is, in the strict sense, prohibitive.

So in a short time—perhaps a century, certainly nothing like the fifty centuries during which Nile agriculture prospered before the dams were built at Aswan—in a short time the dams themselves will be useless and then the silt-laden waters of the Nile will once again enrich the river bottom.

Will history start over again then? Certainly not. Too much will have happened to Egypt in the meantime, most of it bad; and perhaps much to the rest of the world, as the Egyptian people struggle desperately to free themselves from the net in which their well-wishers have unwittingly ensnared them. Things will never again be the same. History does not repeat.

It's tough to be a hedgehog. You take a simple little idea—the right one, you hope—and "thinking on't constantly" (as Newton said) you discover it has wide and unexpected ramifications. In the variety and disunity so cherished by foxes the hedgehog finds a unity, knit together by his one big idea. Being the first to feel its power, and alone with his insight, it is not surprising if he doubts his sanity. Darwin, his mind big with the idea of natural selection, suffered grave self-doubts. Writing to a fellow naturalist just after the publication of the *Origin of Species* he confessed, "When I think of the many cases of men who have studied one subject for years, and have persuaded themselves of the truth of the foolishest doctrines, I feel sometimes a little frightened, whether I may not be one of these monomaniacs."

Rachel Carson, both before and after she published *Silent Spring* in 1962, must have had similar doubts. She took the great idea from ecology, the idea of a system, and by constantly thinking on it, discovered innumerable instances of the harm done by supposing that we can ever do merely one thing. By 1962 many reports of ecological errors were in print, but the diffuseness of the literature minimized the impact. *Silent Spring* concentrated it. Among the accounts of system disruption retold by Miss Carson is the following:

Justice William O. Douglas, in his recent book *My Wilderness: East of Katahdin,* had told of an example of ecological destruction wrought by the Forest Service in the Bridger National Forest, in Wyoming. Yielding to the pressure of cattlemen for more grassland, the Service sprayed some ten thousand acres of sage lands. The sage was killed, as was intended. But so was a green, life-giving ribbon of willows that traced its way across these plains, following the meandering streams. Moose had lived in these willow thickets, for willow is to the moose what sage is to the antelope. Beavers had lived there, too, feeding on the willows, felling them, and making strong dams across the tiny streams. Through the labor of the beavers, a lake backed up. Trout in the mountain streams were seldom more than six inches long; in the lake they thrived so prodigiously that many grew to five pounds. Waterfowl were attracted to the lake. But with the "improvement" instituted by the Forest Service, the willows went the way of the sagebrush, killed by the same, impartial spray. When Justice Douglas visited the area in 1959, the year of the spraying, he was shocked to see the shriveled and dying willows—the "vast, incredible damage." What would become of the moose? Of the beavers and the little world they had constructed? A year later, he returned to read the answers in the devastated landscape. The moose were gone, and so were the beavers. The principal beaver dam had gone out for want of attention by its skilled architects, and the lake had drained away. None of the large trout were left, for none could live in the tiny creek that remained, threading its way through a bare, hot land.

Dimly, we have always known something of the interconnectedness of things. Shakespeare's contemporary, George Herbert, gave form to this insight when he wrote, "For the want of a nail the shoe is lost, for want of a shoe the horse is lost, for want of a horse the rider is lost." This expresses the idea that little things can matter greatly and that there are causal chains—a first step toward perceiving causal networks.

The poet Francis Thompson, whose life was sandwiched between Darwin's and Carson's, took the conceptual step from chain to network:

> All things by immortal power
> Near or far
> Hiddenly
> To each other linkèd are,
> That thou canst not stir a flower
> Without troubling of a star.

In general, one does not put poetical statements under a microscope, but it is worth doing so with Thompson's lines, for they throw light on an important historical question: Why did most scientists take so long to accept the idea of a system? Physicists were at the top of the peck-order of scientists until about the middle of the twentieth century, and their habits of thought set the fashion for all science— and these habits did not include systematic thinking. Narrowly analytical thinking was the mode. Engineering, a child of physics, seldom departed from this pattern; much of the harm that engineers have unwittingly done to the environment is an inevitable outcome of nonsystematic thinking.

Curiously, the systematic approach is implicit in classical physics, but it was not often made explicit. We need to see why. Thompson's statement that we cannot "stir a flower without troubling of a star" is one that a Newtonian physicist would have to agree is literally true —though it would never occur to him to say it. Newton's universal law of gravitation specifically says that nothing in the universe can be moved without changing the trajectories of every other thing:

> *Every body attracts every other body* with a force that is directly proportional to the product of their masses and inversely proportional to the square of the distance between them.

Faith in the validity of Newton's view produced the discovery of the planet Neptune in 1845. Until that time the most distant known planet was Uranus. Measuring its orbit, astronomers found that Uranus was sometimes as much as one minute of arc away from where it "should" have been—about one-thirtieth of the diameter of the moon as seen from the earth. Evidently its trajectory was being "troubled" by a planet still farther out. The position of this body was calculated and lo! Neptune was discovered—first by theory and then by observation. The motion of an unknown body had "troubled" that of a known, though the distance between them was never less than a billion miles.

I have a flower before me. As I lift it "up"—away from the center of the earth—it is literally true that I alter the position and motion of the earth, the moon, Uranus, Neptune, and every other body in the universe, out to the farthest galaxy. That so much is implicit in Newton's scheme is undeniable; and yet neither he nor any other physicist in the next three centuries developed the idea of a system.

Why not? Basically because of the quantitative significance of that phrase "inversely proportional." If two bodies (like Uranus and Neptune) are a billion miles—10^9 miles—apart, the attraction between them must be multiplied by a factor of 10^{-18}. If the distance is 25 million million miles—2.5×10^{13} miles, the average distance between stars—then the attraction between them must be multiplied by a number only a little greater than 10^{-27}. The attenuation of forces by the distances of astronomy is so overwhelming that physicists are quite justified in using the words "insignificant" and "negligible," as they so often do—and in ignoring Francis Thompson's poetry.

The words "insignificant" and "negligible" play a much lesser role in the vocabulary of biologists. For one thing, the objects of the biologists' study are all on this earth and not very far apart. For another, they move around. More important, they reproduce, and this brings in the word "exponential" with its overpowering implications. With exponential reproduction, fewness of numbers and smallness of size cease to be "negligible."

A single bacterial cell lands on the lining of the throat of a man. Does it matter?

A Newtonian physicist, after determining that the bacterium weighs only 10^{-18} times as much as the man—only 0.000000000000-000001 as much—would dismiss the event as inconsequential.

A biologist would not. He would ask first, "Is it alive?" If the bacterium is alive and capable of reproducing on the lining of the throat, the population of its descendants may double every 20 minutes. In 4 hours there may be 4096 cells; in 8 hours 16,777,216; and in a day . . . well, in a day, if the cells could keep up so brisk an exponential rate (which they cannot) there would be more than 10^{21} bacterial cells in the man, and the aggregate weight of them would be 5000 times that of the host. (Now we see why the exponential rate of increase cannot be maintained.) All this from only one cell . . . increasing exponentially.

If the bacterium is a disease-producer it may kill its host, the man; and if the man is a king, and an important one—and if the crown prince is an imbecile—then the falling of a bacterial cell that weighs only 7×10^{-14} grams on the royal pharynx may literally change the history of the world.*

There is a Danish proverb that says: "Do not despise a small wound, a poor relative, or a humble enemy." Biologists would add: ". . . or *any* thing that increases exponentially, no matter how small." Even one DDT-resistant mosquito in a population of billions will, by increasing exponentially, make a mockery of DDT-control. Every chemical control program selects for its own failure.

"Inverse square" phenomena are encountered over and over again by physicists; by contrast, exponential relationships are the daily fare of biologists. By habit, the two kinds of specialists look at the world differently. Where physicists habitually—and safely—dismiss most

* Herbert J. Muller, in *The Uses of the Past* (p. 34), remarks that history is made "philosophically absurd" by trifling, fortuitous events of this sort. "In 1920, for example, the pacific King Alexander of Greece died of blood-poisoning, due to the bite of a pet monkey; a general election led to the recall of King Constantine, who thereupon started a disastrous war on the Turks. Winston Churchill observed, 'A quarter of a million persons died of that monkey's bite.'"

of the things of the world as unimportant, biologists have learned that they must at least try to keep all of them in mind, even the humblest. Significantly, Darwin's last great research was done on earthworms, which proved to be genuinely important in the "economy of nature," small and hidden though they be. Soil is made more fertile by their plowings, and the foundations of abandoned buildings are buried under their intestinal castings, thus being saved for the delight of archaeologists of a later age.

If you keep everything in mind, the image of a chain does not suffice; your mind must move on to a network or web, in three dimensions (four if you include, as you must, the dimension of time). Visualization becomes difficult, so you have to settle for two-dimensional simplifications. Figure 2 shows one such, a *partial* representation of "the web of life"—Darwin's phrase—in an aspen parkland. The arrows indicate who feeds on whom. Plainly, anything that happens to any one element in this web of life will affect, more or less, all the other elements.

In recent times the contrast between the attitudes of physicists and biologists has lessened. Physics, the older science, began with the simplest problems which, paradoxically, concerned the largest bodies at the greatest distances, i.e., the heavenly planets and stars. Wisely, physicists long avoided tackling some closer problems, like the weather. There was good reason for this avoidance: the atmosphere *is* a system, not unlike the systems of biology, though orders of magnitude simpler. Even so, it was much too complex for physics until powerful modern computers became available—though the best computers still may not be powerful enough.

It may be just as well if the technology of weather prediction and control lags for a while, for the minds of many physicists and technologists (some in positions of political power) still have not adjusted to the ecological revolution of thought. Many of them are only too anxious to control the weather—"for the good of mankind," they say. They do not yet realize that in the weather system, as in all systems, "we can never do merely one thing." When they gleefully report that they have been able to cause more rain to fall in Texas, they do not ask what effect this had on New York. Capriciously, they talk of reversing the flow of rivers or ocean currents in order to make

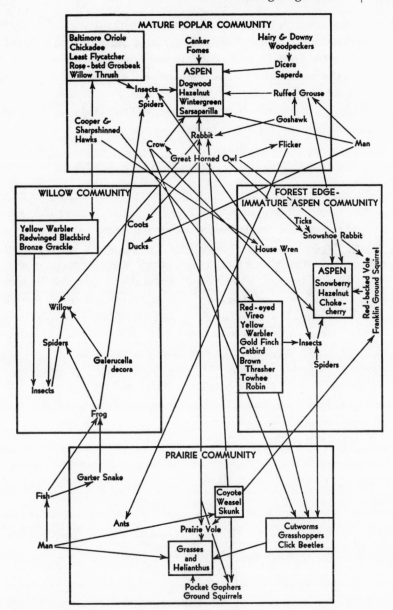

FIGURE 2. A small part of the web of life. Part of the ecological community of an aspen parkland in Canada. Each arrow points toward a prey or food organism. (From Richard Hesse, translated by W. C. Allee and K. P. Schmidt, *Ecological Animal Geography.* New York: Wiley, 1951)

what they see as a desirable local change, without seriously asking what the effects will be on the other side of the world, or a decade later. Their enthusiasm is the enthusiasm of the "practical man," that is, a man who is blind to the complexity of the web of the world (perhaps willfully so).

As always, a poet saw the danger first. William Blake, early in the nineteenth century, made this prayer:

> . . . God us keep
> From single vision, and Newton's sleep.

A poetical biologist, the French physiologist Claude Bernard, later in the century foresaw a growing together of dangerously diverging lines of thought: "I am convinced a time will come when the physiologist, the poet, and the philosopher will all speak the same language and mutually understand each other." That language is proving to be the language of ecology. It is also the language of "systems analysis" and "operations research," disciplines whose roots lie entirely outside biology. The branches of all three disciplines are now converging, casting a shadow over Newton's single vision. The language of these disciplines has a grammar that is complex and subtle. The minds behind this language, as well as the habits of thinking it brings into being, are Darwinian in essence, not Newtonian. No more can small beginnings, the incrementals of time, and the web of the world be ignored.

Not on a spaceship.

CHAPTER 6

Evil: State or Process?

"A civilization that can put men on the moon," it has often been said, "can surely solve the problems of poverty, the city, mass transportation, and crime in the streets." Nothing could be further from the truth. It was a Newtonian civilization that put men on the moon; but only a civilization guided by Darwinian minds can solve the really important problems remaining before us.

Focused on the malfunctioning of systems, the Newtonian mind can be worse than no mind at all. "The people who do the most harm," said Oscar Wilde, "are the people who try to do most good." Consider the way poverty has been attacked in our time, by those who see the problem of poverty as a problem in the redistribution of wealth. This approach is admirably summed up in a statement made by Dr. George A. Wiley on behalf of the National Welfare Rights Organization, addressed to the Democratic Platform Committee in Chicago, 1968:

> The basic cure for poverty is money. We believe that the way to do something about poverty is to give people the money they need. . . .

This statement was reprinted in *I. F. Stone's Weekly* under the admiring heading: AUTHENTIC VOICE OF THE POOR AT CHICAGO. It may indeed be the authentic voice of the poor—but is it the voice of wisdom?

The question we must ask is this: Is poverty—

a state?

—or—

the symptom of a process?

The distinction can be made clear by changing the example. A man has a fever. Is the fever a state? Or the symptom of a process?

If it is merely a state, the answer to the problem of fever is simple: turn on the air-conditioner and the fan and cool him off, until the state of his body is lowered from 104° Fahrenheit to 98.6° F. A state is easy to change—by direct means.

But if his fever is the symptom of a process, the solution to the problem is much more subtle and far harder to find. Actually, fever is, as everyone knows, the symptom of a process. Or, more exactly, of many different processes. No doctor says, "The way to do something about fever is to give the patient the coolness he needs." Physicians try to get at the processes rather than the symptoms.

Paradoxically, the best treatment for an elevated body temperature is usually to elevate the temperature even more. This works because it favors curative processes that attack the microbes that cause the fever.

Note: *A true solution may be counterintuitive*—that is, it may be exactly the opposite of what uninformed "intuition" would suggest to us. Counterintuitive solutions are common when we are dealing with pathological processes.

Common, but not universal, unfortunately—if they were, there would be an effective stereotyped response to every ill: "Be counterintuitive." (This would become the new "intuition.") A stereotyped counterintuitive treatment of poverty would, I suppose, be to rob the poor, making them still poorer. But no one seriously proposes this attack on poverty, so we can ignore it. The problem is much too subtle for simple approaches. Some other counterintuitive approach must be sought.

Sometimes the simply intuitive response is, in fact, the best one. If, for example, a man's fever soars to 106° F., the best thing to do is to pack him in ice immediately to get his temperature back to the "normal" abnormal range before his brain is irrevocably damaged. Then you may once again apply counterintuitive measures.

Is it true that "the way to do something about poverty is to give people money"? Occasionally it may be. But it is obvious that this is not usually a solution, for, if it were, the well-to-do could solve the problem of poverty by themselves, by giving *their* money to the poor —who would promptly become nonpoor and would remain so, according to the implicit hypothesis. But those who recommend money for the poor do not volunteer *their* money; thus they show how little they believe in their own theories.

One of the accompaniments of poverty is poor housing. Circular processes are common, almost universal, in social affairs and it is undeniable that poor houses handicap the people who live in them and add to the difficulties of their escaping poverty. It is quite understandable if the mind of a well-to-do and well-meaning person, after a visit to the slums, generates this implicit argument:

1. Poverty is found in slums.
2. Therefore let us destroy the slums, and thus:
3. We will destroy poverty.

Some such implicit argument underlies the Housing Act of 1949. Since unassisted private enterprise offered no solution to the urban slum problem, the federal government was to step in and make it possible. Because it was unthinkable that this should be done entirely outside the free enterprise system (that would be socialism), the Federal Housing Agency, after condemning, buying, and clearing the land in the inner city, was to sell it to private "developers"— "development" always sounds good—for a fraction of the cost, thus enabling them to make their rightful profit, without which they would not do their part.

Some of the land cleared for development cost the public $1 million an acre. All of it was fantastically expensive—to taxpayers, not to "developers."

At this point it is tempting to view the whole project as a gigantic steal by greedy capitalist pigs. But that would be missing the point. Private enterprisers were dealt into the hand because that's the way we play the game in the United States (most of the time). Their profits, on the prices they had to pay, were not exorbitant: the extravagance came in the "write-down" of prices made by the federal government to get them to enter the game. The "write-down" was done for the noblest of motives—to break the circle of poverty. If the Housing Act had been successful, few would have quibbled about private profits. After all, if we could, by letting private contractors make a $10 billion profit, forever abolish poverty, wouldn't we jump at the opportunity?

Any do-good legislation, to be passed in the United States, must appeal to two motives: the philanthropic and the egotistical. The second is most commonly served by profit-making, but gain in political power motivates many men more. Our national self-image is such that probably no far-reaching legislation can be passed by pointing *only* to the profits and power that can be gained from it. Only a few can gain in this way, whereas many can bask in the glow of national generosity. Idealism legitimates profits. Whatever the hidden balance of motives, it is the do-good aspect of the legislation that figures most heavily in the public debate. Unless the arguments seem plausible in this area, far-reaching legislation will not be passed. So it is precisely on the do-good features that we must focus our attention.

It is now obvious that the Housing Act of 1949 was essentially wrong because it was based on a simplistic Newtonian view of the world. "Slum clearance" is a Newtonian response to slums and poverty. "Urban renewal" is the euphemism that was coined to sell the idea. By the late 1950s, when the results began coming in, "urban renewal" was bitterly identified as "Negro-removal." (The term "black" had not yet replaced its etymological equivalent, "Negro.")

And black-removal it was. By the time the renewers were through with their pretty work, rents had doubled and a different class of people had moved into the renewed area. The slums had been removed—and so had the slum-dwellers. Where were they now? Not in the nice new buildings, but in some other ancient buildings which were now decaying faster than ever, creating new slums for the next generation of urban renewers to "develop"—at a profit.

That was one pattern. The housing program evolved as its faults became apparent. In some areas, to make it possible for poor people (relatively poor—not the poorest) to live in the new housing, upper limits were set on the amount of income a housing-project-dweller could have. The poor could live there; lower middle class could not. This sounded like a just scheme, but it introduced selection into the picture, and Darwinian logic took over. The community evolved.

Remember that the aim of the Housing Act was to "break the

cycle of poverty" at the housing link, thus enabling some of the newly housed poor to climb up the economic ladder. But the "income test" of eligibility for housing meant that those who in fact behaved as the reformers hoped they would, those who bettered themselves, were compelled to move out of government housing (often into worse housing at higher rents, incidentally), leaving behind only those who apparently did not have what it took to improve their economic situation, thus depriving the others thereafter of the daily vision of their example. Perhaps also those left behind may have had their springs of action weakened by the feeling that they were the rejects of society. Whatever one thinks of the relation of income to human quality, it is difficult to believe that the average quality of the slum community is unaffected by such a selection process. Variety—which itself is part of the quality of life—certainly is diminished. Pursuing this path, city after city has replaced unsightly old tenements with a moderate amount of juvenile delinquency and crime with sleek new tenements where crime and disorder are at such high levels that policemen refuse to answer calls for help, except in groups.

Before the experiment was made, most well-to-do outsiders, appalled at the visual appearance of old slums, probably assumed that life could not be worse so it was justifiable to carry out almost any large-scale experiment without making a careful study first. Inhabitants of old slums, particularly ones that have been stable for generations, do not always see things the way outsiders do. Listen to Sophia Loren recalling her childhood:

> The roots of my life are in Naples and in the neighboring town of Pozzuoli, where I grew up. A guidebook describes this area as being one of the most squalid slums in all Italy, but it never seemed that way to me. Life is open in Naples. There is vitality in Naples—warmth and comfort in the streets. In Naples you have a feeling that all humanity is very close and loving.

The camera deceives us. Those who have no personal contact with life in the slums can easily be persuaded of the beneficent effects of urban renewal by "before" and "after" photographs. They see ramshackle wood dwellings with flaking paint replaced by smooth concrete and big windows. But what happens to the lives of the people therein? They may be uprooted from genuine communities, in the best sense, and scattered to the winds to find substitute housing wherever they can, housing that is almost invariably farther from work, more expensive, and often even more crowded. Juvenile delinquency always increases when the sense of community is destroyed. But the camera, organ par excellence of Newtonian single vision, tells us nothing of this. Unfortunately, our information-gathering systems are ruled by the tyranny of the camera.

Poverty is only one of the many evils that we have tried to eliminate by Newtonian means. Table 3 lists several others, with some of the typical Newtonian responses. Some of these may be inherently sound, even though inadequate. For example, traffic lights do make congestion more bearable. Others may actually contribute to the evil itself. Responding to the high price of land by building skyscrapers results in a further increase in land-price (given our taxing system), thus setting up the vicious circle that is a root cause of the hypertrophy of cities.

TABLE 3

Responses to Evil

Nonsystematic attempts to solve evils
that are the symptoms of pathological processes

CODE NAME OF EVIL	NEWTONIAN RESPONSE	DARWINIAN RESPONSE
High price of land	Build skyscrapers	?
Scarcity of time	Build supersonic transport planes	?
Congestion	Buy more traffic lights	?
Waste of commuting	Build superhighways	?
Racism	Buy more school buses	?
Crime	Buy more patrol cars	?
Drugs	Buy electronic "dope sniffers"	?
Anything	*Buy hardware*	*First,* THINK

The responses listed in the second column of Table 3 might be called the "B responses"—*Buy* or *Build,* without thinking about the systematic consequences of the response. B responses require a minimum of information and planning. Our economic system is already set up for such responses. Contractors and purveyors compete to furnish their services; only a minimum of bureaucratic overseeing is needed.

Table 3 is unusual in that one of its columns is essentially a blank. Ordinarily, for esthetic reasons perhaps, one does not include blank columns in a table; but I think the inclusion here serves a useful purpose. A mapmaker in earlier days often had to include a large white area on his maps, which he labeled "Terra Incognita." It was better than faking detail, or reframing a map to omit it. It served to call people's attention to what was yet to be learned. It no doubt stimulated exploration. In mapping the problems of our time it is a wholesome discipline to indicate clearly their Terrae Incognitae, with the same end in mind.

The Newtonian response to almost any social evil is to *buy hardware* in the hope that the problem will somehow be solved by the mere magnitude of the expenditure. It seldom is. The Darwinian response is to *think* before acting—i.e., to study and to analyze, on the assumption that we are dealing with a complex web of causes and effects, and that intuitive responses will probably do more harm than good. The evils listed in Table 3 are certainly united in a network that includes the characteristics of a finite environment as well as those of a limitless ability to reproduce. A general analytical framework for dealing with environmental problems is given in Part Two of this book. In Part Three it is shown that the same analysis applies to problems of reproduction and population growth as well. For the present, in this chapter in which so much attention has been given to poverty, let me point out that the word "proletariat" has a literal Latin meaning of "those with many offspring." Its etymology suggests an ancient hypothesis about the source of poverty. This suggestion was ignored by Marx, who had spoken eagerly and often about poverty and the proletariat, but reluctantly and seldom about population. His example has been faithfully followed by most liberals in the twentieth century.

In the last ten years there has been a great increase in the number of investigators looking at social evils with a Darwinian eye. Land-use and the great complex of problems called "the urban problem" (which includes all the ones listed in Table 3) are now being subjected to searching systems analysis by teams of investigators headed by Jay M. Forrester and Dennis L. Meadows at the Massachusetts Institute of Technology, Kenneth E. F. Watt of the University of California at Davis, and C. S. Holling of the University of British

Columbia. Most of the men on the roster are engineers and biologists who have seen the relevance of systems analysis to society's problems, as many men trained earlier as "urbanologists" do not. Unfortunately, many urbanologists of the old sort are still influential politically. For some time to come we will be beset with extravagant proposals to cure poverty, crime, or what have you by people afflicted with Newton's single vision.

CHAPTER 7

Guilty Until Proven Innocent

It is arguable whether being a king in the old days was preferable to being a commoner, most of the time; but when it came to dying there is no doubt that a king had the worst of it. The trouble was that he was given the best medical care available in his time. His commoners were lucky enough not to be able to afford it.

Consider what Charles II was subjected to, as he lay dying in 1685.

A pint of blood was extracted from his right arm; then eight ounces from the left shoulder; next an emetic, two physics, and an enema consisting of 15 substances. Then his head was shaved and a blister raised on the scalp. To purge the brain a sneezing powder was given, then cowslip powder to strengthen it. Meanwhile more emetics, soothing drinks and more bleeding; also a plaster of pitch and pigeon dung applied to the royal feet. Not to leave anything undone, the following substances were taken internally: melon seeds, manna, slippery elm, black cherry water, extract of lily of the valley, peony, lavender, pearls dissolved in vinegar, gentian root, nutmeg, and finally 40 drops of extract of human skull. As a last resort bezoar stone was employed. But the royal patient died.

Died of what? Of the medical treatment itself more than likely—an "iatrogenic" death, as the medical profession delicately puts it ("physician-generated," literally). Kings could afford such a death; commoners could not. The biochemist L. J. Henderson reckoned that until about the year 1905 calling in a physician to attend the sick *decreased* the patient's chances for survival; after that time medical attention gradually became of positive value. With the coming of sulfa drugs in the 1930s and the antibiotics in the 1940s, the balance swung definitely in favor of medical treatment.

We deride the flounderings of the physicians treating King Charles's ailment (whatever it was): but are we any more intelligent or effective in treating the ills of society? Posterity may conclude not. In both instances an ailing and little-understood system is treated as if it were merely a state that was awry. The measures used are all too often merely a form of sympathetic magic: removing blood to cure high blood pressure, or applying money to cure poverty. As Oscar Wilde said of the social do-gooders, it is much easier

> to have sympathy with suffering than it is to have sympathy with thought. Accordingly, with admirable though misdirected intentions, they very seriously and very sentimentally set themselves to the task of remedying the evils that they see. But their remedies do not cure the disease: they merely prolong it. Indeed, their remedies are part of the disease.

That was written in 1891. Are we more successful today? Have we, in treating the ills of the body politic, yet passed the equivalent of Henderson's 1905 line for human medicine? Do we yet have the capability of doing more good than harm by social interventions that *intend* good? ("But we just have to do *something!*" says the do-gooder when faced with suffering. But suppose that that something increases suffering? Are good intentions then an acceptable excuse?)

When ignorant, what is the best thing to do? If a would-be physician offers us a nostrum, whether for the human body or for the body politic, should we try it? Should we be adventurous or conservative? Should the peddler be allowed (or encouraged) to peddle his pills?

Where does the burden of proof lie? This is the fundamental question. In criminal law, as practiced in Britain and America, a man is "innocent until proven guilty." Quite naturally this policy has been carried over to the realm of medical nostrums. It is in the interest of the peddler that this extension of the law is made. Patients, clutching desperately at straws, often acquiesce (and if they die, their second thoughts don't matter).

Scientists, however, see things otherwise. Science is an occupation in which most experiments fail. Those who cleave to science in the face of constant disappointment expect failure and disappointment as a matter of course (though naturally they hope that the usual outcome will fail to appear once in a while). Confronted with any new, untried nostrum, a scientist, if called upon to place a bet, will bet that it won't work. Such is the conservative judgment.

The overwhelming probability is that any newly proposed remedy won't work. More: experience shows that there is an almost equally high probability that the new nostrum will cause actual harm.

The most intelligent way of dealing with the unknown is in terms of probability. Therefore we should assume that each new remedy proposed will do positive harm, until the most exhaustive tests and carefully examined logic indicate otherwise.

Guilty until proven innocent—this should be our assumption regarding the value of each newly proposed remedy. The law regarding remedies should be sharply differentiated from the law governing human beings accused of crimes.

Although understood for decades by almost all scientists and a great many laymen, the principle of "guilty until proven innocent" was not given effective legal status in the United States until 1962. The change would not have been made even then, in all probability, except for the fortunate tragedy—if such a paradoxical expression is permissible—of the thalidomide babies. The newly discovered tranquilizer thalidomide was used by millions of people before one of its dreadful "side-effects" was discovered: taken by a mother in early pregnancy, it produced badly malformed babies, typically with stumps for arms and legs. Thousands of deformed children were born in Europe before the causal connection was uncovered in America, where the drug had not yet been approved for release. The delay on this side of the water was probably due less to prescient suspicions than it was to normal bureaucratic delays. There's something to be said for inertia and conservatism.

In the wake of the thalidomide tragedy the Kefauver-Harris amendments to the Food, Drug and Cosmetics Act were passed in

1962. These amendments put the burden of proof on the proposer of a new remedy, who, before his product could be licensed for distribution, had to show that it was:

a. effective

b. harmless (or, more exactly: did more good than harm).

This was a revolutionary change in the assumptions of the law. That it should be made first in the area of medicine is understandable: the common man's fear of sickness and death is so intense that the usually effective cries of "socialistic," "un-American," and "a step down the path to the police state" fall on deaf ears. "Better dead than Red"? Not in the mind of John Q. Citizen when he is confronted with the real possibility of death. Moral perfection in death is a luxury most men can do without. In 1962, through their elected representatives, the American people decreed that there are some areas in which they are willing to assume "guilty until proven innocent." Will this attitude spread to other fields? We shall see.

Bringing about an administrative revolution is more difficult than merely passing a revolutionary law. Only gradually did the Food and Drug Administration alter its attitude toward newly proposed nostrums. Administrative minds had been too long biased in favor of the profit motive. Not until about 1970 did retirement and reform bring the FDA personnel to the point of carrying out the aims of the Kefauver-Harris amendments in the vast area of re-evaluation of old remedies.

A European pharmacopoeia of the seventeenth century listed some 6000 drugs in use. In 1960 a similar list in the United States boasted about 3000 drugs, in over 10,000 different formulations. Not much of a reduction in three centuries. Undoubtedly most of the 3000 nostrums are worthless; probably most are more or less harmful. But they were protected by tradition until the Kefauver-Harris amendments were directed at them. Now they must stand on their own feet—i.e., pass a gantlet of rigorous and objectively controlled tests before they can continue on the approved list.

The FDA has begun to remove whole blocs of traditional remedies from the approved list, to the acute discomfiture of drug houses, which are fighting back. Some of the delaying tactics are successful. The long-term results will be determined by the extent to which the scientific attitude has permeated the public mind. Those who understand the connection of probability with intelligent action in the face of the unknown are necessarily conservative and assume *guilty until proven innocent*.

A word of warning is in order. It is always dangerous to take a rule that is good in a limited context and generalize it widely without careful point-by-point testing. The doctrine of "innocent until proven guilty" is no doubt the best of all general rules in criminal law, where the treatment of *people* is at stake. Extending it to *things* led to widespread deception of consumers. It would be at least as unwise to extend the doctrine of "guilty until proven innocent" from the area of things to that of people (i.e., to the criminal law). Generalizations should not be escalated.

The passage of the National Environmental Policy Act of 1969 (enacted into law on January 1, 1970) moved the nation significantly closer to applying the guilty-until-proven-innocent principle to the environmental realm. It did not go so far as to spell it out in general, but it did specify that any proposal of any agency of the federal government must be examined in minute detail for its effects on the environment.

Later in 1970 a small step was made toward applying the same principle to nongovernmental agencies. Henry Reuss, a Congressman from Wisconsin, had unearthed a still valid law governing the discharge of materials into inland waters, the 1899 Refuse Act. Surprisingly, considering its antiquity, this law said that nothing can be discharged into a navigable water without federal permission. Needless to say, consternation greeted the discovery of this old act. To enforce it immediately would be impossible both practically and politically.* A compromise scheme was put forward.

---

* The developing shift in the assumption of the law has not slipped in without notice by commercial interests. Shortly after he came into office President Nixon established a National Industrial Pollution Control Council, made up of some threescore presidents and board members of the wealthiest corporations in America (hardly the most promising group to monitor life on a spaceship). In 1971 this group alerted the President to a dreadful danger they saw looming on the horizon: "The view that no material should be permitted to be released into the environment unless it can be shown to be harmless to man and his environment . . . could be likened to a requirement of proof of innocence by

The Army Corps of Engineers was empowered to issue effluent licenses. Were it not for the changing temper of the times, this arrangement would have been rather like setting the fox to guard the chickens; but the corps is changing, and it worked out an agreement with the newly established Environmental Protection Agency whereby the EPA is to advise the corps on major requests. Because of the sheer volume of the new monitoring to be done, drastic changes in effluent discharge should not be expected soon; but the requirement that businesses reveal what they are discharging, and how much, moves industry a giant step toward initiating rigorous accounting for the flow of materials through its plants. A foundation is laid for environmental decisions to be made later from the standpoint of the general public.

Like the human body, the environment is an enormously complex system of interacting elements and processes—and most of the interactions are unknown. Disrupt this web of life with a random intervention: What is the probability that harm will *not* be done? It is surely vanishingly small. The conservative approach is, therefore, to make no change at all without an exhaustive investigation first.

That is not the way we have treated the environment in the past. Take as an example the detergent problem. We used to wash clothes with soap. It got them clean enough, and caused no great harm to the environment. But we didn't leave well enough alone: we replaced soap with detergents. In terms of the single measure "getting clothes clean," this was an advance. Detergents got them cleaner, and they worked better in hard water than did soap.

Unfortunately the detergents lasted almost indefinitely. Discharged into the streams and the ground water, they proved unsuitable as bacterial food and so they accumulated. Ponds below dams were often covered by billowing mountains of froth. It wasn't certain that detergents were particularly dangerous, but when a glass of water drawn from the tap had a "head" on it like a stein of beer, the public became alarmed. People did not like to be reminded that they drink sewage, more or less modified by time and treatment, but

---

the accused rather than proof of guilt by the accuser." Their (external) vision is excellent; what they signally lack is insight into the problem. What they abhor deserves praise. Will they ever see this? Considering that their average age is probably greater than sixty, and taking account of the fact that they are *very* busy men, one would guess not.

sewage none the less. The "hard detergents"—called "hard" because they are hard for the bacteria to decompose—made it difficult to forget the origin of the drinking water.

Faced with a mounting public outcry, the cleanser companies, at considerable expense, changed from hard detergents to soft. The soft detergents had phosphate compounds in them. Phosphates are required by all living things. Soft detergents are easily decomposed by bacteria, releasing phosphate ions that are utilizable by anything that lives. They're food. . . . It looked as though the cleanser industry had found the perfect solution.

Unfortunately, it's possible to have too much of a good thing. Our cleanly housewives require about two and a half million tons of detergents a year, which (on decomposing) add about a million tons of phosphates to the ground water, the streams, the lakes, and coastal estuaries. That's a lot of phosphate. Phosphate is quite often the limiting factor in algal growth, so if you double the phosphate concentration you double the amount of algae. Ten times as much phosphate, ten times as many algae.

Is that bad? Not necessarily. Algae are part of the food chain, so a small increase in phosphate can increase the production of desirable fish. But when the increase is large, the picture changes. Great mats of algae are produced, and the species composition of the algal mats swings over in favor of blue-green algae, which are not readily eaten. The mats grow so thick that they cut out the sunlight to the lower algae, which die, setting up anaerobic conditions that favor more death. The water stinks and fish die. "Eutrophication" sets in—"perfect feeding," literally, but the practical meaning is perfectly terrible overfeeding of the aqueous world.

As they perceived the disadvantages of phosphates the cleansermen looked around for something else. This time they came up with enzymes—digestive enzymes gotten out of fractured bacterial cells, which can easily be grown by the millions of millions. The proteolytic enzymes—protein-digesting—were touted for their ability to remove resistant stains, of blood for example. Enzymes were added to other cleansing agents. Whether they were or were not effective is disputed, but the dispute soon became of only academic interest because it was discovered that the new formulation had a very serious defect.

All enzymes are proteins. Foreign proteins—proteins derived from flesh other than human—can produce allergic reactions in humans who are repeatedly exposed to them. There are great individual differences is susceptibility to allergic reactions, but if millions of people are exposed to an allergen, thousands will react adversely. Soon after the introduction of enzyme-detergents, housewives started turning up with rashes and respiratory symptoms. Workers in the factories where the detergents were packaged were even more affected, being more exposed.

What next? Next came NTA, or nitrilotriacetate, to give it its full name. No phosphate in it. Unfortunately there is some evidence—not conclusive—that it causes birth defects, perhaps only when combined with heavy metal pollutants like cadmium or mercury, which (however) are not unknown in our environment. . . . Obviously the cleanser-men never thought of *that*.

What's the moral of this long and unfinished story? NTA has been phased out (before being really phased in), and phosphates have been retained while the industry looks for another chemical compound.

Why don't the cleanser-men test the compounds before they market them? *Test them for what?* There's the rub. They have R & D departments—Research and Development—that are constantly testing, but the focus of their investigations is narrow, Newtonian: to find something that will clean. They are not public-health researchers; they are not ecologists; they are not systems analysts. It never occurred to them that a good cleanser might, in time, raise rashes; or cause birth defects; or kill fish; or put a head on tap water. These are not obvious eventualities: why should anyone even think of looking for them?

The next chemical candidate for the cleanser market will no doubt be checked for all these evils—but it may well turn out to have yet another disadvantage that no one dreamed of looking for.

The cleanser industry R & D is looking for just one thing: a better way to clean. But we can never do merely one thing—this is the basic ecological wisdom. Every innovation is an intervention in the entire ecological system. Ideally, we should check every one of the millions of elements in the web of life, every one of the unnumbered trillions of relationships, before adopting any innovation. This is impossible. So we check a few of the most obvious and then hold our breath as we make the change. A small pilot-plant experiment may fail to reveal results that appear only when the change is expanded to a large scale. Perhaps only a few percent of the people exposed may be affected—but a few percent of a population of 205,000,000 is millions. Or the adverse affects may take time to develop—and time inevitably passes.

Just thinking about it is enough to make a technology-liberal into a technology-conservative. At times one wonders if one shouldn't go back to using soap. Or pounding clothes on a rock in the creek.

In this, as in almost every other unsolved problem of our time, population plays a role. Suppose the United States had only twenty million inhabitants instead of over two hundred million. Remembering that phosphates are a good thing if not too concentrated, we realize that with the lower population density there would probably be no reason to become concerned with the disadvantages of new detergents. We would know only the advantages.

The disadvantages of each new intervention in the web of life increase with population size. Recycling can remove the pollutant—but not if its concentration passes a critical value, as it will at some level of population.

A small population can be cavalier in its assessment of the disadvantage of new technology, and get away with it. Not so a large population.

The larger the population grows, the more conservative it necessarily becomes in its attitude toward technological innovation. Either that, or it suffers more.

CHAPTER 8

Word Magic

The official function of language is to facilitate thought and communication. One of its unofficial functions, just as real, is to *prevent* thought and communication.

Living in a time when machine-gunning unarmed peasants in a primitive village is called "pacification," a time when a Secretary of Defense says that our objective, in subjecting a country smaller than Oklahoma to a greater weight of bombs than fell on all the bombed areas in Europe and the South Pacific during the entire World War II, "is not a military victory but . . . the right of self-determination" —living in such a time, we surely do not have to be told that language can be deceptive. But it is a perpetual source of wonder how often what purports to describe reality in fact aims to coerce our perception of reality into delusory channels. Language is a coercive weapon.

But coercive language never announces itself as such: if it did, its coercive power would vanish. Successfully coercive language *always* appears to be merely descriptive.

Nevertheless, he who unmasks coercive language does not earn the prompt thanks of those whose illusions he destroys. We feel such fools to have been taken in. We resent having the mask pulled away; and, for a while, we deny the corrected vision.

Rachel Carson appreciated this after she published *Silent Spring* in 1962. The vindictiveness of the criticism to which she was subjected strongly suggests that she had hurt people's pride—as indeed

66

she had. She showed people that they had been hookwinked by vested interests who had used the nominally descriptive term "pesticide" to coerce their perceptions of the true and total effects of such chemicals as DDT.

Definition: "Pesticide"—something that kills pests. . . . Implicit in the definition is the black-and-white view that organisms can be divided into pests and non-pests, and that pests are wholly and always undesirable. Likewise, since nothing else is mentioned, the word implies that a pesticide kills nothing but pests. A Newtonian view.

The *subject—predicate* structure of our language makes it all too easy to assume that the world is composed only of (*one cause*)—(*one effect*) logical pairings. But it isn't. The world is a network, the "causes" of any effect are multiple, and the effects of any "cause" are likewise multiple (and seldom predictable). Language, perfected no doubt a hundred thousand years before ecology was discovered, does not routinely mirror the poet's ecological truth that we cannot stir a flower without troubling a star. . . . Language is so linear, so sequential.

We can never do merely one thing. How should we speak of the substances now called "pesticides," to come closer to the ecological truth? At the very least, DDT should be called an avicide, since it kills birds. Inserted into the web of life, any so-called "pesticide" will have widespread repercussions. Miss Carson gave publicity to the large, but not widely known, literature on the repercussions. Facts discovered since 1962 have strengthened her case. Any new "pesticide" really should be called a "biocide," until it is proven otherwise. Guilty until proven innocent. The word "pesticide" coerces the hearer to be blind to its unwanted effects. By contrast, "biocide" coerces us into suspiciously looking for them. (Of course, such intelligent suspiciousness may be bad for business.)

It should not be thought that coercive terms are introduced only by vested interests that have something to gain by our blindness. All of us use coercive terms to fool ourselves. We want the world to be simple so that we can easily control it. Like the people we call "primitive," we unconsciously hope to control the world with words. Like our fellow primitives, we are taken in by word magic.

"Side-effects" is most potent word magic. The Zambezi River in Africa was dammed, with World Bank financing, to create the 1700-square-mile Lake Kariba. The effect *desired:* electricity. The "side-effects" *produced:* (1) destructive flooding of rich alluvial agricultural land above the dam; (2) uprooting of long-settled farmers from this land to be resettled on poorer hilly land that required farming practices with which they were not familiar; (3) impoverishment of these farmers and (4) the migration of many of them to city slums; (5) social disorder of uprooted, impoverished people; (6) creation of a new biotic zone along the lake shore that favored the multiplication of tsetse flies; (7) trypanosomiasis (sleeping sickness) among humans; and (8) over-all diminution of protein supply of the region.

"Side-effects"? What does the term mean anyway? Is trypanosomiasis any more a "side-effect" than electricity?

Definition: "Side-effect": any effect we don't want, and the existence of which we will deny as long as we can.

We can never do merely one thing. Does this mean that we can never do *anything?* Not at all. It might have been possible to get electricity out of the Zambezi River without producing all those "side-effects"—*might*—but if so, it would have been because damming was combined with many other operations, all of them based on a great deal of preparatory investigation. Which would cost a great deal of money.

In any event, the consequences of a project should be followed closely, from month to month and year to year. Which also would cost money. When unwanted "side-effects" turn up, new projects should be promptly instigated to mitigate these consequences—in the hope that the new projects do not cause yet other unwanted and serious side-effects!

More money.

In the last analysis, if a thorough ecological study is made beforehand it will not infrequently turn out that the total projected costs—of main project plus subsidiary projects required to minimize so-called side-effects—are greater than the realistically projected benefit. If the projected costs are greater than the projected benefits, rational men will abandon the project.

Those who stand to gain financially from a project—dirt-moving

contractors, construction engineers, manufacturers of heavy equipment and the like—always (quite understandably) try to coerce us
into embarking on the project. One of the most powerful weapons in
their armory of word magic is the word "development." Let's put this
word under a magnifying lens.

What does "development" mean anyway? Its basic meaning de-
rives from embryology. A fertilized egg develops into an adult. A
tadpole develops into a frog. An acorn develops into an oak tree. A
simple-looking thing develops into something complicated, and often
surprisingly different. And more valuable.

Small becomes large. Potential becomes actual. . . . And (under
normal conditions) this development is *inevitable*.

We bow down before the inevitable. We respect it. In dramatic
literature, the high esteem in which we hold tragedy is related to this
fact. (There's nothing inevitable about comedy—it's just a happy
chance. We love it; but it doesn't move us inwardly.) He who would
persuade us of the correctness of his views is well advised to foster a
feeling of the inevitable. Karl Marx understood this: he discoursed
ad nauseam on the inevitable victory of communism.

Embryological development, given the normal conditions for life,
is truly inevitable. The program of development is written into the
genes from the earliest moments of selfhood. The all but valueless
little blob of tissue we call a salmon egg is programed to become a
delightfully valuable big fat salmon a few years later—if nothing
interferes with its development. Somehow it seems immoral even to
think of stopping development.

This is the feeling the big real-estate operator plays upon when he
calls himself a "developer." "Let me take this icky old swamp of
yours," he says, "and *develop* it into a beautiful community of lovely
homes." Or handsome factories. Or a colossal airport. Or high-rise
tenements.

If we say yes, he puts an end to thousands of ducks and geese, to
magic mornings of waiting in the blinds—shivering from the cold,
perhaps, but also getting goose pimples all over from the eerie
beauty of the wild bird calls piercing the gray dawn. The exquisite
but "undeveloped" natural beauty is pushed aside to make room for
whatever it is he has baptized as "development"—perhaps ticky-
tacky houses and all the shoddiness of mass-produced suburbia.

Development? Not on your life. *Destruction. Defacement.* These, if we must settle for single words, are just as likely to be true.

Inevitable? Not if we say *no.*

Row houses are not development. Dams are not development. Draining marshes is not development. Filling in bays is not development. Building six-lane highways is not development.

Change, yes; alteration, yes; intervention, yes.

It may be either good or bad. But it is neither inevitable nor natural. *It is not development.*

"Development" is word magic, designed to keep us from thinking.

CHAPTER 9

Sweet-Singing Economists

If you make us meet your unrealistic air-pollution standards, said Union Carbide to the Environmental Protection Agency, we'll just have to close our Marietta plant and put 625 workers on the relief rolls.

It will ruin us if we have to treat the discharge from our Port Angeles pulp mill, said Rayonier: we'll have to close down.

Impossible! said U.S. Steel. We'll go out of business if we can't dump ten million gallons of acid waste each year into San Francisco Bay.

The EPA was adamant; and all three industries gave in. They spent millions of dollars on pollution-control and stayed in business. They had threatened to use their workers as hostages in an environmental shoot-out. But they had been bluffing.

When it comes to the environmental shoot-out, not all businesses are bluffing. Sometimes the imposition of higher standards *is* followed by the closing down of a factory. Cause and effect? Not necessarily. The factory may have been marginal anyway, and the occasion merely made a convenient excuse for reaching a decision that was inevitable sooner or later.

Or, to put it another way: Which straw breaks the camel's back?

The imposition of external standards is sometimes a blessing in disguise. When U.S. Steel realized it really had to do something about its acid waste in San Francisco it found a user for it and saved the costs of dumping. It was money ahead. This is the sort of success

71

story that technological Pollyannas cherish, but it is rare. (If it were the rule, pollution would be no problem.) Once, a long time ago, a factory that was forced to clean up the suffocating sulfur dioxide in its flue-gas found it could convert it to sulfur and sell it for more than enough to pay for the cleaning process. The story is often cited. But that was a long time ago. In the meantime the market has changed, and it now costs $30 a ton to extract sulfur from flue-gas—and the sulfur then can be sold for only $15. You don't get rich that way. That's typical.

Businesses fight pollution-control for economic reasons—but that doesn't account for the vigor with which they resist. In the long run, there may be no real economic reason for opposing a clean-up, because management can pass the costs on to the consumers. The vehemence of the resistance springs from moral fervor. Management feels it's being screwed. Moralistic hang-ups often prevent managers from even looking for a way to turn a penny by cleaning up. Indignation interferes with economic judgment.

Why the moralistic stance? Is it really unfair to demand that a business clean up the mess it makes? We can hardly expect a businessman to be objective enough to give an unbiased answer; but then, perhaps neither can an environmentalist, who has a vested interest of a different sort. How can we acquire the objectivity needed to answer this question?

Objectivity may be a gift of grace (as theologians might say)—something unsought, conferred on one as if from the outside. But it may also be won by seeking. There are psychological tools for cultivating it. One of the best of these is the "man from Mars" gimmick, an invention (I believe) of the nineteenth-century philosopher-essayist Ernest Renan.

The trick is this: suppose I were a man from Mars, visiting the earth, observing it, and reporting back home to my people. I am (by hypothesis) perfectly rational, keenly observant, and admirably intelligent. I have no preconceptions. I have no vested interest in earthly affairs, and no reason for softening my speech to spare earthmen's feelings, since I am reporting only to my fellow Martians. . . . Looking at the pollution-control problem, what do I write to the folks back home? Let's see how a Martian's report might read.

I've stumbled [says our Martian] across a rather puzzling situation. In this town there is a factory called the Acme Widget Works. It turns out two products: (a) widgets, for which there seems to be a great demand (though I haven't yet figured out why); and (b) smoke, for which there is no demand whatever.

Black fumes fan out over the town, darkening paint on the workers' homes, killing the more delicate plants in their gardens, soiling their clothes, and in a hundred ways making more work for the housewives. Furthermore, it shortens the lives of all by increasing the incidence of asthma, emphysema, and other respiratory disease.

It's obvious to any Martian that the situation borders on idiocy; but it's not obvious to Earthlings. In fact, the most vocal ones are divided into two groups: the "ecologists" and the "economists." Ecology is the study of the relation of all living things to each other and to all the nonliving things in their environment. (There are over three million living species on Earth.) Economics is a study restricted to the mutual relationships of the members of a single species, *Homo sapiens*, with a cursory glance at only a few of the nonhuman components. The names of both sciences are derived from the Greek word *oikos*, which means home or household. Logically, it is obvious that economics is but a small specialty in the much larger science, ecology.

Sociologically, it is quite otherwise: the tail wags the dog. My studies show that the average salary of ecologists is $12,643 per year, while that of economists is $29,078, or 2.3 times as much. By a well-known Law, the social power of economists, relative to ecologists, is given by:

$$e^{2.3} = 9.974182$$

In round numbers, the social power of an economist is ten times as great as that of an ecologist. There are 73 times as many economists as ecologists, so the *total* social power of economists is 730 times that of the ecologists. Understandably, the public listens to the economists.

Whom do the economists listen to? When I asked several of them they said, "Truth!" or something like that; but this didn't jibe very well with their actions, so I carried my investigations further. Fortunately I was helped in this by stumbling across the work of a natural philosopher of the untouchable caste called

"Poets." I neglected to make a note of his name, but here is his theorem:

> Whose bread I eat,
> His song I sing.

This has been checked against reality and has been found to be 99.44 percent true. (The rather large discrepancy of 0.56 percent is yet to be explained.)

The bread of the economists comes from the factories; the song they sing is true.

I asked an economist who specialized in widgets: "What does a widget cost?"

"In today's market, $3.98, or $41.79 a dozen."

I asked the same question of an ecologist.

"The *price*," he said, "is $3.98. The *cost* is unknown, but includes the cost of repainting homes, cleaning clothes, paying for the time of housewives, making recompense for illness and shortening of lives as well as the much more difficult problem of paying people for the enjoyments they are denied—for instance, the scent of delicate flowers, the intoxicating smell of clean air, and the heavenly vision of crystalline skies. The cost is quite unknown but it must be very great. A helluva lot more than the $3.98 on the price tag of a widget."

I took this distinction back to the economists to see how it grabbed them. Their mouths looked as though they had bit into a green persimmon. "Where'd you get that idea?" asked one: "From an econut?"

"Must have been some damn dickey-bird-watcher," said another.

"Or a flower-plucker," said a third.

"You don't speak very clearly," said yet another, and they all went off into gales of laughter.

In my small sample I found only one economist, Milton Friedman by name, who agreed that the distinction between price and cost was sound. The others didn't argue with him. They just went back to their factories for more bread.

Had the man from Mars carried his investigations further, he would have discovered that the run-of-the-mill economists *do* have a way of dealing with this situation. They distinguish between "external costs" or "externalities," and "internal costs," which, significantly, are usually just called "costs" *period*. In the making of widgets, this is the way they divide up:

Costs (i.e., internal costs)	External Costs
Raw material	Repainting houses
Labor	Cleaning clothes
Amortization of factory	Medical care
Workmen's compensation insurance	Compensation for shortening of life
Social-security contributions	Compensation for loss of amenities (pure air, pure water, pleasant surroundings)
Taxes	

I don't know who first coined the term "external costs," but it is quite obvious that he was an economist sitting in the factory manager's office, looking out. A genuinely objective economist standing in the town square, looking in every direction, would not think of this dichotomy, *internal—external*. It is a company-oriented dichotomy, not a community-oriented one.

What is objectivity? The concept is subtle and easily perverted. Much professional jargon that poses as objective is merely euphemistic. The implicit logic seems to be this:

a. That which is objective is unemotional.
b. Euphemisms are unemotional.
Therefore, euphemisms are objective.
A couple of examples will suffice to illustrate the point.

(1) *Statement:* "While his personal intellectual capacity is limited, he rarely hesitates to absorb knowledge from others around him in order to enhance his image as a well-rounded pupil."
    Translation: He cheats.

(2) *Statement:* "The President was less than candid."
    Translation: The President lied.

Posing as objectivity, euphemisms sap the springs of action. If the economist's "external costs" had, from the outset, been called "larcenous costs" or "the costs of business larceny," we would not have tolerated them. Larceny *has* been perpetrated: clean air, clean water, and good health have been stolen from us. The economists should have told us so. Bluntly. A few have: William Kapp, Ezra Mishan, Kenneth Boulding, and Allen Kneese, for example. And a few others.

But most economists have just sung sweetly.

CHAPTER 10

How Did We Get Here?
Where Are We Going?

Few pains hurt quite so unremittingly as the dull ache of realizing that we have been wrong, wrong, wrong—for a long time. The psyche seeks to protect what it takes to be its integrity by refusing to acknowledge past error: "face" must be saved. Error is corrected only after a way is found to restructure the memories into a less threatening pattern.

Psychologically, historical investigation is a sort of compulsive rubbing of the wound created by the discovery of our shortcomings in the past. It hurts; but it feels good too. Given intelligence and courage, we may be able to avoid repeating the errors of the past in the future.

For generations we have had a society shaped by the larceny of "externalities." It is not too much to say that Western society was founded on larceny. How could we have been so blind as not to see the contradiction between the larceny of "external costs" and the system of ethics to which we were officially committed? History, I think, gives an explanation.

Let us go back three or four thousand years, to the Attic peninsula, to look at the mining of copper, out of which bronze was made. How did the bronze industry deal with its "externalities"? The answer is obvious, but more extreme than we might have guessed. At the earliest date even the cost of the copper ore was an externality. The private enterpriser simply went to the nearest green-rock hillside and scratched out whatever ore he wanted and set to work on it. He didn't pay a cent for it. The cost of the raw material was an external cost.

This couldn't last long, of course. With the increase in population, particularly with the increase in the number of private enterprisers interested in making money out of copper, crowding at the mine sites led to squabbling. The animal instinct of territoriality soon created the human tradition of private property in real estate. Private property could be passed on from father to son; and it could be sold. Once this stage had been reached, the only way a new enterpriser could join the game was by buying in. With this act, the hitherto externalized cost of the raw material became internalized in the bronze industry. The price of the product had to reflect this internalized cost.

In passing we might ask this question: Was justice served in the historical act of internalizing the cost of ore? We have no records of this momentous event. It is doubtful if we will ever know. But if an omniscient being promised to give you the answer as soon as you placed your bet, how would you bet?

Is there any doubt in your mind? The internalization was undoubtedly achieved with great injustice, with the strong taking from the weak. Force, deceit, treachery, cupidity—these were rewarded, no doubt. Decency, altruism, temperance, consideration for others were doubtless suicidal virtues.

The end result—internalization of the cost of raw materials—was good, however, and necessary in an increasingly crowded world. The internalization of this cost by the creation of the concept of real property decreased overt bloodshed, once the transition had been made. But it is probable that this end result was achieved by means that were almost wholly evil.

Did the good end justify the bad means? This is a tempting question to ask—but what does the question mean? What does "justify" mean? It is not at all clear.

We have benefited from that historic occurrence. Many of the participants in the act of change may well have suffered. These are factual statements about people widely separated in time. It is not easy to say what logical connection there is between the two historical statements.

Perhaps we should not ask.

What next? Probably labor was the next cost to be internalized. For something like a hundred generations men of power tried to externalize the cost of labor through the institution of slavery. The slave-owner is a prisoner of fantasy: he dreams he is Aladdin and has only to rub his lamp to get a genie to appear and do his bidding. Reality is rather different, because the genie who appears is human too, and capable of forcing diplomatic negotiations upon the slave-owner, albeit subtly. Slaves aren't altogether amenable and reliable. It's no bed of roses being a slave-owner.

Nevertheless, so great is the superior power of fantasy over reality that slavery persisted for many centuries. Its death knell was sounded about 1000 A.D. when some unknown genius invented the horse collar. The connection of this with the demise of slavery is not obvious, but it is real.

Remember the pictures of Ben Hur's chariot race? Each chariot is drawn by three horses. Why *three* horses? Three can't go three times as fast as one. And that's an itty-bitty chariot. But small as it is, it is an abomination to the horse when his owner hasn't been smart enough to invent the horse collar. In Ben Hur's time the load-bearing trace of the horse's harness passed around the neck of the horse, with the result that every time the horse pulled hard he cut off his wind and had to slacken up on his effort. (As a matter of fact this old harness was unintentionally an admirable cybernetic device that insured against excessive speed—not too different from the governor on James Watt's steam engine.) Before the horse collar the horse, though fine for riding, didn't amount to much for pulling.

Economically oriented historians have reckoned that the cost of food per unit of work performed at the time of the Roman Empire was just about the same for man and horse. The horse ate more, but cheaper, food. Horses weren't given to staging revolts like slaves; but neither could they understand as well. It was a toss-up which the prudent man should use, horse or slave.

Then, to judge by medieval drawings, the horse collar was invented about 1000 A.D., no doubt by some clever freedman rather than by any of the slave-owners, who were corrupted by the "externality" of slave labor. Suddenly a horse became far more valuable than a slave, at least for a great deal of field work (pouring the afternoon tea in the garden was another matter). From that day on, slavery was on the skids, since the rational excuse for it had been torpedoed. It was just a matter of time.

(Of course history moved more slowly in those days, so the demise of slavery took several centuries. The Emancipation Proclamation came in 1863 in the United States.)

With the abolition of slavery the cost of labor was internalized. The transition was not painless. Every new internalization of a so-called external cost is fought bitterly not only on rational or selfish grounds but also on moral grounds. Students of ethics like to think of their subject as somehow being prior to, and superior to, mere selfish interests, but when we dig back into the archaeology of the discipline we cannot help being struck with the way ethics adapts to the Establishment. Dwell on this noble statement by James Boswell, opposing the English abolitionists of the eighteenth century:

> To abolish a status which in all ages God has sanctioned, and man has continued, would not only be robbery to an innumerable class of our fellow-subjects; but it would be extreme cruelty to the African savages, a portion of whom it saves from massacre, or intolerable bondage in their own state of life, especially now when their passage to the West Indies and their treatment there is humanely regulated.

In the end, when slavery was abolished in the United States, the masters were robbed by the state, as Boswell had foreseen. . . . Again questions about ends and means rise to the surface. . . .

The pattern becomes clear. The remaining steps can be passed over more quickly. Table 4 shows the historical sequence of the internalization process, so far as we can see it now.

The labor-cost that was internalized with the abolition of slavery was, in many places, merely the minimal cost—the cost of paying for the food needed by the laborer to prepare himself to work one more day. Wages were not generally adequate to pay for rearing laborers

TABLE 4

Internalization of So-Called "External Costs":
The Historical Sequence

COST	WHEN INTERNALIZED (APPROX.)
1. Cost of raw materials	Before Christ
2. Cost of labor	From about A.D. 1000 to 1862
3. Cost of raising and educating labor force	From about 1800 to 1900
4. Cost of industrial accidents	From about 1875 to 1925
5. Cost of industrial diseases	From about 1900 onward
6. Cost of cleaning up polluted environment	[Yet to be internalized]
7. Cost of preventing pollution of the environment	[Yet to be internalized]

to manhood, or for supporting them in old age; or to pay for their womenfolk if the latter did not go into a factory or become prostitutes. These costs were externalized onto the community and paid for in innumerable ways: private charity, public poorhouses, and all the apparatus for dealing with crime when the more enterprising of the poor elected to take matters into their own hands. These costs did not appear on the ledger books of the factory-owners; they were allocated, unsystematically, to society as a whole. The history of the labor movement of the last hundred and fifty years can be viewed largely as an unconscious process of internalizing the whole cost of maintaining a labor force in reasonably good health, from birth to death. The struggle for good wages and shortened working hours was bitterly fought every inch of the way. Opponents of internalization always act, to hear them tell it, from the highest of motives.

Toward the end of the nineteenth century the internalization process began to encompass the cost of industrial accidents. The classical attitude toward an accident in the factory is that it is the worker's fault. "He shouldn't have been so careless." "He should watch what he is doing." "Clumsy lout!" "*His* accident is certainly not *my* fault."

The word "accident" is a bit of word magic. It is akin to the word "miracle"—a name for an event that is somehow outside the framework of rational discourse. One does not *expect* accidents or miracles —so how can one prepare for them?

The justification for this attitude began to crumble in the middle of the seventeenth century, when Fermat and Pascal laid the foundations of the theory of probability. The connections of the theory with the practice of insurance was obvious and by the nineteenth century had been thoroughly enough worked out to furnish a basis for the prudent management of accidents (strange as that phrase may sound).

It may be all right to call a single event "an accident." But when a million workers are working year in, year out, accidents cease to be mere accidents: they become predictable events. We can prepare for them. An accident ceases to be a miracle-like event; it is merely an event that has a low frequency of occurrence. Accidents become "rationalized," to use this word in an unfamiliar and nonderogatory sense. Insurance is a multibillion-dollar industry based on the rationalization of accidents.

Once accidents are rationalized, all justification for externalizing their cost disappears. This is now widely recognized. In highly industrialized countries, the comforting title of "externality" is no longer conferred on industrial accidents. The cost of accidents appears on the ledger books of the accident-generating industries.

Internalizing the costs of diseases produced by industrial processes took a longer time because cause-and-effect relationships were harder to demonstrate with a rigor that would stand up in a court of law. The pathological consequences of working with lead, asbestos, radioactive materials, and countless other substances often take years to make their appearance. Because workers are subjected to many other influences as well, large-scale and sophisticated statistical studies are required to establish causal connections. Many industrial diseases have yet to be brought under the protective umbrella of the law. Nevertheless, in principle, it is now generally acknowledged that the costs of industrial diseases should be internalized.

Which brings us to the costs of pollution control, the most aggravating of the externalities now waiting to be internalized. It is obvious that this internalization is going to be at least as painful as the others; and it might take just as long, unless we become adequately frightened by the escalating rate of pollution. The escalation is very real because pollution is a product of three factors:

1. population growth,
2. growth in per-capita income,

3. shift to more extravagant, and more polluting, technologies.

What can we learn about the process of internalization from past instances that may help us in the future? *First of all* it should be quite clear that treating a cost as an externality is the primitive approach. It springs directly from the ego-centeredness of the individual, who jolly well isn't going to pay any bills he can evade. The natural course of evolution is from externality to internality; our problem is to hasten the evolution and ease the pain of transition.

Second, we must always expect internalization to be vigorously resisted by those who have frozen the externalities into their accounting system. Opposition will arise even when we can show, as we sometimes can, that in the long run the enterprisers will not be hurt by the change. Any demonstration of this sort is necessarily only a theoretical demonstration until the change is actually made. The successful enterpriser got where he is by being skeptical of merely theoretical demonstrations. "A bird in the hand . . ."

Third, the status quo will *always* be defended by moralistic arguments. Many practical men cherish the belief that they are concerned only with empirical facts, that their approach to the world is wholly pragmatic. Their behavior belies this belief: when challenged they always try to show that their actions are not only pragmatically right but morally so.

"Man, by his nature, wants to know," said Aristotle. The consequences of this impulse are shown in Figure 3. We may grant, for the sake of argument, that the solution to a problem presented by an objective situation is found largely by "threshing about"—random trials—with the successful response being psychologically "reinforced." Wholly pragmatic men would be satisfied with that. Real men are not. Turning their experiences over in their minds they go on to elaborate a SET—a Supporting Ethical Theory that makes what they do seem right and serves as a guide for future action. The psychological mechanism underlying this process is called "dissonance resolution."

Whatever words we use, it is a fact that the human mind secretes theory as a gland secretes hormones. The necessity is undoubtedly connected with the fact that we are a verbal animal. The verbal secretion is called (variously) theology, law, alchemy, or science.

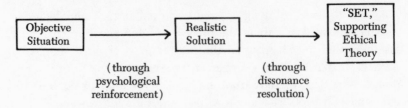

What happens if the Objective Situation changes?
Two possibilities:

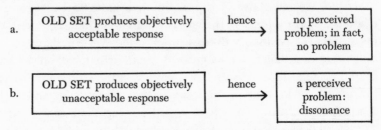

FIGURE 3. The origins and functions of SET, Supporting Ethical Theory

Those who have not the intellectual ability to create the sort of theoretical framework required in these disciplines make do with crude typological images about personalities—"stereotypes"—that explain a world awry as the fault of thieves, hypocrites, devils, infidels, bolsheviks, imperialists, or racists. Such stereotypes, which vary from age to age, are always available to the unscrupulous who seek to manipulate the minds of others cheaply.

What happens if the objective situation changes? The word-bound SET will be applied to the new situation. Sometimes it may "work," sometimes it may not. It doesn't matter much what the proportion is between these two outcomes, because we selectively notice only the times when the SET fails. In such a situation we start threshing around for a different solution, which, when found, starts the process of dissonance resolution and the elaboration of a new SET. This time of change is frequently bloody, with cries of "selfishness," "hypocrisy," "radical," and "reactionary" filling the air. The battle cries used are almost wholly moralistic: verbal pragmatism simply does not grab the heart.

Although it is true, as Aristotle said, that man by his nature wants to know, yet thinking is such hard work that we are usually willing to settle for the shadow of knowledge by routinely applying some old SET to each new problem. In fact, the law assumes that there is always an old SET that is applicable to any new problem, distrusting all novelty. The result is frequently chaos. Consider the SET embodied in the Fourteenth Amendment to the American Constitution. Created for the protection of the persons of former slaves it was adapted by verbal magicians to the defense of dangerously powerful corporations, through the legal fiction that a corporation is a person and hence entitled to all the protection the law gives to real, nonfictional persons. We still have not undone all the harm of this clever extension of the SET of this amendment.

Fourth among the lessons we should have learned from past internalizations is this: whenever we change the rules of the game, some people are likely to be cheated. When we internalized the cost of labor in the United States by abolishing slavery, wealthy slaveowners by the thousands were made paupers overnight. There was no move to recompense them for their losses. Yet economic calculations show that a generous legal recompense would have been far cheaper in money (not to mention lives) than the Civil War, the real purpose of which (though not its nominal one) was to put an end to slavery.

Purely rational men might have opted for buying out the slaveowners; but the new SET that supported the internalization of labor costs produced a moral stance that precluded thoughts of being fair to those operating by the SET under which they grew up. Indeed, it is characteristic of those who embrace the new SET that they deny the very existence of a Supporting Ethical Theory for that which they loathe. (Who recalls now that Saint Thomas Aquinas quite seriously defended slavery as the will of God? Or is willing to recall?)

In our own day some of the more radical environmentalists, in the act of changing the rules to internalize the costs of pollution, quite obviously hope that industrialists—"Big Business," "the Establishment," "Capitalists," "Polluters"—will have to pay for the clean-up, and that it will hurt. They do not recognize that, in the final analysis, the cost will have to be passed on to either the consumer or the taxpayer. Recent converts to a new SET do not want change to be painless to those whom they see as the enemy, i.e., the people with vested interests in the old order. The moralistic attitude of such environmental reformers is understandable; but it need not be encouraged.

Fifth, virtue comes easier to the rich than to the poor. When it became clear that the PCBs (polychlorinated biphenyls) used in making many plastics were harmful to the environment, the company principally responsible for supplying PCBs to the European market voluntarily stopped the manufacture. It was a rich company, making many products. It could afford to take the long view. A small, one-product company cannot afford to be so altruistic or long-sighted when its product is attacked.

Similarly, in the control of pollution rich nations find it easier to "grasp the nettle" than poor nations. In fact, many of the poor coun-

'Gad, sir, reforms are all right as long as they don't change anything.'

FIGURE 4. Colonel Blimp

tries now look with suspicion at any request that they control pollution; they think rich countries are trying to make them even poorer. They say they can't pay for pollution-control. Poverty narrows the options.

Sixth, the need to internalize costs increases with population size and population density. There was nothing wrong with the first bronze-maker's helping himself to copper ore from the nearest hillside. The plume from a single factory smokestack in a large valley may be picturesque and almost harmless. Daniel Boone had no need for a toilet and a sewage system—but the hordes of city-slickers now taking conducted "wild river" rides down the Grand Canyon are in danger of turning it into a Cloaca Maxima. Toilet paper litters every sandbar, like confetti on Wall Street after a parade.

Seventh, the internalization problem can be put another way: if you don't want to give up all the freedoms implied by the externalization of costs, you can have your wish if you will consent to giving up just one freedom: the freedom to breed. If population were kept controlled at a very low density we could, for the most part, safely and enjoyably forget about taking care of the environment. But if we aren't willing to give up the freedom to breed . . .

Let's let the late David Low's Colonel Blimp have the last word (Figure 4).

Part Two

On Board the *Beagle:*

The Dawn of Responsibility

Inside the mountain of the *Beagle* the dozen inhabitants are assembled in a living room of baronial size. The glass wall is tilted
inward at the bottom like the window of a dirigible: it gives a view
of the plain, on which hundreds of people are seen moving around
amidst the ruins of abandoned factories and dead trees. One observer, leaning against the glass, looks idly out. Most of the others
are facing a wall which is covered with a battery of small TV
monitors surrounding one big screen, which, at the moment, is
blank. Outside, it is a landscape by Dali; inside, despite the technological appurtenances, it is a clean, light-suffused interior by
Vermeer.

In a corner, somewhat removed from the others, two men sit
huddled over a book. They both appear to be about thirty-five years
old, but one of them is strangely childlike in attitude, actions, and
speech. As he runs his finger over the lines of the book he speaks
hesitantly.

" 'Run, Dick, run,' said Jane.

"Dick ran.

" 'Run, Spot,' said Jane: 'You run, too.'

"They bowf ran."

"No, no," interrupted the other. "Not *bowf,* Jerry. *Both.* B-o-o-oth.
Try saying *both,* like me."

Jerry made several tries, succeeding fairly well, and then beamed
as his teacher praised him.

"I think that's enough for right now. You're coming along. You'll
be reading big folks' books in no time."

Jerry blinked, puzzled. "Why do you say 'big folks,' Allen? I weigh thirty pounds more than you do. Aren't I big?"

"Yes, that's true, Jerry. Just custom. But learners used to be little folks. Back on Earth. Hadn't you noticed how short the learners were in that Dick and Jane book?"

"Well . . . they look a little funny. But I can't tell how big they are, not in the pictures. . . . Tell me again where I came from, Allen."

"Oh, you nuisance! Okay, here goes. Now, listen, because someday you will have to tell this story to me when we have changed places and I am no longer a big folk."

Allen settled himself back in his chair while Jerry curled up on the floor, his chin cupped in his hands, which were supported on the speaker's knee.

"When people realized that Earth would be destroyed someday, they decided they had to do something about it. Obviously the thing to do was to make a big spaceship, fill it with people, and blast it off toward other stars to look for a planet to settle on. So that's what they did.

"The scientific problems of the spaceship were difficult, but the solutions were completely known. The energy for this ship comes from what's called a Zwingli-Dyson Pack. This is a continuously exploding hydrogen bomb on the other side of the ship, the side you never see, the side under our feet. You never see this for a good reason: the radiation would kill you. The cup-shaped underside of the ship both protects us and absorbs the energy of the explosion. That's what pushes us forward. The Zwingli-Dyson Pack is a long way behind us—twenty or thirty kilometers, I think.

"The pack also supplies the energy for our daily needs—heat, light, synthesis of food, recycling of wastes. Everything. The energy is channeled to us along a plasma conduit and is automatically processed down below.

"That's all just technology, and it's simple enough. The real problem of a spaceship is its people. How can thinking, changeable people keep going for the centuries the trip takes without fighting with each other, or losing their ability to solve new problems? How can they keep knowledge alive so that when they finally reach a new planet they can colonize it successfully? Obviously the people on a spaceship need a government.

"That's a pretty big word, Jerry; but it means that the people have to meet and talk things over. They have to have leaders, people who can tell them what to do. And they have to have National Goals, too. That's a pretty big word, too; but the idea is the people have to decide what kind of government they want, what they want to do eventually, how they want to change. . . .

"Well, change is the problem. Things were changing very fast on Earth at that time, but it wouldn't do for them to change on a spaceship that was going to be traveling all by itself for several hundred or even several thousand years. Suppose the people on the ship changed their minds about what they wanted to do and turned around and headed back to Earth? That wouldn't do. Yet that was the way people on Earth had acted for a long time—changing their minds every few years. They were very fickle."

Allen's language was getting pretty fancy for a five-year-old— Jerry's true new age—but he seemed to be talking more to himself, dreamily running the tape through his mind once more.

"Earth people never learned how to create a stable government. Some countries changed governments several times a year. No nation lasted very long. One of the longest-lived was Byzantium; it lasted just fifteen human lifetimes. America, where we came from, had lasted only about four human lifetimes when we left, and it wasn't at all sure it would make it to five.

"But the spaceship would be at least ten lifetimes on the way to a new planet, and maybe as much as a hundred. Maybe more. How could we make sure the people on board would keep steady in their goals for so many generations? How could the people on Earth furnish the spaceship with a reliable government when they themselves had none to give? That was the question.

"It's hard to keep ideas and ideals constant through the turnover of generations. What I have to say now is pretty complicated, but you'll understand it someday.

"People get their ways of doing things from the generations before them—their fathers and mothers, grandfathers and grandmothers— by two sorts of heredity. One is called genetics. Each of us has a microscopic message inside his cells called DNA. It's sorta like the words you've been reading in your book, Jerry, only much smaller and much more complicated. Your DNA tells you how to walk when you're old enough. Older people try to help you, but you'd learn without the help. You're programed to walk. It's written in your DNA.

"The other sort of heredity is called 'culture.' It's all the things you've been told by the old folks who lived most of their lives before you. Things like reading: you learn that from us. If we weren't here you'd never learn it. If you never saw a book you'd never make one yourself.

"The trouble with both sorts of heredity is that they change. The change is particularly fast with cultural heredity. To put it another way, heredity is very fragile. That's the problem. How could a small spaceship, where change was dangerous and perhaps fatal, be supplied with people who could be relied upon not to change?

"Change takes place most rapidly when one generation succeeds another. This is because inside a person's head there's a process called the 'Oedipus process,' which requires a son to kill his father before he can be free. Symbolically speaking, that is—he doesn't really kill him. But he has to renounce the ideas he got from his father, even if they are the best ideas. Then he gives birth to his own. They may really be the same as his father's, but they are *his*. A poet named Goethe put it this way: 'We must earn again for ourselves that which we have inherited.' That's what the Oedipus process is— a process of earning for ourselves.

"The earliest processes of development have to take place successfully or the individual dies. A primitive pulsating blood vessel has to contort itself into a four-chambered heart or the embryo will never make it. But late processes are not so essential. Some people never get their wisdom teeth. Some people never go through the Oedipus. They survive. Are they normal? Well . . . Complete? Mature? Words are tricky, Jerry. Defective in some way—yet there was a President of the United States who had never made the transit through the Oedipus. He fastened his affections on one scoundrel after another because his father died before he could kill him. Caused no end of grief for everybody else. But etiquette kept people from speaking of his embryological problems.

"The Oedipal transit means change, and not all of it is for the good. 'If all my father's ideas were good, then I'll have to embrace bad ones'—this seems to be the motto of the mind. You can see what an unstabilizing force this process would be on a spaceship.

"So it was decided that no one would be put on board the spaceship who had not passed through the Oedipus process and stabilized. That minimized the principal unstabilizing force of cultural heredity. But what about biological heredity? In the formation of a new generation new assortments of DNA are made, and sometimes mutations—completely new kinds of DNA—are produced because of a passing cosmic ray or whatnot. So genetic heredity isn't stable either. So what should be done?

"The obvious thing to do would be to put people into deep freeze before loading them onto the spaceship, and not thaw them out until just before time to touch down on the new planet. That way they could be reliable carriers of civilization. Unfortunately, for basic geometric reasons, it isn't possible to deep-freeze so large an object as the human body and have it survive. So that was out. Some other way had to be found to prevent the appearance of new generations, to keep the basket in which civilization was being carried from changing. Fortunately, a way was found just a few years before the *Beagle* took off—eternal life. By the time this breakthrough was made, Science was a secret thing, so the common people never knew about the discovery, but the Leaders did. They knew they could treat the passengers of the ship so they would live forever.

"Well, they didn't really *know*—they couldn't know for sure until hundreds or thousands of years had passed; but they didn't have time to wait for that. The *Beagle* had to leave soon. So they'd just have to give the passengers the immortalizing treatment and hope for the best.

"Then another problem was raised. The succession of generations causes change, and change is what is needed if circumstances don't stay the same. Or if you don't have the right answer in the first place. There's no evolution if there's no succession of generations. No progress without death.

"A real dilemma. There was no way out of it, so the Leaders compromised. They divided the *Beagle* into two parts. Here in this room we have the immortals, the Argotes, the ones who will live forever. That's us. We represent stability. We are the custodians of the best Earth had to offer. But that may not be enough. So out there"—he waved his hand toward the window—"are the other half of the compromise, the ordinary people, the Quotions, selected for many fine qualities, but left with their mortality and their changeableness. They don't even know immortality is possible. They don't know we exist. They've passed through five generations since we left Earth—already they've changed a great deal.

"Someday we'll reach our goal and disembark. Who's *we*—the Quotions or the Argotes? Them or us? We don't know. We'll see how things look then. We may have to re-educate them. Or we may have to destroy them. We'll see. We've got more than one string to our bow."

Allen paused thoughtfully. Jerry's mind had obviously been wandering. The silence brought it back.

"I'm an Argote and you say Argotes live forever. But I can't remember all the things you can. I don't remember getting on board. Where did I come from?"

Allen chuckled. "If I were a lawyer and this was a law court on Earth I'd prove to you that you *did* get on board a long time ago. We have records to prove it. We have the fingerprints of Jerry Wood, a reporter, who got on board at the beginning. They are identical with yours.

"That brings up another problem. When scientists discovered the secret to physical immortality, this raised a question about psychological aging. Does a man's mind become inflexible and ultimately senile because the brain becomes physiologically old? Or is it because the sheer volume of experience overloads the mind and leads to the malfunction we call senility? Scientists divided into two camps on this question. The argument wasn't settled before the *Beagle* left the earth, so the ship was equipped with a Psychic Decorticator just in case perpetual youth—physiological youth, that is—wasn't enough.

"Good thing, too. For it turned out that as we Argotes got old our minds *did* age. Not physiologically. Just a matter of having an overload of information in them, a tangle of irresolvable strains set up by an accumulation of warring cathexes, producing the ultimate stalemate of mental senility. So, though the body doesn't need renewing, the mind does. That's what the Decorticator brings about. Without damaging a single brain cell, it destroys all the functional changes that have accumulated since birth. Like pushing RESET on a computer. Then you start over again. In the same body you become another person. On earth they would have called it reincarnation."

"But I can't remember ever being a reporter."

"No."

"Then I never was!"

"You are right. You are wise beyond your years. . . . Who knows" —Allen laughed—"maybe I used to be Abraham Lincoln, Napoleon, and Caesar. Since I don't remember, I never was."

"I heard a couple of the guys say we'll have to kill old Jorgensen soon," said Jerry, nodding his head toward a strikingly young-looking man. Jorgensen, almost as if he had heard, looked their way. Belying his face, his eyes had a haunted, old look in them.

"Not kill, Jerry: *reset.*"

"What's the difference?"

"It sounds nicer."

"Will you tell him?"

"I don't know," said Allen, looking at the candidate meditatively. "He's pretty skittish. We may just have to grab him and put him in the hopper.

"But not yet, I think. It won't do to have too many young folks around at the same time. Look, Jerry, you remember when I took you down into Stores last month?"

"Boy, I'll say! Gee, I'd like to be able to play with all those things."

"In your lifetime you'll use a little bit of them. It's a great hodge-podge of the impedimenta of Earthly civilization, put on board here on the remote chance that some of it might be useful someday in some unforeseeable way.

"But those physical stores are nothing compared with the information stores we have on board. They don't take up more than a fraction as much space, but by any method of reckoning the number of items is orders of magnitude greater. It isn't enough that this information is there: we Argotes have to be able to use it, to know how to get access to it, if we are ever to fulfill our mission of colonizing another world. Just knowing how to get into the information stores takes years and years of education. It takes thousands and thousands of adult man-hours to re-educate each reset Argote. If we fail in this, all is lost.

"It turns out that a highly technical civilization like ours cannot afford to have more than about one person in six under the age of eighteen. If the proportion of young rises above that, the information-transmittal scheme breaks down and civilization goes *pfft!* Those who don't know overwhelm and corrupt those who do. We found that out the hard way: we almost lost our civilization in the early days, when we reset our senile members at too fast a pace. We know better now. The senile just have to wait a while sometimes. Gradually, we are getting the age groups spaced out in time. Old Jorgensen will just have to wait a bit, I'm afraid."

"Let's look at the pictures," said Jerry suddenly and skipped over to the bank of TV monitors, arranged as neatly as apothecaries' jars on the wall. Each one silently displayed a moving picture from a different part of the world below. Jerry looked along the rows, seeking something of interest. His eyes stopped at a couple caressing each other.

"What are they doing?" he asked in disbelief.

"Making love."

"Do they have to?"

"No, they *want* to," answered Allen.

"Yu-u-uch!" Jerry sounded as if he might vomit.

"I don't understand it either," said Allen, "but it's all written up in the books in our library. There are two different kinds of Quotions, male and female, and they like to play with each other. Our records tell us that we Argotes were treated with two different potions before we were put on board, because we couldn't function as stable trustees of civilization if we were assaulted by the emotional storms of the Quotions. One potion destroyed something called 'desire.' The other one removed the desire of desire.

"That's what the records say. I haven't the foggiest notion what it means. . . . Here's something interesting," said Allen. "Lot of activity there. Look at the mob! Someone must be making a speech. Let's get this on the big tube and hear what they're saying."

He pushed a button beneath the monitor. The scene shifted over to the big screen in the middle, and the sound came on. It was a sort of pig-Latin.

"Hey, you forgot to push TRANSLATE," said Jerry; running to the other side of the control board to beat Allen, he did so. "You can't understand them if you don't." The sounds took on form.

". . . based on selfishness cannot long endure. Our forefathers knew not what they were doing, nor why they were here. No wonder. We—"

"Yu-u-uch!" said Jerry. "Let's get something interesting." And he reached for another button.

Allen grabbed his hand. "No, you don't. I want to hear this. Go play with your dolls."

Jerry started to argue, but then, discouraged by the choice of pictures, abruptly left, pulling a ball out of his pocket and bouncing it as he ran. Allen returned to the screen, as others gathered around.

"The trouble with them was that they had no sense of responsibility." The speaker had a florid face surmounted by a shock of wavy white hair. His great jowls shook as he emphasized a point with a pounding of his fist. The side lighting revealed an explosive burst of fine droplets of saliva as he spat out the word "responsibility." Rich, juicy speech: the gift of the demagogue.

"It's responsibility that will save us, the responsibility that every decent man feels stirring in his bones from the time he's a babe in his mother's arms. Responsibility for *others,* not selfish concern for himself. We are nothing except insofar as we are a part of the great common soul. The selfish men of yesterday brought on their ruin because they thought only of themselves. They believed in *competition.*"

The speaker rolled his eyes dramatically. The crowd picked up the cue. Cries of horror filled the air.

"But we know better. We know that man is born for cooperation, not for competition and conflict. [Cries of "Right on!"] In a spaceship there is no room for competition. It's all for one and one for all."

Immediately the chant began, "All for one; one for all. All for one; one for all." This continued wildly until the speaker, after mopping his brow with a great handkerchief, signaled for silence again.

"No force. No compulsion. No coercion. We *trust* each other. We must trust each other; so we do. Freedom. Each man has to do his own thing, guided by his own God-given sense of responsibility. We must be free to develop our sacred souls. And in this freedom there can be no limits, no limiting, no limitation, no limitabulation! Freedom is indivisible. Mark my words, *freedom is indivisible.* Let no man, at the peril of his life, try to divide it. *Responsibility*—that's the inner light that will enable us to live in a peace and prosperity the like of which this spaceship has never known before. The old order goeth; the new one is at hand. It will last a thousand years, and forever. Let no one doubt it.

"Only freedom and responsibility can create harmony on a spaceship. Coercion, force, laws—these are powerless to create what the bound soul cannot encompass.

"*Freedom and Responsibility*—let these be the watchwords of our God-chosen community from now on. Thank you, Brothers. Thank you, Sisters."

A pandemonium of sound washed over the speaker as the audience wildly voiced its approval. The orator waved, beamed, turned around and shook hands, and turned around again, his left hand held up in a clenched fist, his right making a Y with thumb and forefinger.

One of the viewers turned down the volume. "Well, what do you think?" he asked: "Do you think they'll make it this time? Freedom and Competition before. Now Freedom and Responsibility. Is that the formula?"

"It's an improvement, anyway," said Allen. "Maybe they can breathe from now on."

"Did you say *breed?*"

"Good God, no. They can do that all right. No, I said *breathe.*"

There was a long silence as each of the Argotes apparently ran the thoughts through his head, trying to predict the future. The silence was broken when one of the men, who had not taken his eyes off the screen said, "Hey, look at that guy standing off there, at the edge of the crowd. He hath the lean and hungry look of one who thinks too much. The world is too much for him. Let's see what he's going to say."

He turned up the volume.

"Woody, I like what you said. It's beautiful. That's where I want to be. Free—that's for me. There's only one thing that bothers me. There's a lot of us here, you know—several thousand. We're not all alike. Now *I* have a sense of responsibility, and *you* have a sense of responsibility, and so do almost all our Brothers and Sisters here.

"But suppose someday we find that one of our Brothers doesn't have a sense of responsibility; and while the other Brothers and Sisters, guided by Freedom and Responsibility, hold back on the meat and potatoes, this honky Brother with just Freedom to guide him, and no Responsibility, takes more than his share? Coercion is unthinkable. So what happens then, Mr. Woodstock?"

As the drift of the critic's argument became clear, the blood rose in Woodstock's face. Almost before the lean one had finished speaking, the orator signaled to two burly men dressed in leopard suits. They descended on the questioner, knocked him to the ground, and jumped up and down on his body with spiked clogs. Cries of pain gave way to a crunching of bones; then silence.

The scene shifted to Woodstock, who stood with raised arms and blazing eyes, gathering the attention of his people to him. He spoke slowly, his voice deep with emotion and threat.

"Our Pseudo-Brother mocked us. Let all other Pseudo-Brothers beware. Mockery is the one unforgivable sin in a Brotherhood."

CHAPTER 12

A Piece of the Action

Percy W. Bridgman (1882–1961), a Nobel Prize-winning physicist now remembered chiefly for the light that he threw on scientific methodology, once remarked that "the conjuring up of 'responsibility' is often only a device of a lazy man to get someone else to do for him something of vital concern to him which he should be doing himself." Was he merely being cynical?

Hear this story told by Danilo Dolci, an engineer who abandoned his profession to study and try to help the desperately poor people of Sicily. He has recorded an account given by the father of five children. Both parents have tuberculosis and are in and out of the "san" —the sanatorium. The father speaks:

> But it was no good; they told me the Council was short of money and couldn't afford to pay for the board and keep of five kids.
>
> "They're too young to look after themselves," I said. "They just can't be left there like that."
>
> "Go apply to the Child Care Committee," the official said to me. But I drew a blank there too.
>
> "Do I have to kill somebody before I get any help?" I shouted at the director.
>
> "If you 'kill somebody,' you'll be sent to prison," he said in a cold voice.
>
> "All right," I said, "I have to go back to the san, so there's only one thing for me to do—bring the kids here and leave them."
>
> As soon as I left, the director, a shrewd-looking egg, went

101

around where I lived and asked the neighbors about my case. One of them said how sorry she was for the children.

"*I'll make you responsible for them, Signora,*" the director said. [Italics added.]

"I'm only a poor woman—I'll take them in and feed them, but I can't do it without the maintenance money," she said. Well, she did take them in, but a month went by and the maintenance money wasn't sent to her, so she went to see the director.

"If you'd let me have the money—" she started to say, but he never let her get any further.

"Go away, Signora," he said, "but remember, if any harm comes to those children, you'll be to blame."

Obviously, Bridgman was not cynical: he was merely a good observer who was not easily taken in by word magic. He recognized the coercive power of language. Once one is sensitized to the coercive power of the word "responsibility," one finds countless instances of its being used as a weapon to control others—without bloodshed and often without the victim's realizing that he is being controlled. It is a favorite weapon of successful leaders. American presidents love to use the word "responsibility" to get their way without having to invoke the more blatant weapon of statutory law.

But words mean whatever we want them to mean, and among the many discernible meanings of "responsibility" there is one that is honest and useful. This meaning can be reconciled with cybernetic principles, and it can be used with profit to analyze the political basis of environmental problems. The roots of the cybernetic concept of responsibility are worth exploring at some length before taking up its connection with political problems.

As an egoistic animal—as the descendant of an unbroken line of ancestors who survived because they were sufficiently egoistic—*I want my way.* Suppose that what I want is to keep my apartment at the right temperature: how can I bring this about?

The most direct way is by taking care of it myself. As needed, I can open the valve to the furnace so that it produces more heat, or close it. Nobody else is responsible for controlling the heat; I am responsible. The definition of the word implied by this usage is that given by the Columbia University philosopher Charles Frankel:

A decision is responsible when the man or group that makes it has to answer for it to those who are directly or indirectly affected by it.

In the example cited the decision-maker and those who are affected by the decision are the same: *me*. I am *intrinsically responsible*. There's no need to lecture me in high-flown language on my "responsibilities." If I must neglect my "duties" I suffer for it; and that's that.

If each of us took care of all his needs there would be no need for the concept of responsibility. But for a variety of reasons too obvious to enumerate, we don't. We seek to get some of our needs taken care of by others.

Suppose, feeling that I'm too busy to take care of the heating system myself, I grab another man and say, "Hey, take care of the temperature control for me: *I make you responsible for this task.*" How does he react?

As another egoistic individual, he gives a short and sweet reply: "Like hell you do!" He will accept the responsibility only if there is something in it for him. He will not perform for others unless he is made "answerable" to those who are affected by his actions.

Slavery is one way of making a man answerable for his actions. Where slavery is a tradition, a slave who behaves himself is given food and lodging; one who misbehaves is whipped, or perhaps killed. The slave is responsible.

A "free" man can be made responsible by a system of wages. If he performs well, he is paid his wages; if poorly, he is fired and must then find some other way to live. If the second alternative means, in practice, that he dies of starvation, there are reasons to doubt that he is really free; and so we sometimes speak of "wage slaves." Wage slave or free man, he is responsible.

Whippings, wages, and threats of death are contrivances whereby responsibility is imposed on a man who is not intrinsically responsible. We subject him to *contrived responsibility*.

By definition, intrinsic responsibility is that kind of responsibility that cannot be evaded; but contrived responsibility can be—and the egoistic animal called man constantly seeks to evade contrived responsibility.

Suppose I hire a furnace supervisor whose duty it is to keep my

apartment (among others) at the right temperature. Suppose he lives
in the building next door and must come over periodically to see how
my heating system is working. This is a nuisance in *his* life, of course.
If there is a heavy snow he may not want to go out; or an old crony
may come over to play checkers with him and he may lose track of
time. Whatever the reason, ego continually fights against contrived
responsibility.

I might, of course, fire him for a single shortcoming, but I won't,
and he knows it. Two? Three? Ten? . . . I don't fire him without
"adequate cause" because his replacement may be even less reliable.
But what is "adequate"? Neither of us knows. In the twilight region
where I am unwilling to make a hard decision I try to augment contrived responsibility with *jawbone responsibility*—tongue-lashings
and lectures about his "responsibility," his "duty"; and—if the situation warrants—about his "patriotism," his "honor," or some other
high-flown abstraction.

Is jawbone responsibility effective? Sometimes, if the person has
been conditioned right (or "educated," "trained," "disciplined"—
what have you). For a while. But seldom for long.

Jawbone responsibility is effective only if it carries an implicit
threat of force. The implication may be subtle; but it must be sensed,
at least at the subconscious level. An iron hand within the velvet
glove.

A system that depends on contrived responsibility is never wholly
reliable. "Other things being equal," it is always desirable to replace
contrived responsibility by intrinsic responsibility. How can I achieve
that and keep my apartment at the right temperature?

One way would be to invite the heating supervisor to live with me,
in my apartment: that would give him "a piece of the action." If the
temperature is too hot or too cold, he suffers along with me. Without
any lectures on my part, he does what *I* want because it is what *he*
wants. To have a piece of the action is to share in the losses or gains:
this is what "intrinsic responsibility" means.

This is fine in one sense. But it is not likely that I want the man for
a housemate. I want his intrinsically responsible actions, but not his
ever-present personality. A dilemma. So what am I to do?

The answer is obvious: get a thermostat. A thermostat, placed in my apartment, also has a piece of the action. *My* temperature is *its* temperature. Its standards are my standards. It is made to shut off the heat when it gets too hot, and to turn it on when it gets too cold; and I adjust the "set point" to suit my idea of comfort (which the physiological set point of a human supervisor might not match). The inanimate thermostat does not play checkers or go fishing; it has no egotistic ambitions, nor any tender feelings to be hurt. It will not complain that it is either a slave or a wage slave; and I will have no moral qualms about exploiting it. And it is much cheaper than a man. Even at the same price, I would prefer it. One of the principal aims of the automation revolution is to purge control systems of ego.

Should we seek to bring the revolution of automation to an ultimate conclusion, with the expulsion of ego from all control systems? So radical a change evokes an instinctive and conservative *no*—and can be supported with weighty arguments; but these must be deferred to another time. For the moment let us focus on the behavior of some widespread human control elements and see how well they meet Frankel's criterion of responsibility, i.e., of being answerable to those who are affected by the decisions they make.

Few occupational groups are invested with so much "responsibility"—let the word be ambiguous for the moment—as the medical profession. For the most part, we are satisfied with this state of affairs. But now and then the arrangement is onerous—as it has proven to be in the area of elective abortion. A common attitude toward abortion among many medical men has been expressed by one of them as follows:

> The responsibility for interrupting a pregnancy is a joint responsibility of the surgeon, the psychiatrist, the patient, and the prospective father. To abrogate this responsibility to the decisions of the patient would be a violation of the basic standards of medical practice. In no other medical situation do physicians permit patients to assume such responsibility.

The statement begins with a fine flourish of diplomacy, getting everybody into the act. But then the second sentence gives the show away: the physician obviously sees this only as a struggle for power between himself and his patient: "To abrogate this responsibility to the decisions of the patient would be a violation of the basic standards of medical practice."

In brief: you are pregnant, you want an abortion—but it is I, the physician, who has the power to make the decision. The speaker says it is his "responsibility"; but is he talking about Frankelian responsibility? Let's see.

We must begin with the fact that the woman is pregnant: the past cannot be remade. The question is, what about the future? Moralists often talk as if her options were these: to have an abortion, or to do nothing. *But we can never do nothing.*

Her real options are these: to have an abortion, or to have a child. What are the costs of these two options—to her (if she can pay them); or to society, if society must pay? Table 5 lists the more important costs.

TABLE 5

The Costs of Abortion and Its Alternative
Data for deciding the responsibility for a decision
to abort; the cost of alternative actions.
The key question: who pays these costs?

COST OF EARLY ABORTION	COST OF CHILD
1. About $250	1. About $1000 for prenatal care and birth
2. Loss of day's time	2. Loss of at least a week's time
3. Minimal physical pain	3. Considerable physical pain
4. Negligible psychological pain	4. Variable psychological pain
5. Very slight risk of death	5. Risk of death 8 times that of abortion
	6. Allocation of 16 years of life to caring for child
	7. About $30,000 for rearing child to age 18, with no college

The estimates are, of course, only approximate, but they are in the right ball park. Item 4 under abortion deserves comment. In the days of abortion-prohibition, much was made of the supposed psychic trauma following abortion. This has turned out to be a ghost. If a woman *asks* for an abortion she has already resolved the moral problem satisfactorily in her mind. The psychological trauma will then be greater if she does *not* get the abortion. Experience in the states where abortion is now legal amply confirms this statement.

Prenatal care and childbirth cost far more than abortion, but that is not even half the story: with nonabortion there is a child to take care of. As a minimum, this will require fourteen to sixteen years of the woman's life; and the cost, exclusive of any college education, will be in the neighborhood of $30,000. If the woman and her child end up on the welfare rolls, the cost to society (as determined in California in 1970) will be about $54,000.

The increase in cost, if she has a child instead of an abortion, will be more than a hundredfold.*

The physician can be responsible *in Frankel's sense* only if he has a piece of the action. In the nature of things he cannot bear the child himself, or any fraction of it. But he could responsibly shoulder part of the financial burden. Every time he refuses an abortion to a woman he could give her a check for, say, $3000, thus accepting a tithe of the financial burden. Only if he did something like this could he claim to be a responsible agent, in Frankel's sense. If he does not—and no physician ever does—all his fine talk about "responsibility" is just a blowing in the wind.

Intrinsic responsibility is not possible for a physician in matters of abortion. Only contrived responsibility is possible—paying part of the cost, changing a few hundred diapers, taking the child on weekend trips, and so on. It would be interesting to create such contrived responsibility and see how rapidly physicians' attitudes and language changed!

What the physician wants, of course, is power (called "responsibil-

---

* Some would say that the cost analysis is not complete unless we include also the cost *to* the "child," meaning the fetus (which loses its life in abortion). This is contrary to law. In law, there is no person until a living child is born; at this point it has retrospective rights and can sue for damages *in utero*, e.g., by industrial X-rays. No live birth, no child—no human being. Abortion is never defined as murder. Where the law regards abortion as a crime, it is a crime in a class of its own—"criminal abortion." Thus legalists sidestep the awkward question of classifying the embryo.

Whether a fetus of *Homo sapiens* is or is not a human being is not a scientific question. It is nonetheless gratifying to report that scientific practice is consonant with law. In all biology, embryos and fetuses are specifically distinguished from the definitive, more completely formed stages. An acorn is not an oak tree, an egg is not a hen, a human fetus is not a human being or person. Smashing acorns is not deforestation, scrambling eggs is not gallicide. The cost analysis given in the text above is, therefore, defensible.

ity") and no real responsibility. Power without responsibility—that's an operational definition of a god. The physician wants to be god (and to a considerable extent he succeeds)—but then, isn't that what we all want? Each of us, as an ego-centered reaction system, strives for godship. The members of a profession succeed better than most because the power of special knowledge enables them to strike a hard bargain with the laity. To guard against their own striving for power (which may evoke defensive backfire on the part of their clientele), professions establish codes of ethics, which are only moderately effective. There is always some truth in George Bernard Shaw's saying that "all professions are conspiracies against the laity."

In spite of its dependence on expertise, now and then the general body politic strikes back at the professionals, when egregiously serious errors have been made. A particularly heartwarming instance took place in Russia in 1968. It seems that an architect had failed to make provision for an elevator in a twelve-story apartment building he had designed. When the matter was brought to the attention of a judge, he condemned the absent-minded professional to live on the twelfth floor of his own building. At least, that's what a news report said.

If an American judge were to make a decision like that, it would undoubtedly be overthrown by a higher court on the grounds that it violated the constitutional injunction against "cruel and unusual punishment." Yet what is more effective than "to make the punishment fit the crime," as W. S. Gilbert put it in *The Mikado?* The ego, seeking to evade responsibility, constantly evolves new and unusual ways to do so; why should the general public be forbidden to reply *in kind?* The more complex the society, the greater its need for creativity in the contrivance of operational responsibility.

Jawboning is not enough.

CHAPTER 13

The Third Political System

Robinson Crusoe had no political decisions to make; the rest of us are not so fortunate. Each of us faces a dichotomy: *ego*—and everybody else. Ego wants its way. *I would if I could* dispose the power of the world asymmetrically—"heads I win, tails you lose." But all the *others* are egos too, and would do likewise. So each of us must curb his desires and accept a symmetrical political system, must agree to general rules that restrict the freedom of *ego* in order to restrain all *others*. I do unto me as I must do unto others. . . . Regrettable, but inescapable.

"I accept the universe," said Margaret Fuller.

"By God, you'd better!" retorted Thomas Carlyle.

The environment produces riches, and we want to utilize these riches—you and I, ego and others. There will be work and harvests: how shall we divide these up among us? Who shall do the work? And who reap the harvest?

It takes too much imagination to deal only in abstractions; we need a concrete model to help us absorb general truths. For our model let us take a pasture, photosynthesizing in the sun. Less than one part in a thousand of the radiant energy that falls on the land is captured by the chloroplasts of the plants and turned into plant tissue. But only a fraction of that is available to man as food. We can't eat grass; we have to employ an intermediary. Cows will do. By human economic standards cows, like plants, are "wasteful." They follow the rule of the Ecological Tithe: only about 10 percent of the

109

energy resident in plant cells is converted to the chemical energy of cows' cells. "Wasteful"? Perhaps: but we can't do better, so it won't help much to "call names." Perhaps, following in the footsteps of Miss Fuller, we should accept the cow.

But how shall we manage this enterprise? Whose cows shall harvest the grass? And who shall harvest the cows?

As for the first part of the problem, there are basically only two possibilities: either each of us individually owns some cows and sees to it that they are set to grazing; or we band together into a group and turn our group-owned cows loose in the pasture. Two possibilities.

When it comes to distributing the results of this environmental utilization—the beef—again there are two possibilities: either the proceeds go to individuals, or they go to the group as a whole.

The total number of possible arrangements is $2 \times 2 = 4$, and is exhibited in Table 6. Let us explicitly describe how each of these arrangements works in terms of our model.

Case I. We could divide up the field with fences, assigning each fenced area to one herdsman. This land would then be his "property," or he would have exclusive "rights" to it. At the end of the season he would butcher the cows and the meat would be his alone. This political system we call "private enterprise."

TABLE 6

The Four Conceivable Political Systems of Environmental Utilization

	RULES OF THE GAME				
	UTILIZATION OF ENVIRONMENT BY:		PROCEEDS GO TO:		*Name of the Game*
CASE	INDIVIDUAL	GROUP	INDIVIDUAL	GROUP	
I	√		√		*Private Enterprise*
II		√		√	*Socialism*
III		√	√		*System of the Commons*
IV	√			√	?

Case II. The undivided field is owned by everyone, as are the cattle. The harvest belongs to the community and (presumably) is divided up according to some system that takes account of age, physical condition, etc. This we call "socialism."

These two systems are well known, but our analysis reveals that there are two others, which have not previously been explicitly identified as political systems. There is, first:

Case III. The field is not fenced, but the cattle are privately owned. Each herdsman drives his branded cattle onto the common field. When harvest time comes each man reclaims his cattle and enjoys the proceeds of a season's fattening. This political system we call the "system of the commons." The model, as described, was a reality in England until the middle of the nineteenth century. Each village had its "commons," open to all the individual cattle-owners of the region.

Case IV is included in the table only for logical completeness. There seems to be no real-life example of it—not in the national realm, at least. Perhaps parenthood is an example: parents capture (as best they may) environmental riches and then distribute them to the group, their children. Private philanthropy might qualify. The Scotsman Andrew Carnegie made a fortune of $400 million and then gave all but $1 million of it to his adopted nation through the intermediaries the Carnegie Corporation, the Carnegie Institution of Washington, etc. But the basic stories of parenthood and philanthropy are hardly captured by our model; the rewards, the motivations are not deducible therefrom. In any event, there is no nation, no enduring group, that systematically and habitually plays the game according to the rules laid down in Case IV. As a political system it is a *nul class*—a class with no members. It is hard to imagine seriously proposing to found a nation on this system. For the most part we will ignore this hypothetical system from here on.

Before exploring the properties of the three real political systems —their advantages and disadvantages—a few *caveats* are in order.

First caveat: the focus of the analysis will always be on the effectiveness of each system in utilizing the environment. Obviously, other aspects of political systems are also important—their ability to evoke moral fervor, for example. The analysis here given is only partial and does not dictate the final choice.

Second caveat: a reminder. No real nation corresponds exactly to any of the three systems. Every nation is a "mixed economy." Russia, which calls itself a socialist state, has many subsystems run by the rules of private enterprise. The United States, officially committed to private enterprise, in fact has many socialistic features about it. Water systems and sewage systems are almost everywhere run socialistically—by the group as a whole, through appointed managers. This is a fact of life that the more rigid of our economic conservatives —such groups as the John Birch society—would like to erase from their consciousness. It is notable that the superconservatives do *not* propose setting up competing private enterprises to handle the sewage of their communities. Every time John Birch sits down on the toilet, he becomes a socialist.

As has often been remarked, socialist Russia, since the 1918 Revolution, has been gradually increasing the number of its subsystems governed by the principles of private enterprise; and the United States, during the same period, has become increasingly socialistic. There may be some place in the middle where they will meet. Rigid doctrinaires have lost the battle in both countries. On our side of the fence, the nineteenth-century English philosopher Herbert Spencer (who had many followers in the United States) explicitly called for doctrinal purity, proposing that we desocialize sewage systems, water systems, road systems, postal systems, etc. Fortunately, John Q. Citizen is more interested in what works than in doctrinal purity.

Third caveat: we are concerned with what things are, not with what they are called. A telephone system is necessarily run socialistically. How would you like to live in a city with five competing phone companies, each with its own lines? Which one would you subscribe to? You would want to find out first which one your best friends had joined. If you were a businessman you would have to join all five. The waste would be monumental.

Although the telephone system is frankly set up as a socialistic entity everywhere in Europe, it is nominally run by private enterprise here. But it is only nominally so. The phone company is a monopoly, supported by law; and the rates and the profits are regulated by community agencies. A regulated monopoly is only the ghost of private enterprise. The man from Mars would see no substantial difference between American and European phone companies.

In actuality there may be slight differences between a regulated monopoly and a socialistic enterprise, at any particular time. In the past the American telephone system has functioned conspicuously better than the French, and this fact has been cited as evidence of the superiority of a nominally free-enterprise system over one that is frankly socialistic. Perhaps it is; but we should not lay too great weight on the evidence now that the quality of our phone service is decaying. We have recently converted our postal system into one that is nominally a semi-private enterprise. It will be interesting to see if it in any way—in cost, efficiency, or honesty—becomes better than the frankly socialistic enterprise that preceded it for almost two hundred years.

With these caveats in mind, let us examine the three political systems to see how well each can be expected to work in helping man utilize the environment intelligently. Cattle grazing in a pasture will continue to be the concrete model used to reveal the properties of political systems.

Every pasture has what ecologists call a "carrying capacity." The meaning of this term can be shown by a quantitative example. Suppose we say that "the carrying capacity of this pasture is 100 cows": what do we mean?

We mean that if we pasture 99 cows on the land we will not get as great an annual yield as if we pasture 100. (This is hardly surprising.)

But we also mean this: if we pasture 101 cows we will get *less* productivity than we would with 100. There are many possible particular reasons for this decrease. There may not be enough grass for 101 cows, so individual cows become thinner and the aggregate amount of beef is less. Or 101 cows may trample the ground too much, stunting the grass. Soil erosion may take place, decreasing plant growth in subsequent years. Since cows eat the "good" grass, leaving the "weeds" (by their standards), they selectively favor what they don't want, and the field may become weedier and weedier as the years pass.

Notice that many of these effects do not take place immediately. Implicit in the concept of "carrying capacity" is the assumption that the accounting will be continued into the indefinite future. The carrying capacity of a portion of the environment is a measure of the maximum exploitations it will permit, year after year after year, without diminution. The carrying capacity is the level of exploitation that will yield the maximum return, in the long run.

As long as we utilize a portion of the environment at *less* than its carrying capacity we really have no problem. The problem arises when we are fully utilizing the environment and now are about to stress the environment by going just beyond the carrying capacity. At this point, the inherent differences between the three systems become important and even critical.

Table 7 displays these properties. *Note that all the signs in column (1) are negative:* this is a way of indicating that the carrying capacity has been reached and that the decision-maker is now proposing to add one too many cattle to the pasture land. The key question is this: Will the decision-maker suffer if he makes the wrong decision? Does he have a large enough piece of the action to make him responsible? Clearly, we must first identify the decision-maker.

In the system we call private enterprise the decision-maker is the man who owns both the cattle and the land. It is assumed this ownership will continue indefinitely. If the owner makes a bad decision he will suffer—hence the minus sign in column (2). In other words,

TABLE 7

Properties of the Three Real Political Systems
Consequences of bad decisions when carrying capacity
is exceeded, producing a negative over-all gain

| | RESULTS OF THE GAME | | |
| | GAIN FROM STRESSING THE SYSTEM: | | |
NAME OF THE GAME	OVER-ALL GAIN (1)	GAIN TO THE DECISION-MAKER (2)	INTRINSIC RESPONSIBILITY (3)
Private enterprise	—	—	+
Socialism	—	0	0
System of the commons	—	+	—

he has a piece of the action. In terms of the definitions given in the preceding chapter, he is intrinsically responsible—hence the plus sign in column (3). We do not need to lecture the individual in such a system; nature will punish him if he is stupid.

Socialistic systems work differently, principally because of a size effect. We have to identify the decision-maker. In a small socialistic community it might be possible to assemble everyone in a "town hall" meeting every time a decision had to be reached (e.g., about adding one more cow to the pasture). In such a case the *identity* of decision-makers and recipients of the proceeds would make the signs in the second line like those in the first.

But if the socialistic community is of appreciable size—say, more than a hundred people—calling a town meeting every time a decision has to be reached becomes impractical. A manager is designated and empowered to make decisions. This act changes the properties of the game completely.

Suppose the socialistic community consists of a million people. Now suppose the manager of a 100-cow-capacity pasture mistakenly adds another cow. What happens to him personally? Since, by hypothesis, the total beef production is now slightly decreased, he suffers some, *but not much.* The loss is shared by a million people. *For all practical purposes* the decision-maker's share of the loss is *zero.* It is shown as such in the second line of the table. The decision-maker does not have a piece of the action. He is not intrinsically responsible.

Where there is no responsibility we cannot expect "duties" to be conscientiously fulfilled. Such a situation is obviously intolerable to the socialistic community, so the people seek to make up for the lack of *intrinsic* responsibility by developing mechanisms of *contrived* responsibility—e.g., rewards for good management and penalties for poor. These contrivances in turn raise other problems, which will be discussed in another chapter.

For the present let us go on to an examination of the third political system, noting the striking and significant ways it differs from the other two. Again our model is a pasture land with cattle in it. This time we consider what will happen when each herdsman owns his own cows but the land is shared by all: the environment is utilized by the group, but the proceeds go to the individual, as shown by check marks in column (2) and column (3) of Table 6 on page 110.

Such an economic system for the exploitation of pasture lands actually existed in England for hundreds of years. It was not gotten rid of until a long series of "enclosure acts" enclosed the commons of one village after another, converting it to private property. Toward the end of this historical period, a logical analysis made by William Forster Lloyd (1794–1852) showed why the system of the commons was becoming intolerable.

Lloyd is a very obscure figure in the history of Western thought. He seems to have been something of an amateur mathematician, but beyond that we know almost nothing. His most important publication is entitled: *Two Lectures on the Checks to Population, Delivered before the University of Oxford in Michaelmas Term, 1832.* These lectures were published in 1833, but they seem to have attracted little attention and were cited only occasionally in economic literature during the next century. Finally, in 1968—one hundred and thirty-five years after their publication—the message of the lectures was resurrected and put into circulation again.

Picture yourself as a village herdsman trying to make a living in the days when the commons still existed. You are, by hypothesis, perfectly rational. You are ego-centered and seek your own good, working for the good of the community only when it encompasses your good too. When it is a question of what appear to you to be mutually exclusive alternatives—the community's or yours—you always choose yours.

(To choose otherwise is, in the long run, to eliminate yourself from the community. This is, in the strict sense, a suicidal policy and can scarcely be called rational. Self-selection has produced a world in which the majority of its members at any moment in history are ego-centered. Theory must be built around the behavior of the majority type, for it persists.)

Very well: *I* am a herdsman using the common. It has a carrying capacity of 100 cows. At the moment it happens to have 100 cows on it, of which 10 happen to be mine. Now I have a chance to acquire an eleventh cow. I wonder if I should do so. I debate the decision with myself in roughly the following way.

"If I add one more cow to my herd that will make a total of 101 on the common, which is one too many, and so all of us will lose a bit. On the other hand, 11 cows is 10 percent more than 10 cows, so I gain. The over-all loss I would estimate at about 1 percent, and that is shared among all us herdsmen. *My* gain is about 10 percent, and I don't have to share it. Clearly I stand to gain from adding one too many cows to the commons, so I shall do so."

As shown in Table 7, the sign in column (2) is the opposite of the sign in column (1); and because of this, the sign in column (3) is negative. It is logically correct to say that *The decision-maker in the commons enjoys*—the word is used advisedly—*a negative responsibility.* It is to his interest to make bad decisions.

But (you may say) in the long run . . .

Ah! But *I can't wait for the long run:* my competitors won't let me.

Suppose I take the long view and do *not* add to my herd. Fine. Public-spirited. But I may wake up to discover that another herdsman has just seen the logic of the commons and *has* added to *his* herd. Then another herdsman gets the idea. And another. . . . What have I gained by my restraint?

One: I have made my competitive position in the community worse—this, in the short run.

Two: In the long run I have not prevented the ruin of the commons.

Each herdsman, musing to himself, says (in effect): "If 11, why not 12? If 12, why not 13? If 13, why not . . . And if I don't add to my herd, my competitors will add to theirs. I have to get my share before the pigs take everything."

All rational herdsmen *must* reason in the same way.

"But if only everybody would take the long view," says the idealist, "then they wouldn't be such pigs."

Yes: if *everybody.* But if *one less than everybody* takes the long view, then the implied system of voluntary restraint breaks down. Everybody would have to be perfect for a voluntary system to work. No political or economic system can be judged viable if it requires perfect human beings to keep it running. *A system is judged to be good only if it will work with imperfect components.*

The system of the commons can work in a limitless world, a world in which the carrying capacity has not been reached, a world in which the signs are + in column (1) of the table. But it cannot possibly work in a world that is reaching its limits, in which the decisions being made overstress the carrying capacity of the environment—in a word, in the world of a spaceship. On a fully populated spaceship, all signs are negative in column (1) of Table 7.

It is the essence of the system of the commons that the members are free to make their own decisions. It is also crystal clear that in a limited world—the only world we will ever know—freedom in a commons brings ruin to all.

Inevitably. Remorselessly.

The great twentieth-century philosopher Alfred North Whitehead pointed out that "the essence of dramatic tragedy is not unhappiness. It resides in the solemnity of the remorseless working of things. This inevitableness of destiny can only be illustrated in terms of human life by incidents which in fact involve unhappiness. For it is only by them that the futility of escape can be made evident in the drama."

Following Whitehead, it is rigorously correct to speak of *the tragedy of the commons*.

CHAPTER 14

Commons, Cryptic and Overt

Had the commons vanished from the world with the enclosure of the last common pasture land of an English village in the nineteenth century, the properties of the system of the commons would be of antiquarian interest only. Unhappily, such is not the case. A multitude of commons surround us, most of them masquerading as other political systems.

To begin with, there is the ocean. Despite national ambitions, more than 99 percent of it is claimed by no one. It is a commons in which anyone can fish. The "freedom of the seas" means the freedom of a commons, which leads inexorably to ruin. Fishermen of many nationalities, trying to increase their take from declining stocks of fish, buy ever more sophisticated gear to locate, to capture, to preserve, and to transport their catch back to market. A society "hooked" on technology accepts this as the right way to do things; it happens also to be the inevitable choice under the logic of the commons. The consequences have been trenchantly described by Paul and Anne Ehrlich in their *Population, Resources, Environment:*

A single Rumanian factory ship equipped with modern devices caught in one day in New Zealand waters as many tons of fish as the whole New Zealand fleet of some 1,500 vessels. *Simrad Echo,* a Norwegian periodical published by a manufacturer of sonar fishing equipment, boasted in 1966 that industrialized herring fishing had come to the Shetland Islands, where 300 sonar-equipped Norwegian and Icelandic purse-seiners had landed undreamed-of

119

quantities of herring. An editorial in the magazine queried, "Will the British fishing industry turn . . . to purse-seining as a means of reversing the decline in the herring catch?" Another quotation from the same magazine gives further insight: "What then are the Shetlands going to do in the immediate future? Are they going to join and gather the bonanza while the going is good—or are they going to continue drifting and if seining is found to have an adverse effect on the herring stocks find their catches dwindling?" The answer is now clear. In January 1969, British newspapers announced that the country's east coast herring industry had been wiped out. The purse-seiners took the immature herring that had escaped the British drifter's nets, which are of larger mesh, and the potential breeding stock was destroyed.

The April 1967 issue of *Simrad Echo* contains another example of activities in the modern fishing industry. In an article discussing a newspaper item about a purse-seiner that was being built by a Norwegian shipyard for Peru, which has one of the world's major anchovy fisheries in the rich Humboldt Current, *Simrad Echo* says:

"Fish-rich Peru nurses an ever-growing apprehension. Increasingly it is asked: surely the anchovy stocks off the coast—seemingly limitless at present—cannot sustain catch losses running into millions of tons year after year?

"Behind the news item lies what many people consider to be the answer to the Peruvian question—bigger and better equipped boats to augment the hundreds of small 'day trip' purse-seiners engaged in the stupendous coastal fishery.

"They theorize that if the present abundant stocks *do* start to get scarce there will be boats on the scene able to go much further afield and be suitably equipped to track fish down.

"They theorize further that *now* is the time for action, while things are still relatively good, not at the last moment of truth. In the meantime valuable experience can be gained in operating the latest fish-finding devices, such as echo sounders and sonars."

One wonders whether the author of these words (and the captains of industry who promote these electronic marvels) ever heard of the fable of the goose that laid the golden eggs.

Obviously we should not look to technology to solve the "problem" of increasing the take of the ocean fisheries. Political change is what is required. Technological improvements merely hasten the day of ruin.

The first response to the prospect of ruin in the commons is always an appeal to conscience and "responsibility"—a meaningless term as used in this context (since the "responsibility" is clearly not Frankelian). The appeal, of course, has no effect.

Some 7000 blue whales were caught in the 1950–1951 season. The following year the catch was down to 5000. In 1955–1956 it was less than 2000; three years later it was down to 1200 and still falling. The history of all other species of whales is following a similar course, at a few years' remove. The stocks are so depleted and the competition is so fierce that all nations except Japan and Russia have given up fishing for whales on the high seas.

Each year the International Whaling Commission studies, meets, and *recommends* what the take should be for the following year, if there is to be a sustained yield year after year. Each year Japan and Russia ignore the recommendations, exceeding them many times over. The next year stocks are lower and the recommendation is still lower—and the downward spiral continues.

The only weapon the International Whaling Commission has is an appeal to conscience. Should we condemn Japan and Russia because they ignore this appeal? Should we vilify them for their "selfishness"?

If we do we have not learned the lesson of the commons. Each nation implicitly defends its behavior thus: "We've got to get those whales before our competitor does. The whales will not be saved by our restraint. Such unilateral action on our part would merely assure that our competitor got the last of the riches at our expense."

In the commons, rational men are helpless to behave otherwise.

Faced with the tragedy of the commons, we can have only one rational response: change the system. To what? Basically, there are only two possibilities: free enterprise and socialism. Free enterprise in the oceans would require some sort of fences, real or figurative. It is doubtful if we can create territories in the ocean by fencing. If not, we must—if we have the will to do it—adopt the other alternative and socialize the oceans: create an international agency *with teeth*. Such an agency must issue not recommendations but directives; and enforce them. Either such an agency must be invested with the necessary power or the whole world must reconcile itself to giving up all but a small fraction of the potential production of the seas. Near-shore fisheries, protected by the territoriality of national waters, can survive in part. (Even these will be somewhat diminished because fish, in their breeding and movements, do not recognize national boundaries and so are susceptible to depredation taking place in the commons beyond the limits of national waters.)

Can an international agency with teeth be created *de novo?* The history of the late lamented League of Nations and the currently unhappy United Nations gives small cause for hope. Nations do not want to give up even a fraction of their sovereignty, for fear, no doubt, of "the camel's nose." Yet in the area of oceanic fisheries the risk is probably minimal. The size and type of international navy that would be needed to monitor fishing boats would offer a minimal risk of escalation into an international military force that could seriously threaten the sovereignty of nations in other respects. On the contrary, saving the oceanic fisheries by replacing the system of the commons with the necessary international system might be a fruitful first step toward the international cooperation we will need for the much more critical problem of eliminating the possibility of thermonuclear war.

But this first step will be vigorously opposed by almost all existing national governments, whether socialistic or capitalistic.

It is easy to see that problems of air pollution and water pollution are also problems of the commons. Air and water are treated as commons into which anyone can dump his trash. The reasons for this are historical, of course; but they are also practical—it is difficult to put fences in the atmosphere or in streams, lakes, and oceans. In the absence of real fences there is no intrinsic responsibility, and our problem is to contrive ways to make polluting agencies responsible for what they do. Various contrivances have been proposed, with varying degrees of seriousness and prospects of success.

Proposal: that the sewage outfall pipe of a city be required by law to be *upstream* from the intake for its water supply. The reverse arrangement is the rule now. St. Louis's sewage is part of Memphis's drinking water, an arrangement not conducive to a responsible attitude toward the treatment of sewage.

Proposal: that the effluent from the smokestacks of a factory be piped into the homes of the president and all the officers, thus achieving Instant Responsibility.

Proposal: that the government sell "licenses to pollute" the air and water, payment to be a function of the quantity of air and water polluted, and of the concentration and kind of pollution. Many environmental enthusiasts are appalled at this suggestion because licensing pollution seems to them to be sanctioning pollution. We must, they say, set a *zero tolerance level* for all pollutants.

As concerns the engineering aspects, a zero tolerance for anything is unrealistic. Dilution, precipitation, solvent partition, adsorption, or any other method of removal of pollutants always leaves some residue. As the concentration of pollutants in the residue comes close to zero, the costs of further purification skyrocket, increasing as a "power function." Money spent for superpurity cannot be spent for other amenities. Since we are not infinitely rich, we must compromise and set a standard for pollution that is somewhat above zero.

Does charging for pollution sanction pollution? Not necessarily. It depends on how much society charges. It's possible to adjust the charges to get the performance society wants. At that point the pollution tax becomes less a means of raising money than one of coercing people without the appearance of harshness. A manufacturer who is offered the alternatives of buying better pollution-control equipment or paying for the pollutants he discharges may feel that he has more freedom than he would were he to be flatly ordered to clean up. The feeling may be justified. At any rate, the Army Corps of Engineers' administration of the 1899 Refuse Act (page 61) is moving in this direction. By setting the price of "pollution rights" sufficiently high, any desired degree of cleaning up can be achieved.

Proposal: that we make the legal basis for pollution control more secure by a constitutional amendment that begins with this Declaration of Interdependence:

> We hold this truth to be self-evident, that the media of the world belong to everyone and to no one. Everyone has the right to use them; no one has the right to pollute them.

Sounds like a wonderful idea. Too bad we didn't think of it in 1787.

Viewing the desecration of the environment here in the United States, many of our reverse-chauvinists put the blame for pollution on the capitalist system, i.e., on free enterprise. The charge is disproved by facts. Marshall Goldman, reviewing the massive Russian literature, has shown that this nominally socialist nation is every bit as much polluted as our nominally capitalist nation. Lake Baikal is an exact parallel of Lake Erie, and the Volga River of our Hudson. Why so?

The answer becomes obvious when we ignore the nominal principles of the two countries and observe the real system under which their decision-makers operate.

The United States. A paper-making factory discharges its untreated wastes into a river, ruining it. Asked to change the practice, the manager says, "I cannot internalize the cost of effluent treatment because if I do so our product will cost more. We will then lose business to some other factory that is not internalizing this cost. I am responsible to the board of directors, and they in turn to the stockholders. They will fire me. I need free access to the commons to survive."

Russia. A paper-making factory discharges its untreated wastes into a river, ruining it. Asked to change the practice, the manager says, "I cannot internalize the cost of the effluent treatment because if I do so our product will cost more. It will be noticed in Moscow that my factory is not as 'efficient' as other factories that are not internalizing this cost. I am responsible to a Commission, which in turn is responsible to the Central Committee. They will fire me. I need free access to the commons to survive."

It is not capitalism that creates pollution problems.

It is not socialism that creates pollution problems.

It is the system of the commons, unlabeled and not widely understood, that is at fault.

Always in human affairs one must be alert to camouflage, and not use the wrong analysis because one has mistaken the nominal for the real. Don't mistake American Telephone and Telegraph for private enterprise; a publicly regulated monopoly is only marginally different from a socialistic bureau. Better or worse, perhaps; but not essentially different.

Variation makes a continuum of the world. In the final analysis it is seldom possible to divide phenomena into Black—White; Present —Not Present; Go—No Go. Reasoning is facilitated by "atomic" conceptions, by mutually exclusive alternatives; but it must finally come to grips with realities that are not so agreeable as to sort themselves into clear-cut classes.

The time has come to take account of the fact that responsibility is not as simply related to political systems as Table 7 (page 114) implies. Daniel Fife has descried limits of this analysis and has shown how the next step in the progress toward truth must be a quantitative one.

Suppose a man who owns a forest decides to sell the trees for lumber. This sounds like a free-enterprise system; and according to our table the man is intrinsically responsible. We might therefore expect him to act in what the rest of the world would call an ecologically responsible manner; that is, to cut down the trees in such a way as to permit soil conservation, clear-stream preservation, and reforestation on a scale that would permit a stable sustained yield, year after year, into the indefinite future.

In fact, free-enterprise lumbering often works quite otherwise. Knowing full well all the facts, and behaving responsibly in a narrow Frankelian sense, the owner may "clear-cut" the forest, polluting the streams, eroding the soil, and making reforestation all but impossible. Then he gets rid of the land, selling if he can; but if not, simply abandoning it.

Why does the nominally responsible man behave so irresponsibly, ecologically speaking?

As he is a rational man, what he does depends on the quantities involved in the total situation. How much does he pay for the land? How much can he sell it for in the ruined condition? How much does partial cutting cost as compared with clear-cutting? What is the cost of reforestation? What is the tax on mature forested land? What is the tax on land while the process of reforestation is taking place? What is the interest rate on money?

Taking all these into consideration results in a rather complex analysis, so let's examine a highly simplified example which is quite adequate to show the logic involved.

Suppose the value of the timber in a mature forest is $1,000 per acre, and that it takes 40 years for a forest to reach maturity. Let the interest on invested money be 5 percent. Neglect all other variables.

A rational man is debating whether to maintain his forest land on a sustained-yield basis or take his profits and get out. He analyzes the alternatives thus:

Sustained forestry yield: "I can harvest one-fortieth of my acreage per year. Put another way, I can get this *sustained yield from my land:* $1000 ÷ 40 = $25 per acre per year."

Cut and run: "I clear-cut all the land, yielding $1000 per acre. This is a one-time operation, following which I abandon the land rather than pay taxes. I can then invest my money at 5 percent, getting a *sustained yield from my investment* of $1000 × 0.5 = $50 per acre per year." (Paradoxically, the yield can be expressed as dollars per acre, even though the man no longer owns any acres.)

Conclusion: "Cut and run."

The rational decision of the free-enterpriser in this situation is no different from that of Japanese whalers destroying the whale populations. Quantities matter. If we want to change the end result of lumbering, we have to pay attention to quantities. High taxes on land that is many years away from being timbered encourage cut-and-run. Taxes on newly felled logs discourage cutting, particularly if the nth tree removed from the same holding pays more taxes than the $(n-1)$th tree. Taxes can be assessed on stream pollution and soil destruction (though administration of them presents difficulties). The basic point is this: what happens to the land must never be construed as "natural development." What happens is the consequence of rational men seeking their own interest in a field of forces defined by manmade laws. What happens can be changed.

There's another way to look at the matter. We often speak of the "rights of private property," but what is "property"? The word has many meanings, among which are the following.

If I say, "I own this land" I imply that:

    a. I can use the land;

    b. I can abuse the land;

    c. I can sell the land (i.e., I can break the tie of responsibility between my land and me).

In an uncrowded world there may be no reason to restrict a person's freedom to do all three. But in a spaceship, where land is forever limited, there is a limit to our tolerance of the misuse of the heritage which our generation has received from our ancestors and which we hope to pass on to our descendants. Flagrant abuse is, indeed, almost certain to provoke us to limiting our neighbor's freedom to do what he wishes with *"his* property." An acute and abiding awareness of the imminence of posterity leads us to conclude that private property is not so much something that a man owns as it is something for which he is a trustee. His enjoyment of certain rights with respect to "his" property is—or should be—conditional upon his acceptance of the implied obligations of trusteeship.

Beyond the limits of his confining skin, no man can own any *thing.* "Property" refers not to things owned but to the rights granted by society; they must periodically be re-examined in the light of social justice.

CHAPTER 15

Reconciling Freedom with Coercion

The logic of the commons should be plain enough. In a crowded world the freedom of the commons leads to an intolerable and tragic end; we can avoid the tragedy only by relinquishing that kind of freedom. This we find hard to do. Rhetoric stands in the way of reason: "freedom" sounds so good, "coercion" so bad.

"Why can't we just let conscience be our guide?" This, the last defense of the unthinkingly tender-hearted, is seductive. Paradoxically, as we shall see, it leads inescapably to cruelty.

Let's look at the general problem of socially controlling human behavior by the alternatives of coercion and conscience. To lay bare the logic, let us use a model that does not arouse much in the way of emotion because it is so commonplace. Let us imagine an unsigned automobile crossroads, long regarded as safe, but at which lately there has been an increasing number of collisions. Desiring to prevent the loss of human life, we wonder what we should do about the crossroads. We see various possibilities.

First (as always), we can "do nothing," by which imprecise language we mean "make no change." With the increase in population of both people and cars, we can expect to see an increase in accidents and killings; in fact, a disproportionate increase. (Congestion is a power function of population.) Put another way, it is the very increase in population that has forced us to consider restricting freedom, since the cost of "doing nothing," namely increasing the death rate, seems too high.

Second, we can try education. We can put up DANGER signs. We might place a mangled wreck at the side of the road near the crossing, leaving drivers to make their own inferences. Or we might plant a conspicuous white cross every time someone loses a life at the intersection. Educational gimmicks sometimes work: but usually not for long. People become inured to them.

Third, sooner or later we must call for definite action, namely STOP. How shall we "call" for it—by persuasion or coercion? Shall we rely on conscience or force? Which of these two signs should we put at the intersection?

a. PLEASE STOP. Meaning: no force will be used, no punishments handed out; we're appealing to your conscience.

b. STOP. Meaning: you have no freedom of choice; society has the power to punish you for infractions. You are being coerced.

Rhetorical stereotypes lead many people to think that conscience is a gentler rein than coercion, but analysis casts doubt on this automatic conclusion. It is the *new* restriction that people are tempted to enforce by conscience alone, forgetting that most long-standing restrictions are enforced by coercion (and not thinking to ask why).

What are we asking when we ask a man to PLEASE STOP, for conscience' sake? He would prefer not to stop. By putting up the sign we create a psychological conflict inside the driver between what he really wants to do and what his conscience tells him to do. The conflict will resolve itself differently in different people. Some will stop, some won't. Those who do stop sacrifice some perceived good that is not given up by those who don't.

In other words, *a system that depends only on conscience rewards the conscienceless.*

As those with stronger consciences perceive what is happening, many (not all) will change their behavior, and the PLEASE STOP signs will become increasingly less effective. Ultimately we bow to the obvious and put up new signs that say simply STOP, with all that implies of force and coercion.

No one wants to be coerced into doing something. But, in a crowded world, each of us wants to keep others from doing certain things. (I don't want to be kept from robbing banks myself; but I do want to keep all others from doing so.) Seeing the counterproductive results of voluntary compliance with guidelines, we finally admit the necessity of coercion for all—*mutual coercion, mutually agreed upon.*

For all societies more populous than Robinson Crusoe's, this is the nearest we can get to freedom. "Mutual coercion, mutually agreed upon"—this is what we mean by "freedom through law."

This is all terribly obvious, but only because it is concerned with solutions reached in the past and accepted as unthinkingly as we accept breathing. It is when we perceive the need for a new restriction that the issue of conscience versus coercion is raised—and usually wrongly solved at first because of the emotional power of words like "freedom" and "conscience."

Consider the commons. We have seen that it is to society's interest that we give up the commons of the air and water and the marine fisheries. But how shall society control the individuals of which it is composed? By an appeal to conscience? If we ask pulp-mill operators to buy expensive pollution-control equipment as a matter of conscience, we reward those operators who are conscienceless. Similarly for steel mills and every other business that generates polluted effluents. Likewise for municipalities that must raise tax money to pay for sewage-disposal systems. The only reason we even think of trying to control pollution by "voluntary" compliance is because we have only recently become aware of the problem.

Coercion is the only means that will achieve the ends desired. A PLEASE STOP sign will not work: we must say STOP.

The word "coercion" is itself coercive. When we free ourselves of the paralysis engendered by its magic spell, we see that when coercion is the necessary choice it is also the kind one. The tender-hearted preference for an appeal to conscience is psychologically cruel. Let's see why this is so.

If we ask a man who is exploiting a commons to desist "in the name of conscience," what are we saying to him? What does he hear —not only at the moment but also in the wee small hours of the night when, half asleep, he remembers not merely the words we used but also the nonverbal communication we gave him unawares? Sooner or later, consciously or subconsciously, he senses that he has received *two* communications, and that they are contradictory:

1. (Intended communication) "If you don't do as we ask, we will openly condemn you for not acting like a responsible citizen."

2. (The unintended communication) "If you *do* behave as we ask, we will secretly condemn you for a schlemiel, a sucker, a sap, who can be shamed into standing aside while the rest of us exploit the commons."

In a word, he is damned if he does and damned if he doesn't. He is caught in what Gregory Bateson has called a "double bind." Bateson and his co-workers have made a plausible case for viewing the double bind as an important causative factor in the genesis of schizophrenia. The double bind may not always be so damaging, but it always endangers the mental health of anyone to whom it is applied. "A bad conscience," said Nietzsche, "is a kind of illness."

Should it not be regarded as evidence of the underlying psychological unhealthiness of our society that our leaders so often seek to control us by putting us in a double bind? Has any President during the past generation failed to call upon labor unions "voluntarily" to moderate their demands for higher wages, or upon steel companies to honor "voluntarily" the government's guidelines on prices? I can recall none.

We customarily perceive persuasion and coercion as mutually exclusive alternatives, but in fact they merge into a continuous spectrum. At the extreme of effectiveness, persuasion becomes coercion, as the following example shows.

In August of 1971 President Nixon called for a "voluntary" freeze on wages and prices. A few days later the economist Walter Heller was asked whether the "voluntary" freeze would work. His first reply was worthy of the oracle at Delphi: "We must pray to the deities that it works." Then, approaching the problem more substantively, he said that what was needed next was a wage-price review board "to put the pitiless spotlight of public opinion on the bad guys and praise the good guys."

When the velvet hand of persuasion is wrapped in so hard an iron glove, how does it differ from coercion? The urge to control others by an appeal to conscience in the hope of arousing guilt feelings in them is widespread. The desire to arouse guilt feelings is surely pathological. Paul Goodman has said: "No good has ever come from feeling guilty, neither intelligence, policy, nor compassion. The guilty do not pay attention to the object but only to themselves, and not even to their own interests, which might make sense, but to their anxieties."

Conscience versus coercion. We tend to see this as a choice between tender means and cruel; yet now we have shown that the choice is between two cruelties. Is there no better way to view our options?

I think there is. Let's look once more at the idea of tragedy. As Whitehead said, the *essence* of dramatic tragedy lies not in its content of unhappiness but in the tonic thrill we feel at the revelation of the remorseless working of things. The scientific equivalent of dramatic tragedy is the body of inescapable natural laws—what the mathematician Edmund Whittaker called "impotence principles," because they are beyond our ability to alter or escape. Unlike dramatic tragedy, they need not involve unhappiness—unless we foolishly build our lives on the wish that they be not true. Scientific thinking is, as Whitehead said, permeated by a recognition of the remorseless inevitableness of things: "The laws of physics are the decrees of fate."

The law of gravity defines some of our impotence. Should we weep because we cannot fly—not as a bird flies, which is really flying? Should we be heartbroken because we fall and skin our knee, or explode with anger because we sweat when we climb a mountain? Those who react so are rightly labeled "immature." We would have scant patience with anyone who said, "Freedom is indivisible; if I cannot be free of the law of gravity, then freedom is not mine."

The philosopher Hegel was wiser: he said, "Freedom is the recognition of necessity."

We are not free to violate the laws of nature. We become free when we recognize their necessity. The laws governing human interactions are not yet so clear, but as they emerge we can become free in proportion as we correctly identify the necessities. When we see clearly the consequences of exponential growth, of selection, and of responsibility mechanisms—when we can, like Margaret Fuller, accept the world (all of it!)—then we become free.

CHAPTER 16

The *Quis Custodiet* Problem

It's a dramatic photo: a wiry European in a safari jacket, a floppy hat on his head (no one dares wear a sensible pith helmet now that colonialism is over in Africa); in the near distance—too near for comfort—an elephant charging, a great beast with wrinkled proboscis raised high in threat; and, at the man's shoulder, an elephant gun, ready to fire.

Moral? Immoral?

We don't know. It's only a photograph. Morality cannot be deduced from a photograph. Of course if you believe, with the Jains of India, that all killing is immoral, then you have no doubts. At the other extreme, big-game hunters also have no doubts. The rest of us are not so sure. Thinking not of the individual animal but of the good of the species as a whole, we wonder (when we see a photo) if it is moral to kill this particular animal.

No answer. No answer is possible until we know the total situation. If the elephant we see in the photograph is a pregnant female, the last of her species, then it is certainly immoral to kill it, if we regard the continuation of the species as an intrinsically desirable thing. But if the elephant in the photo is one of the elephants of East Africa today, then the killing of it may actually be beneficial for the species. Virtually without natural enemies, elephants are multiplying out of control, destroying native trees in their search for food, diminishing the carrying capacity of their environment, diminishing their numbers by their own activities, and potentially even extinguishing

133

the species. To save the species "elephant," man must kill elephants. Not all—just the right number. A photo may be evidence of a killing, but it shows nothing about the right number. A photo may be emotionally moving—but it is of no help in reaching a moral decision.

The morality of an act is a function of the state of the system at the time the act is performed—this is the fundamental tenet of "situation ethics." It deprives us of the comfort of simple dogmatic directives like "Thou shalt not kill elephants." Directives become conditional: "Thou shalt not kill elephants *if* . . ." Killing an elephant may be moral this year, indeterminate two years from now, and immoral in five years. It is the state of the system, and our knowledge of the state of the system, that is determinative—and this does not show in a photograph, which (at best) freezes a moment in time.

"A picture is worth a thousand words," says an old Chinese proverb: *but it takes ten thousand words to validate it*. The tyranny of the camera penetrates everywhere into the fabric of modern life. We thoughtlessly suppose we can tell good from bad in a photograph, and beauty from ugliness.

No doubt Hell photographs beautifully.

The alternative to situation ethics, namely absolutist ethics—the ethics built upon *thou shalt nots*—renders lawmaking easy. The spirit of situation ethics is more difficult to capture in the laws. And more difficult for the individual to follow. "When the stock of elephants falls below x number, then thou shalt not kill elephants." But how is an individual to know when the number is less than x? As an *interested* party he may unconsciously bias his observations slightly; for that must he go to jail?

Whenever the state of a system needs to be taken into account before an act can be approved or disapproved, an administrative agency is needed. Ideally, an administrator should be *disinterested*. As a human being he may fall short of the ideal, but the thrust of the legal specifications is clear. The administrator who decides when elephants can be hunted should not himself be an active hunter. His rulings should be based on the facts, not on his own desires.

A signal advantage of administrative rulings is that they can be revised more rapidly than can statute law. A medical example illustrates his point well.

Around the turn of the century it was shown that most blindness in newborn babies is caused by maternal gonorrhea, and that the blindness can be prevented by putting drops of silver-nitrate solution into the baby's eyes immediately after birth. Laws requiring this treatment were speedily passed in many states, including California.

In the 1940s it was found that penicillin, discovered a few years earlier, was better than silver nitrate. But medical men could not change their practice because of the specificity of the law. In California, it took almost a decade to make the needed statutory change. There was no difference of professional opinion to confuse the legislators, and it is improbable that the amount of business involved in selling one product or another was enough to support professional lobbyists. It was only the inherent inertia of the legislative process that made change so slow and difficult.

An administrative agency could have moved much more expeditiously. Instead of specifying silver nitrate, the law should have specified merely that the treatment to prevent neonatal blindness should be based on the best medical judgment of the time, naming the agency charged with determining what that was. With a general directive like this, change could have been more rapid.

But legislatures are loath to establish administrative power to create law, and voters back them up. *Quis custodiet ipsos custodes?*—"Who shall watch the watchers themselves?" goes the ancient question. We ignore it at our peril.

At the root of the *Quis custodiet* problem is the issue of responsibility; and coupled with this is the control of information. Table 8 extends the analysis developed previously to include a new component, the temptation to sabotage information, in the last column.

In a private enterprise the intrinsic responsibility of the decision-maker insures that there will be no interference with the gathering and reporting of information. The private enterpriser *wants* to know about any bad decisions he makes, the sooner the better. This is not to say that some enterprisers are not given to wishful thinking, but the aberration is pathological. A competitive system is self-correcting because aberrant enterprisers who are given to fantasy will suffer at the hands of their more rational competitors.

The system of the commons is ambivalent with respect to its treat-

TABLE 8

Characteristics of the Three Political Systems
How temptation to sabotage information systems leads to the
Quis Custodiet problem

	RESULTS OF THE GAME			
	GAIN FROM STRESSING THE SYSTEM:			
NAME OF THE GAME	OVER-ALL GAIN (1)	GAIN TO THE DECISION-MAKER (2)	INTRINSIC RESPONSIBILITY (3)	TEMPTATION TO SABOTAGE INFORMATION (4)
Private enterprise	—	—	+	0
Socialism	—	0	0	+
System of the commons	—	+	—	(0)

ment of information. Since decision-makers gain by bad decisions, it doesn't much matter what happens to information, so long as the system continues. Nevertheless there may be a tendency for those with a vested interest to suppress information *as to the existence of the system itself*. American industrialists, using the commons to dispose of their wastes, always fail to point out that they have departed from the free-enterprise system they praise so highly.

It is in the operation of a socialistic system that the management of information becomes critical. Since the decision-maker in this system has no intrinsic responsibility, he is subjected to contrived responsibility—rewards for good management, punishment for poor. But how can the community tell whether the management is good or bad? Except for gross blunders, it is not easy. It takes an immense amount of information to tell whether the decision-maker is doing well or poorly. This information the bureaucrat needs for his own purposes. When he discovers that he has made a mistake, he will be strongly tempted to suppress information to save his own skin. If he can, he will suppress truth in the name of national security, thus exposing his opponents to the risk of jail sentences if they ferret out and publish any of the information that casts doubt on his competence.

In any nation, whatever its nominal political system, the defense department is a socialistic system, run by bureaucrats, outside the area of competition. Of all agencies of the government, this department can most plausibly hide behind the mask of "national security." Under the circumstances it is no wonder that extravagance and incompetence flourish in *all* departments of defense. Information can be so effectively controlled that a nation may be destroyed before incompetence is revealed—all in the name of "national security"!

Every bureaucrat is threatened by freedom of information; but in the long run the entire administrative system can survive only if information cannot be permanently bottled up. This conflict creates permanent tension. Seeking to survive, bureaucrats continually evolve new ways of sabotaging the information systems. Each such act of sabotage consists of two parts:

a. the suppression of information

b. suppressing the information that information has been suppressed.

In response, the society served by a bureaucracy must continually evolve new probes to penetrate the ever more effective smoke screens of its servants.

We cannot do without bureaus; how are we doing with them? Anyone who reads the daily papers sees ample evidence that we have not done very well in the last half-century. The FAA (Federal Aviation Administration), the ICC (Interstate Commerce Commission), the FCC (Federal Communications Commission), the FTC (Federal Trade Commission), the FDA (Food and Drug Administration), and countless others were, as of the 1960s, in a state that could only be called corrupt. This does not mean that the bureaucrats were necessarily venal. A few no doubt were, but the majority probably were not. But they had been slowly corrupted by their conditions of employment.

Suppose a needed decision involves $10 million a year. If ten business concerns are affected, the manager of each will go to a great deal of trouble to try to influence the regulatory agency. If his potential share is $1 million, he can easily afford to make several trips to Washington, to prepare expensive information brochures justifying his position, to advertise, and to take a few bureaucrats to lunch. (The government employees may even pay their own way, and yet still be affected by the air of friendship.)

On the other hand, the general public that stands to lose $10 million is diffuse, unorganized. As I am one of two hundred million citizens, my share of the loss is five cents. I can't afford to go to Washington to present my case, nor can any of the unorganized consumers, so the bureaucrats hear only one side. This is the greatest danger to administrative rulings, that they will be based on insufficient evidence.

Social factors enter in to worsen the situation. Bureaus need experts. The bureau needs the same kind of experts as do the businesses it is supposed to regulate. The psychological bond between experts is likely to be stronger than the bond between an expert and his employer. Chatting with his counterpart in business, the bureau expert is likely to forget the interests of his bureau, and ultimately of the public.

In addition, if the government expert impresses his business counterparts with his competence, he may at some time in the future be offered a position in the business concern at a much higher salary. Without a word being said about it, this must always be in the back of a bureaucrat's mind. Under these circumstances, even the most honest of men has trouble maintaining his objectivity.

The watchdog role of bureaus has been undermined also by the very pervasive pro-business atmosphere of the first half of the twentieth century. "What's good for General Motors is good for America, and vice versa," a onetime president of the company is reputed to have said. There is some truth in the statement, of course, but probably not when a conflict calls it into question. Unfortunately, most bureaucrats acted as if they believed it all the time. When marine wells of the Union Oil Company spilled crude oil that washed ashore on the Santa Barbara beaches, there was a marked discrepancy in estimates of the quantity. It is not easy, of course, to measure the amount of oil from photographs of an oil slick; but the discrepancy between the estimates of an independent scientist and of the United States Coast Guard was more than could be accounted for by "sampling error." Coast Guard estimates were only 10 percent as great as the scientist's. Of course, he may have been wrong.

Two years later a Navy aircraft carrier spilled oil which washed ashore on southern California beaches, including the beach of the "Western White House" at San Clemente. The Coast Guard estimated the spill at 1200 gallons. Fortunately this time the exact amount could be determined from the loss to the oil bunker of the ship. It was 299,446 gallons. The Coast Guard had reported only 0.4 percent of the true amount—one gallon out of every two hundred and fifty. In this case it was not business the government bureau was protecting, but another branch of the government. No doubt the Coast Guard saw itself as a defender of the peace; it did not want to "arouse the natives" by needless accuracy.

It is undeniable that the great majority of the American administrative agencies created in the first half of the twentieth century had, by 1970, been thoroughly corrupted, though probably honestly so. The regulators had been captured by the regulatees. Chickens, set to guard against the foxes, had been gobbled up.

The principal ray of hope was the appearance of Ralph Nader on the scene. Trained as a lawyer, with the passion of a muckraker, this remarkable man probably had more influence on the day-to-day operations of the American government than any other man in the twentieth century. Pricked by him, bureau after ponderous bureau slowly turned around and walked the other way, away from seductive business interests toward the public they are supposed to serve.

All this has been fine, but it hardly offers a general solution to the *Quis custodiet* problem. Ralph Nader is in the nature of a miracle, and we can hardly build public policy on the assumption of periodic miracles. What we need are statutory provisions of corrective feedback processes designed to keep administrators honest and on their toes.

Recognizing the difficulty of the *Quis custodiet* problem and overwhelmed by the myriads of instances of malfeasance committed by our bureaus, we are often tempted to throw in the sponge and get rid of all administrative decisions by going back to finely detailed statutory law. This plainly won't do. We've got to pay the price of population.

The bigger the population, the faster the rate of growth of knowledge, and the more complex the society to which it needs to be applied. But the greater the population, the slower the legislative process. From these two facts the necessity of bureaus and administrative law follows. If you don't like bureaus, find a way to reduce population.

Bureaucracy increases the citizen's feeling of alienation, of course; but even this is not a valid argument against it. As the population becomes larger, even legislators come to seem remote and unapproachable—only marginally less so than bureaucrats.

We can't get rid of administrators and administrative regulations —not unless we are willing to submit ourselves to whatever legal control would be necessary to reduce our population to a small fraction of its present size. For the foreseeable future the *Quis custodiet* problem—still largely unsolved—will be a major political problem of our lives.

CHAPTER 17

To Kill Progress
that Responsibility May Live

Born   1795
Died   1971

That may someday be the inscription engraved on the tomb of Progress. Insofar as it is possible to assign a sharp date to the beginning of any movement in history, we can say that Progress was born in 1795 with the publication of the Marquis de Condorcet's *Sketch for a Historical Picture of the Progress of the Human Mind.* It died on Wednesday, March 24, 1971, when the United States Senate, treading closely on the heels of the House, denied any more funds to the SST (supersonic transport plane) by a vote of 51 to 46. Let's see what sort of beast it was that died that day.

The idea of Progress is essentially a religious idea. The hypothetical man from Mars would have no difficulty identifying Progress as a religion. As conventional religion waned in power in the nineteenth century, Progress grew. Like every living religion, Progress possessed dogmas beyond doubting. Two in particular need to be noted:

1. *The Dogma of Aladdin's Lamp:* If we can dream of it, we can invent it.

2. *The Dogma of the Technological Imperative:* When we invent it, we are required to use it.

The first dogma cannot be reconciled with the philosophy of impo-   141 tence principles (itself the product of the intensely religious minds of Whitehead and Whittaker); it is demonstrably false. We cannot square the circle (as the problem is defined in Euclidean geometry), nor can we trisect the angle. Neither will we develop an airplane that will fly the 25,000 miles around the world in just 1 hour, for that is the "escape velocity." A plane flying at such a speed would go not around the earth but straight off it.

What about the dogma of the Technological Imperative? *Must* we use everything we invent? . . . Who says so?

Curiously, economic conservatives say so. In our day an economic conservative is one who fights fiercely for the freedom of every private enterpriser to "do his thing," regardless of the good of the community. But the members of the community, though sometimes technically free to use or not use a new technological device, are always looked at suspiciously if they propose to exercise this option by saying *no*. To put the matter parochially, it's un-American to say *no* to technology.

This conservative attitude surfaced viciously when the nation was debating whether or not to manufacture the SST. Since the planes were economically unsound in a free economy, they had to be built with government money if they were to be built at all. The conservative James Burnham concluded a justification of the government subsidy of the SST with what one aerospace industry spokesman lauded as "this clincher":

> There is no point debating whether mankind "needs" supersonic transportation. Mankind is going to get it . . .

—*in the neck,* apparently.

This is not the language of rationality; it is the language of a primitive religion, a religion that requires human sacrifice, only now it is not the icon of an unseen god in human form that requires the sacrifice, but the all too visible and inhuman specter of technology. So compelling is the religious demand for sacrifice to the god of Progress that conservative economists abandoned their habitual defense of the principle of free enterprise (which government-financed manufacture of SST was not) in order that the great god Progress might be served.

The most powerful incantation of the religion of Progress has been this simple affirmation:

You can't stop Progress.

When you stop to think about it, that phrase, "You can't stop Progress," is remarkably revealing. The rhetorical pattern of the sentence is simple; we might expect to hear it used often. But do we?

How often do you hear someone say, "You can't stop gravity"?

Or, "You can't stop raspberry pie"?

The first happens to be true; but it is so very true that one never needs to say it. Gravity is here to stay; it needs no promoters.

Raspberry pie is something else again. I *can* stop eating raspberry pie. In fact, I don't even have to start. If a man tells me otherwise it is because, with coercive language, he seeks to ensnare me and deprive me of my freedom to choose. The compulsion characterizes the speaker—not the pie.

It is curious how the more extreme of the conservative economists prove, in matters of temperament, to be blood brothers of Karl Marx. Both serve their religion *in the same way*—it is only the object of worship that differs. Karl Marx said *You can't stop communism,* and this coercive statement has been a powerful weapon in the hands of his followers. You can't stop communism, he said, because it is historically inevitable.

"You can't stop Progress."
"You can't stop communism." } *What's the difference?*

Any operational definition of "religion" must include something of the attitude of the believer in the presence of those forces that he commits himself not to oppose. Verbalizing, he converts his commitment to personal impotence into an omnipotence of the *other*. Basking in the reflected glow of the Omnipotent Other, the True Believer sings ecstatically of his helplessness.

Since he is helpless, the worshiper is not responsible for what happens. This is the real reason why men intone "You can't stop Progress"—it is a way of escaping the responsibility of thinking and judging. Irresponsibility is the blessed state all men seek—for themselves.

The man who says, "You can't stop Progress," is a genuinely religious man. But is this the best religion on board a spaceship?

The motives of those who voted on the SST in March of 1971 were mixed, on both sides of the issue. Some of those voting against the SST were really voting against President Nixon or the war in Vietnam. Unquestionably some of those voting for were more concerned with supporting the President than with getting that behemoth up into the air. Allowing for all this, I think the vote on that historic day was a genuine expression of revulsion with the sort of progress the SST symbolized. It is not beyond the bounds of political possibility that the project might someday be revived; but if it is, it will be an uphill fight all the way. Never again will the SST, or any other similar large project, enjoy an automatic and unthinking acceptance "because you can't stop Progress."

We can stop Progress.

We have stopped it. At least once: and we can do it again.

Although the SST is part of history now, it will pay to examine several points of the controversy because they involve general principles that will be encountered repeatedly as we continue to dismantle the religion of Progress.

For our purpose, some of the issues can be quickly disposed of. One of the dangers alleged of the SST was that a flotilla of five hundred or more of them spewing forth combustion products in the stratosphere would so alter the properties of this "window" to the sun and outer space that the heat balance of the earth would be disturbed, causing the surface to become either (a) hotter, or (b) colder. The uncertainty of knowledge is indicated by the contradiction of the two possibilities. With a few years' intensive study it should be possible to resolve the issue. The practical question was: Should we suspend the SST program until we learn the answer; or should we go ahead and assume that everything will turn out all right?

It was also alleged that SSTs would increase the amount of cancer in the world. The prediction may sound far-fetched, but is based on the meticulous studies of the chemist Harold Johnston, which predict that the nitrous oxides discharged into the upper atmosphere will catalyze reactions that destroy ozone, which is opaque to ultraviolet light. Without this UV filter the atmosphere will let through more short-wavelength light to the earth's surface, producing more skin cancer. And perhaps other effects. . . . Again, the danger alleged cannot be regarded as scientifically proved.

Then, there is a matter of noise, in the ordinary sense, as it would impinge upon the area around the airports where the SSTs would land and take off. The FAA in 1969 suggested that the level of perceived noise by subsonic planes landing and taking off be kept below 108 decibels. The most optimistic estimate for SSTs is 124 decibels. Because the decibel scale is logarithmic, 124 db is 40 times louder than 108 db. Put in practical terms, one SST taking off would make as much noise as forty of our biggest subsonic jets all taking off from the same runway at the same time. (Imagine yourself living near an SST airport.) The fear of such a noise was countered with the promise that "science will solve the problem." It is true that subsonic jets have been made quieter since they were introduced; no doubt supersonic engines will undergo a similar evolution (though how far is not clear). Again, the debate has no clear-cut result.

Important as they are, these inconclusive matters need not be pursued further because there is another consideration that leads to a completely conclusive negative judgment on the SST. One exclusion on rational grounds is enough.

The decisive issue is the "sonic boom." In physics, sonic boom is related to noise in the ordinary sense. Psychologically, however, those phenomena are utterly different, as anyone who has experienced a boom can attest. Being boomed is like living inside a large drum beaten erratically by an idiot drummer; the sensation penetrates to all parts of the body. Suddenness and unexpectedness are essential parts of the distress.

Improving the engines of SST would have no effect on the boom. An SST with absolutely silent engines would produce the same boom, which is a product of the movement of a solid body through the atmosphere at a speed greater than the speed of sound (which is in the neighborhood of 700 miles per hour). Once supersonic speed is achieved, there is no way to prevent the boom.

Seeking to spike the guns of the opposition, SST proponents promised that the planes would not pass over the continental United States but would be flown only over the "open oceans." What does "open" mean? The implication of "open" in this context is "free of people." But what of all the people in cargo ships and cruise ships? What of the millions of people living on the islands of the Caribbean, for example, who would be flown over by planes going to South America?

Moreover, it was obvious to all that the promise to avoid flying over the continental United States was made in bad faith because the people making it were gripped by the Technological Imperative. Once the SST was in the air, they would argue that it was uneconomic to restrict it to ocean flights. Hence, they would say, to keep the SST from being a drain on taxpayers (through subsidy payments) it would have to be cleared for flights everywhere—and we would be screwed by technology again.

How many people would be disturbed by each flight of an SST across the United States? From the predicted width of the boom-strip, and from the known distribution of the population in the 1960s, it was calculated that a minimum of 20 million people would be boomed by each continental flight, no matter what the route. Who are these 20 million people? What are they doing at the time of the unexpected shock?

To take some special (though not rare) cases first, among those boomed would be:

babies just going to sleep
invalids desperately in need of rest
mental cases in need of peace
artists composing music or writing poetry
surgeons performing delicate operations

And so on. But important as these special cases may be, "hard-nosed" acceptors of the Technological Imperative reject them in favor of the "average man" or the "common man" who is not operating on an eye, composing music, writing poetry; or taking care of invalids, mental cases, or infants. And who presumably is neither young nor old himself, and is healthy. Without arguing about the size of the sample, let's consider the common man. Let's ignore all the special cases and assume everybody is a common man and ask: Is it to his advantage or disadvantage to have the SST?

This is a problem in cost-benefit analysis. It is a rational problem. It can be quantified. It leads to a precise answer.

We look for a rational answer by setting up the following equation:

(Sum of all benefits) minus (Sum of all costs) = Utility.

If the utility is plus, we go ahead. If it is minus, we don't. If the utility is zero, it's a toss-up.

Whenever it is difficult to make exact quantitative estimates of costs or benefits it is often possible to reach a decision by seeing what the "break-even point" is, i.e., the point at which:

(Sum of all benefits) minus (Sum of all costs) = Zero

At which point:

(Sum of all costs) = (Sum of all benefits)

Let's use this approach for the SST. The presumed principal benefit of the plane is that it saves time. We must say "presumed," because it is not clear that saving time is always a good thing. Will Rogers once remarked, "I never yet talked to the man who wanted to save time who could tell me what he was going to do with the time he saved." But this is too fundamental an approach to be widely acceptable; let us not question the conventional wisdom.

The only people whose time is saved are the ones who fly on the SST. The capacity of the proposed American ship is about 240 passengers. Whisked coast-to-coast, they will save 2 hours each at the most optimistic estimate. So 480 man-hours will be saved. What are they worth? Let's assume that everyone who is so eager to save this time is an important executive, making an average salary of $60,000 a year. Such people probably work at least 60 hours a week 50 weeks a year, or 3000 hours a year. Their time is, then, worth $20 an hour. The time saved by a planeload of them is worth $20 × 480,   or $9600. This is the benefit.

Now what is the cost that will exactly balance the benefit at the break-even point? This cost decomposes into two portions:

(Cost per person) × (Number of persons) = $9600.00

Since twenty million people will be disturbed by each flight, we can write:

$$(\text{Cost per person}) \times (20{,}000{,}000) = \$9600.00$$

or:

$$\text{Cost per person} = \$9600.00 \div \$20{,}000{,}000$$
$$\text{Cost per person} = \$0.00048$$

In words, the break-even point is at less than five tenths of a mill.

A priori we might have been hard pressed to say what the negative value of being subjected to a sonic boom was. Five cents? Ten cents? A dollar? Tastes differ. But by sidestepping this difficult question and going directly to the break-even point we find that it is easy to reach a practical conclusion. If you would regard it as a fair recompense to be paid a penny for each twenty sonic booms you are subjected to, then the SST is worth while, on a rigorous cost-benefit analysis.

If you would regard the penny as less than adequate recompense for twenty booms, the SST is indefensible.

The answer is surely obvious.

Remember: this is based on only a partial analysis. Taking into account all the factors would surely lead to a worse showing for the SST. There's the matter of infants, mothers of infants, invalids, insomniacs, mental patients, composers, poets, and eye surgeons. There's the matter of proven structural damage, including damage to irreplaceable national treasures like the cliff dwellings at Mesa Verde National Park in Colorado.

And there is the justifiable doubt that the time of the average SST commuters would be worth $60,000 a year *to society*. Some of them might be society women flying from coast to coast to attend a garden party. Some might be Mafia members on their way to Switzerland to make deposits in numbered bank accounts.

And others might be merely officials of the Federal Aviation Administration flying out to the hinterlands to give service-club luncheon speeches on "American Destiny and the SST."

No rational analysis is ever complete. There are yet a few more layers of this logical onion that need exposing.

Suppose the benefits of the SST exceeded the costs—would that justify the device? Not necessarily. We would then have to ask:

Who benefits?
Who pays?

It is clear that the two "whos" are different. There is little overlap. In a word, Frankel's criterion of responsibility is not satisfied. And cannot be, for the following reason.

Theoretically, one could pipe factory smoke into the living room of the president of a polluting company and make him responsible for his actions. But there is no way we can subject the rider of an SST plane to the boom his plane is producing on the ground. The SST is intrinsically and irrevocably an irresponsible technological device.

It is not beyond the bounds of possibility that some contrived responsibility could be engineered into the system. Before going ahead with the SST I suggest that we subject all airline and aerospace workers, all 45,000 employees of the FAA, and all 535 members of Congress to 20 sonic booms a day, disposed randomly in time, and pay each person a penny for each day he is boomed. Continue this for several months. Then take a vote.

The only remaining semi-plausible defenses of the SST are nonrational.

1. The Technological Imperative, already discussed in general terms. We cannot say *no* to Progress because if we don't go forward we will slide backward. The image is spatial, the logic specious.

2. "It makes work." The same can be said for a heroin factory. Actually, one can defend the idea that a society should have as its primary concern the principle that every able member must always be able to find work. We may someday come to this. But at the present time we are miles from it. Anyone who proposes this as a general principle is quickly labeled a Communist. But it's all right to raise the "makes work" argument to save a particular industry that is rationally indefensible in a free economy.

3. "We need it for National Prestige." National Prestige, whatever it is, cannot be achieved self-consciously. It has to be a "fallout" from activities that are *intrinsically* worth while. Those who woo her hardest win her never.

CHAPTER 18

Progress: The Next Coming

Many commentators instantly recognized March 24, 1971, as a day of historic importance. Those who thought that shooting down the SST was a good thing referred to the day of decision as "a watershed." Those who thought it a serious error—the President's Science Adviser, Edward E. David, for one—referred to it as "a loss of nerve," suggesting that it was the first step in the descent of America to a second-class power. They saw the econuts as the villains in a drama in which innocent Progress was the lovely heroine who was being murdered. It never occurred to them that Progress might have been committing suicide.

At about the same time another child of Progress was expiring without the help of any villains. This one had no government subsidy, so its demise attracted much less attention. But this death, too, suggests the end of an era.

In the 1930s the Du Pont Corporation had a fantastic scientific and commercial success in nylon. It put millions of dollars into the development of this synthetic substitute for silk, and ultimately it took billions out. It was a success story it naturally ached to repeat.

In the 1960s Du Pont thought it had found a repeater: Corfam, a substitute for leather. It put millions into it, and it looked like a sure winner. . . .

But it wasn't. Part of the trouble is hidden in that word "looked"— Du Pont was a victim of the tyranny of the camera. The substance Corfam has a remarkable "memory." After you take off a pair of Corfam shoes at night, the minute alterations in shape that have accumulated during a day's walking slowly disappear and the shoes come back to their original shape by morning. *They take a good picture*—they look like new shoes, day after day, while leather shoes change.

That's just the trouble. Your feet don't want shoes that have a good memory, shoes that take a good picture forever. They want shoes that change, yield; the deformed old boots that Van Gogh painted are closer to the sole's desire than Corfam.

In 1971 Du Pont abondoned its "miracle" product, selling off the inventory for pennies. The company had laid out over $100 million on the gamble that the "Progress" of nylon could be repeated. It had lost. The Dogma of Aladdin's Lamp tells us that since we can dream of something better than real leather, we must be able to invent it. Possibly the dogma is false.

What are the limits of technology? We don't know, and it is unlikely that we will discover a general theorem that will permit us to define the exact limits. Yet it is difficult to believe there are no limits. There's a saying on Wall Street that "no tree grows to the sky," referring to the price of stocks. Why should technology's stock be an exception?

The matter can be put another way. It costs money to invent and perfect a new product. The cost of R & D increases cruelly with the passage of time. The R & D budget for the invention of the safety pin didn't amount to much; the search for a leather substitute cost an astronomical sum. Easy things are invented first. As the field of possibilities is progressively brought closer to exhaustion, the costs of R & D escalate until finally it isn't worth anybody's while to develop one more widget. Technological "Progress" stops short of the theoretical limit, for economic reasons. That we are already close to this practical limit is suggested by the large amount of R & D paid for by the government, i.e., by Santa Claus. Without this nonrational component of the development system, the supersonic transport would never have been proposed.

It wasn't technology that was shot down on March 24, 1971; it was Santa Claus. Not a bad day's shooting.

There are men now living who can remember the day when there were no automobiles, no movies, no airplanes, no radio, and no television. Never in the history of mankind has such diversity of techno-logical changes occurred in one long lifetime.

Will the next ninety years see so great a change in the technology of daily life? Perilous though it is to predict, I doubt it. This predic-tion is based on estimates of opportunity, cost, and demand. The opportunity is now less if we have (as I think) come closer to ex-hausting nature's possibilities. The cost of R & D is certainly increas-ing, probably exponentially. And as for "demand"—who's *demand-ing* another widget? "Demand" is a fiction created by the advertising industry whenever there is no *real* demand.

As we face the future, what are our true needs? Can anyone think of a technological invention that is *needed* to improve the quality of life? Even one? I think not.

But outside of technology the needs—which is to say, the opportu-nities—are immense. Many of our clearly felt needs revolve around information-handling problems. How to broadcast it more effec-tively. How to counteract the spontaneous decay in precision. How to protect the sources of information against corruption. How, in a word, to solve the *Quis custodiet* problem, the solution of which will be immensely more important than discovering how to split the atom.

And how can we minimize alienation in a mass society? What is the best response to tribalization? How can we create a sense of community?

Looking inward, how can we more effectively identify pride and envy, and neutralize their destructive effects?

These are real needs, not "needs" created by Madison Avenue. We are scarcely farther along in solving these problems than were the Greeks twenty-five hundred years ago. There is much wisdom in "lit-erature," but much foolishness also. How does one separate the two? There will be no enduring progress until the theoretical bases of hu-man society are made so clear that we can recognize necessity, and so become free.

The Cassandras of technology who complain of a "loss of nerve" when failing monsters like the SST are shot down miss the point. The ball game has moved to another park. The old game is pretty well played out; a new game is just beginning.

Part Three

CHAPTER 19

On Board the *Beagle:*

Freedom's Harvest

"Migawd, look at them! They look like a skillet of worms! How can they stand it?"

Four men were looking out the mountain window at the plain below. The ground could scarcely be seen for the bodies glistening in the synthetic sun. In constant motion, people chatted with one another, walking arm in arm, jostling, pushing, shoving, reacting—but never separating far from contact with one another.

George spoke: "Harry calculated that there must be something like twelve million of them now on this little old three-kilometer-wide spaceship. One more doubling . . ."

"Why don't they build apartments?" asked a wide-eyed, black-haired giant, obviously the baby of the group. His rebirth age was perhaps thirteen. "There are still some sheets of steel around that they could use for floors, and plenty of building blocks they could stack up to make walls. Then they wouldn't have to worry for a while."

"Peter, you sound like a Quotion," said George with some disgust. "Anyway they're too dumb to think of that. And if they thought of it they couldn't do it now. Couldn't clear enough space to work in. They should have thought of it earlier. Population growth has painted them into a corner. No options open. They're in a sink. All they can do now is go down the drain."

"Who pulls the plug?"

"God—if they're lucky. . . . Only, God is dead. . . ."

Peter spoke again. "Why don't they stop breeding? The Pill Fountains are still working. I saw them myself on the tube the other day."

George spoke sharply. "You know that's against their principles!"

155

Peter persisted. "But they'd be happier if they stopped. Some of them must see that. Why don't the ones who understand set an example for the others?"

George turned to the bookish little man at his right. "Hugh, we still have that tape we made of the Great Debate two hundred and fifty years ago, don't we?"

"I know right where it is."

"Would you be kind enough to dig it out? I think Peter should see it."

Hugh walked off briskly down a corridor to the right. George turned to young Peter again.

"Look, Pete. It's this way. You seem to think that the nonbreeders might shame the breeders—right?"

"Well, yes. But I thought if the breeders saw how much better life the nonbreeders had . . ."

"How much better life would they have, boy? Look out there"— with a sweep of his hand—"what happens if that comical character waving her hat there doesn't have a child, and the skinny woman next to her does? How does that make her life better or even different? They're all together, writhing on a common plain."

"Well . . . at least she wouldn't have the pain that comes when a baby is born. I saw one of the females on the tube the other day having a baby. She was obviously in pain. Surely no one would want that."

"Did you have the sound turned on?"

"Yes."

"What did she say when it was all over?"

Peter wrinkled his nose. "Well, that was sorta funny. She said,

"For babe and ache,
For child and cramp,
For joy and pain—
Dear God, I thank thee."

"Did she look like it was hurting when she said that?"

Peter shook his head slowly, wonderingly. "No, she didn't. She looked positively happy."

A buzzer sounded.

"Hugh's got the tape," George said. "Come on over here. I want to show you something that took place out on that same plain two hundred and fifty years ago."

They drew chairs up to the big tube as the picture went on.

The scene is the Plain of Quo at a time when the wrecked hulks of many buildings were still visible and only about 50,000 Quotions peopled the plain. The camera zeros in on a slightly elevated platform. At the table are four chairs, occupied by two men and two women. They are dressed for the occasion. A white man and a black woman are clothed in green; a black man and a white woman are dressed in yellow. The matronly white woman in yellow is speaking.

"On this great spaceship we must all be as brothers and sisters. There's no room for quarreling or competition on a spaceship: we have to pull together. That means that I must support your right to do your thing when it comes to having a family, just as you must support my right. Freedom is indivisible. Parents must be free to choose the number of children they produce. We Yellows appeal to the consciences of all parents to Stop at Two. Remember, we're living on a spaceship. But we wouldn't dream of forcing anyone. We just set an example and hope that, in time, everyone will follow it. Let no one dare to speak of coercion. True virtue is voluntary. Do Your Thing—Stop at Two—those are our twin mottoes."

The woman in green jumped up with her fist closed and yelled, "Right on, Sister!" She sat down.

The Yellow woman continued. "Our most precious heritage is Unity in Freedom. We must never lose that."

The man in yellow interrupted. "I hate to take issue with my Yellow sister, but I would like to ask a disturbing question. At least it disturbs me. I'm older than most of you. I can remember the time when I was a boy when the Holy Order of the Wearin' of the Green was first formed. For years, I don't suppose one person out of a hundred was a Green. Then somehow we began to notice an awful lot of little green kids running around, and pretty soon there were more and more. Now today as I look out among all you fine Brothers and Sisters"—with a sweep of his hand—"it seems to me that at least one out of every four is a Green.

"Don't misunderstand me," he hastened to add. "You're all fine people. Some of my best friends are Greens, but—"

He was interrupted by a swelling sound of disapproval. Cries of "Shame!" could be heard, and hisses. The Green man on the platform was on his feet, calling for quiet. He turned to the Yellow and said in his most glacial terms, "Do I understand you correctly, my Yellow Brother? Are you calling for GENOCIDE?"

The Yellow became very agitated and stammered, "Oh, dear no.

No, no—not at all. I wasn't calling for anything. I was just reciting some facts. It's always good to have facts, Brother."

It was a lame finish. He mopped his brow. The Green continued his attack.

"Do you believe in the inalienable right to life, liberty, happiness, and a family?"

"Absolutely."

"Would you deny any woman's right to have little children? Would you set a policeman to follow every woman around to see to it that she takes her pills? If she got pregnant anyway would you send a state Baby Liquidator to her home to abort her? *Would you put a policeman under every bed?*"

"Never!"

"Then what are we arguing about, Brother Alan? Let's not bring up irrelevant figures from the past. Let the dead past bury its dead. The world is for the *living!*"

He turned full face to the audience. "Our Brotherhood is built on faith. Faith in man's goodness. Look at the great progress we've made already. Let us not now suffer a loss of nerve. Let every Brother do his thing and let every Sister do her thing, and let every Brother and Sister trust every other Brother and Sister. Trust to the divine goodness implanted in every soul—trust to that and to the wisdom of Nature. Don't be led astray by any honky statistic that some fainthearted Intellectual pulls out of his bag of tricks to try to suck away your nerve. The world is for the living; the more life we create, the better. Those who have not the nerve to create life should not criticize those who do. But those who do should not try to shame those who don't: leave them do their thing.

"Don't believe the nay-sayers among us who say that the old ways aren't best, who say we must give up our God-given Freedom! Freedom has served us well in the long, long past. From time immemorial we have been free. Freedom will serve us even better in the future, if we don't let her down. I say Freedom! Brothers and Sisters —that's the word: Freedom! Freedom!"

A roar of approval came from the crowd as hats—both green and yellow—went flying into the air. The man in yellow, seated, leaned on the desk, holding his head in his hands. The man in green stood erect, arms and legs spread, drinking in the adulation.

The scene faded from the screen. George turned the knob off.

"Do you see what happened, Peter?"

"Yes . . . I guess so. But why aren't those people out there today wearing green?"

"Why should they? The last Yellow died twenty-five years ago. Within a year the Greens stopped dyeing their cloth. There was no point in it. If there's only one color, there's no color.

"But I don't see why there shouldn't be some Yellows left," said Peter. "After all, they were reproducing *some.* Not as much as the Greens, but some. They shouldn't have disappeared entirely."

"Come here, Pete," said George, going over to a blackboard on the wall away from the bank of television monitors. "You've been studying calculus so that you can someday take your turn in Emergencies. You'll need a lot of mathematics for that; and mathematics is useful in looking at the past, too.

"You know that every reproductively isolated group potentially multiplies in exponential fashion. Now the Plain of Quo was occupied by two different reproductively isolated groups, the Holy Order of the Wearin' of the Green, and the Trustful Fellowship for Zero Population Growth. The ZPGers, as they were first called, when it came to family reproduction, believed in stopping at two. 'We believe in family planning,' they said.

"The Greens believed in having as many children as they possibly could. They also said, 'We believe in family planning,' and they sincerely did.

"The Greens planned big families; the ZPGers planned small ones.

"Now let's look at the mathematics."

Writing on the board, and talking: "Let x equal the number of Greens, reproducing exponentially:

$$x = Ke^{gt}$$

"Let y equal the number of Yellows, also reproducing exponentially:

$$y = K'e^{ht}$$

"Obviously g has to be greater than h.

"What will be the ratio of x:y, as time goes on?

$$\frac{x}{y} = \frac{Ke^{gt}}{K'e^{ht}}$$

Since K and K' are both constants, we can replace them by a new constant, say C:

$$\frac{x}{y} = C\,\frac{e^{gt}}{e^{ht}}$$

But, by the laws of exponents, this may be written:

$$\frac{x}{y} = Ce^{(gt-ht)} = Ce^{(g-h)t}$$

And, since g and h are also constants, we can replace their differ-ence by a new constant, say b, giving:

$$\frac{x}{y} = Ce^{bt}$$

and b is a positive number, since g was greater than h.

"Now, Peter: What's the limit of this ratio, as t increases in-definitely?"

"No limit. Infinity."

"Does it make any difference how small b is?"

"None at all. Even the slightest difference between the two group constants produces a positive b, and the ratio goes to infinity."

"So much for the theoretical answer. But in a real world, which is finite, and where the value of y can never be less than one, a fraction of a person doesn't make sense. In fact, you need two, a male and a female. So: What will be the ultimate number of y—of Yellows—with not too great a t, really?"

"Zero, of course." Peter thought a bit. "I can't work out the values of g and h in my head for two children and—what?—twelve chil-dren, but I don't think there's been time enough in two hundred and fifty years for all the Yellows to disappear."

"Good boy! Very good! No, there hasn't. A theory is only a model of reality, and all models are incomplete. The theory we've just worked out is called the Competitive Exclusion Principle. But strong as its conclusion is, it is too weak for reality. At the last, another process came in, a process that requires a different mathematics.

"As the Yellows realized they had shrunk from a majority group to a minority group, a psychological change came over them. Maybe their cultural heritage included the phrase 'survival of the fittest,' we're not sure. But they seem to have reasoned this way:

    a. The fittest survive;

    b. we aren't surviving very well;

    c. therefore we aren't the fittest;

d. therefore it is our duty to stop reproducing.
And they did. They just gave up."

"The logic doesn't sound very good to me," said Peter; "they could just as well have—"

There was a sporting cry from the monitor board, where all the rest of the Argotes had gathered. "Hey, George—Pete! Come on over. One of 'em's going to get it."

Abandoning the blackboard, the two joined the others.

"What's up?"

"Don't know exactly, but evidently that curly-headed guy did something unQuotic. They're tying him to the stake now. How long do you think he'll last?"

"Five minutes."

"Three."

"Three and a half."

"Four."

A hubbub as they made their guesses.

"He's tied! Now let's see how they abandon him. In that crush, they may not be able to. That'd be ironical, wouldn't it?"

But the ringleaders in front turned their backs on the man tied to the stake, locked arms in a circle, and started pushing everyone away from the criminal. As they did so they shouted "Alone . . . Alone . . . Alone . . ." in unison, and the cry was taken up by the multitude, producing a wail that touched even the hearts of the Argotes, spectators though they were.

When the clearing around the staked man had widened to a radius of twenty-five feet, the Status Quotions at the edge of the circle raised their hands and said, "Sh-h-h-h-h . . ." and the sound spread like a wave over the multitude.

Silence.

The ringleaders turned around to watch.

The observers in the mountain were silent, too. One of them started a stopwatch.

Silence.

They waited.

The silence was broken by a sound from the screen. The tied man, after struggling convulsively but quietly for a while, raised his nose to the sky like a dog and began howling, "Alone! Alone! Alone! O my God, why hast thou forsaken me? Don't, don't!" Tears streamed down his face.

Presently he stopped howling; he became rigid as his eyes dilated with horror. Abruptly, he collapsed.

"He's dead! He's dead!" the crowd shouted in glee and closed in about him.

"My God," said the holder of the stopwatch at the monitor board, "just one minute and thirty-eight seconds! A new record . . . What hath Evolution wrought!"

"It's hard to believe they're the same people as we," said Harry, thoughtfully.

"They aren't," said George. "Not now. When we all got on the ship together we were. But not now. All of us in this room are genetically the same as we were in the beginning. But *they* have evolved."

"But why so different?" asked Peter: "And so *horrible?* So unnatural—not being able to stand even the pseudo-solitude of being a few body-lengths away from the nearest companion. It's not natural."

"It's natural now," said George grimly. "For them. When they first started filling up all the nooks and crannies with people, we thought population growth would come to a natural halt when they became too crowded for comfort. They had more food and water and air than they could use—in fact, plenty of everything. Except space. We thought that space would stop them. We thought overcrowding would create a stress reaction that would inhibit their breeding.

"We couldn't have been more wrong. We had forgotten about evolution again. First, the Right to Breed selected for fertility; then overcrowding selected for tolerance of crowding. The crowdability that has evolved is not merely facultative—it is obligatory. The adrenal cortex has been, apparently, completely changed. A distance of a mere ten feet from the nearest human body has pathological effects. Fifteen feet is lethal."

"I don't see how they can stand the crowding," said Peter.

"They can't live without it. They love it. It's *normal.* . . . Funny. I remember you saying, one life ago, Peter, that it's immoral to allow people to adjust to *intrinsically* crowded conditions; and when I asked you to define 'intrinsic' you got mad and threw a book at me."

"Did I? I don't remember," said Peter and winked.

"I think we had better have a council of war." The speaker was a tall, lean man who did not speak often. His hair was clipped in a crew cut, his face lined.

"Harry and I have been looking over the data and extrapolating into the future. It doesn't look good. Remember the point of all this. We Argotes were to be the stable element of the venture, like the nucleus of the cell. We were the trustees of the essential information. Social stability and reproduction aren't compatible, so we don't reproduce.

"The Quotions reproduce. So they change. When this project was planned, it was hoped that they wouldn't change too much in the short time needed to get to Alpha Centauri; but Alpha Centauri was no good, so we tacked off in another direction. And then another. Now the hundreds of years have stretched into thousands, and the Quotions have changed. Evolved. Drastically.

"The question is: in their present form are they fit to become the colonizers of a new planet when—I won't say *if*—we find one? *We* can't because we are sterile. And I submit that they are not fit either.

"A suitable planet must be an empty planet (otherwise we'd have to begin the Brave New World with mass murder). The colonists will have to spread out.

"Those cockroaches down there"—his voice was filled with disgust—"wouldn't spread out as far as you can spit! They'd be useless. They'd huddle together like a bunch of brainless sheep. They're not really brainless; but temperament is as important as brains. Their temperament is utterly unsuited to the task ahead.

"Of course, eventually the counterselective force of great space would select for the adventurous, for the ones who could leave their buddies; but that would take a long time. We might not have that kind of time to spare on the new planet. We don't know what kind of situation we'll encounter.

"So: we've got to bring about that evolution on board this ship, before we land. The only way we can do that is to reduce the population. Drastically."

"How drastically?"

The lean one hesitated a moment before speaking. "I don't know. Down to a tenth of one percent, perhaps. Maybe to a thousandth of one percent. No use trying to answer the question precisely, because we don't know the exact quantitative effect of the agent we're going to use."

Everyone was quiet, waiting for the details. The speaker frowned, regarded his nails for a long time in silence. Then he spoke.

"It will be a harrowing experience for them. There's only one way to keep it from destroying them psychologically. They must think that what is happening to them is the will of God. They still believe in him. Fortunately. This mountain must be the source of the voice of God."

He turned to the man on his left. "Kenneth?"

Kenneth had a broad face reminiscent of the traditional statues of Socrates: flat-nosed, a friendly face with peasant strength. When he smiled, his face became Happy Hooligan's.

"First," Kenneth said, taking up a small object shaped like a gas mask with an electric cord attached to it. "First, we decided the voice of God just has to be deep and resonant. Unfortunately, none of us has a really resonant voice. Certainly I don't. So we engineered this little dilly. Let me show you how it works."

He strapped the gadget to his face, plugged it into the control board, and turned to face the others.

Singing was heard. Deep, resonant—a real rain-barrel voice:

> "Barbasol, Barbasol;
> No brush, no lather, no rub-in—
> Just wet your razor, then begin-n-n-n . . ."

Everybody laughed.

"Where on earth did you get that?"

"Oh, out of the Archives," said Ken, taking off the mask. "It's amazing what we have there."

"What is it?" someone asked.

"God only knows."

The lean man's eyes twinkled momentarily. "I doubt it. . . . . Shall we get on with the show?"

"Okay." Ken became serious. "Now what I'm going to do is this. I'm God. I'm going to call all those good people together with nonsense words first. It won't do for God to waste words, you know. So first I must get their attention. Then when I have their attention, I speak. In real words.

"For the nonsense words I thought I'd use the Gettysburg Address, untranslated. You know, 'Four score and seven years ago our fathers brought forth,' and so on.

"How will that sound untranslated? Well, let's push TRANSLATE and listen to it. Just us."

He pushed the lever, put on the mask, and turned to them. A pig-Latin version of a few sentences of the address, heard through a rain-barrel, came out. He took off the mask.

"Of course that's all wrong. That's the way they'd sound if they talked to you. . . . No. That isn't it. Well, it's like a mirror. . . . Hell, I'm no logician. You know what I mean."

Smiles and friendly laughter met this admission.

"Anyway," said Ken, continuing, "after I've got their attention, I'll shift to the real message. I'll shift these switches so you hear the real message, translated into Quotion, as it comes out of the loudspeaker in the rock, but retranslated back into this room. Clear?"

He looked around.

The lean one, tense, said, "Let's go."

Kenneth cleared his voice, snapped on the mask, flipped the switches, and started in. A pig-Latin Gettysburg Address boomed into the room.

Out on the plain the multitude stopped as if transfixed at hearing this sound which they had never heard before. The Mountain was speaking. Like sunflowers turning to the sun, they revolved and faced the source, mouths open. They were all immobilized in that position by the time Ken finished the address. He flipped two more switches and began again, now understandably.

"Those who will not become as gods must serve God.

"You have sinned greatly. Your iniquity is failing to choose, and the wages of sin is death. I am the Lord thy God. I have spoken.

"I offer you three choices; choose ye now one of them, that I may do it to you.

"Shall seven years of famine come unto you in your land? Or will you flee three months before newfound enemies who will pursue you and smite you grievously? Or would you that there be three days' pestilence in your blessed land?

"You must choose. Take counsel among yourselves and give me your answer on this spot, at sunset."

The sound snapped off. Inside the mountain there was a dead silence as the men thought over what they had heard. Finally one of them spoke to the lean one.

"Let me see if I've got this straight. If they elect famine, we cut off the flow of the food chutes. If they choose pestilence, we select one of the lyophilized microbe cultures we've kept in deep storage all these centuries, take it out of storage, culture it, and distribute it in the air ducts, after first immunizing ourselves just in case there's a slight leak between the two systems. But what if they elect war? Who's going to pursue them—us? On horses? With swords?"

Everyone laughed, the lean one as well.

"Hardly. We'd make pretty damned incompetent soldiers. And only twelve of us against that many million of them!"

"Then how can you make good your threat? Suppose they choose the one option that is impossible."

"No danger. This same experiment was tried once before, about twenty-five hundred years before the *Beagle* took off. I was reading about it in the Bible, in the Second Book of Samuel. The people then chose the third option.

"Look at it this way: they just *have* to. It's the only thing compatible with human nature. First, consider famine. Each man thinks: 'If there's a famine, the little food that's left will be divided equally among all of us. I will suffer just as much as everybody else. That won't do. I don't want to die.' . . . Equalitarianism is a public passion only in prosperous times: *Give me my share of the loot*—that's what the less favored demand when times are prosperous. When things are tough, I don't want my share; I want *more* than my fair share. I will never deliberately choose famine because I am afraid I will get only a fair share.

"Now for the second: war. No one wants war unless he is assured ahead of time that he is Superman, that he has the biggest legions, that God is on his side. But we have just told the Quotions that he *isn't* on their side. They will be the pursued, not the pursuers. No rational man chooses such a fate.

"Lastly, disease. This is not a pleasant thought either, but it has the great advantage that it is a gamble. In his bones, every man thinks he is a little bit lucky, now and then. He is descended from a long line of ancestors who believed that way. His survival is not certain. But if he knocks on wood, rubs a rabbit's foot, or closes his eyes and turns around three times . . . Each one has his own formula for biasing the dice of Fate. Not a nice choice, but the least bad of the three. Inevitable. We don't have to worry what their choice will be.

"Come on. Let's go down to the lab. We can get in several hours of work before the Quotions return with the inevitable answer."

A hundred years have passed. The plain of the *Beagle,* now sparsely populated, once more has a covering of low plants growing almost everywhere: not only grasses but skyflowers nestling among them.

At the foot of the mountain three young women are chasing one another with consummate grace and playfulness. They don't look very bright, but they *are* lovely—straight out of Botticelli. An ash blonde, a brunette with dark and lovely skin, and one with carrot-colored hair. One of them trips and falls against a rock facing of the mountain, which clangs metallically and then springs back against her body, revealing a gaping crack, door-high.

"Oh!" She picks herself up and takes hold of the free edge. "Girls! Come help me."

All three grab hold and pull. By moving a few small rocks from the dirt outside and straining a bit, they succeed in opening what proves to be a precisely fashioned metal door, camouflaged as rock.

"I wonder what this is."

"Let's go in."

"Gee . . . fun!"

Like inquisitive puppies, they fall over each other getting through the door, then stop while their eyes grow accustomed to the dim light. On the wall facing them is a bronze plaque, two by three feet, and a sign. The plaque has many lines of raised letters, too small to read in the dim light. The letters on the sign are large and easily readable: ANTI-ANTI-SEX. Above the letters is a drawing of a hand grasping a lever. Jutting out from the wall is a real lever, identical with the one in the picture, lacking only a hand.

"Hey, look," says Carrot-Top. "Look. If I put my hand on this thing . . . no, the other hand—it's just like the picture."

Without a moment's hesitation she pulls the lever upward. Electric lights turn on and for three seconds there is a muffled sound as of escaping steam somewhere in the distance, succeeded by a recording of the second movement of Beethoven's piano sonata, Opus 10, No. 3.

Three pairs of eyes open in a wild surmise. The young women are held spellbound by the sound and do not notice the slow and inexorable shutting of the door through which they entered.

As the closing notes of the movement die away an inner door ponderously opens, revealing a long hallway curving out of sight in the distance, a hallway brightly illuminated and spotless. An inviting passageway.

The brunette turns to the others, head cocked on one side, eyebrows arched. Formally, with great dignity, she asks: "Shall we?"

Their eyes sparkle.

"Let's!"

CHAPTER 20

End of an Orgy

"From time immemorial" means *for three generations.* If it was so in my father's time, as well as in my grandfather's, and if it is so now—then it has been true always. And will be true forever. . . . So works the human mind.

Most men, having only an imperfect feeling for the inflections of history, thoughtlessly suppose that population growth is normal. It was true in our father's time, and in our grandfather's; and it is true now. It must be an eternal truth. Growth is normal.

Only history and reasoning can correct the error. Let us look backward first to see how fast the human population has grown in the past. (See Table 9.)

The biologist Edward Deevey reckons that there were 125,000 human beings on the earth a million years ago. Obviously there are great uncertainties in this estimate. First, there is the question "What is a human being?" At which stage in the evolution of man do we say our ancestors crossed over the line into humanity? Should our ancestors a million years ago be called "men" or "proto-men"? Only an arbitrary decision is possible. That made, there arises the problem of taking a census nearly a million years before anyone knew how to count. Or write. There is much guesswork here.

Fortunately, these uncertainties don't much matter. The properties of exponential calculations are such that the figures in the last two columns of Table 9 are not much affected if the "beginning" is set at a million years or twice that or half that; or if the "initial" population

TABLE 9

Population Growth in Times Past

World population estimates from Deevey (1960),
Carr-Saunders (1936), and United Nations.
Time reckoned with reference to year 1970 A.D.

YEARS IN PAST	DATE, A.D.	WORLD POPULATION, IN MILLIONS	AVERAGE GROWTH RATE IN INTERVAL, PERCENT PER YEAR	DOUBLING TIME, IN YEARS
1,000,000		.125		
			0.000297	233,333
300,000		1.00		
			0.000439	158,060
25,000		3.34		
			0.00310	22,335
10,000		5.32		
			0.0697	994
6,000		86.5		
			0.0108	6,445
2,000		133		
			0.0840	826
320	1650	545		
			0.290	239
220	1750	728		
			0.438	158
170	1800	906		
			0.514	135
120	1850	1,171		
			0.636	109
70	1900	1,608		
			0.660	105
50	1920	1,834		
			0.911	76
40	1930	2,008		
			0.991	70
30	1940	2,216		
			0.826	84
20	1950	2,406		
			2.14	33
10	1960	2,972		
			2.03	35
0	1970	3,632		

is assumed to be ten times as great or only a tenth as much. The quantitative conclusions are affected very little by these variations, and the *qualitative* conclusions (developed below) are affected not at all.

First of all, what was the *average* rate of growth of the human population for the past million years? It averages out to almost exactly a thousandth of 1 percent per year. Put another way, at this average rate of growth the length of time it takes a population to double is 67,447 years.

At the present time—"present" being assumed to be the year 1970 throughout this discussion—world population is growing at approximately 2 percent per year, with a doubling time of only 35 years. If we compare 35 with 67,447 it is obvious that we live in exceptional times.

The matter can be put another way. A million years ago it was the year 998,026 B.C. (Christ, paradoxically, was born in the year 4 B.C.) If the eighth of a million people then living had multiplied steadily at the *present* rate of 2.03 percent per year, how long would it have taken them to produce the present population of some three and a half billion? The answer is startling:

YEAR	POPULATION
998,026 B.C.	125,000
997,514 B.C.	3,632,000,000

It would have taken just 512 years to reach the present population—and the time would still have been nearly 1,000,000 B.C.

Obviously population increase has not been the major accomplishment of humanity during most of its existence on earth. From the table we see that in the first 700,000 years the doubling time was 233,333 years. Doubling time fell rapidly until it reached a low point of 994 years during the interval of 10,000 to 6000 years ago, then rose again. This low point corresponds to the beginnings of agriculture, one of the three great cultural revolutions in man's history. (The others were the earlier tool-making revolution, and the industrial-scientific revolution in which we are still living.) Agriculture, in effect, increased the capacity of man's world, hence the sudden spurt. Once this revolution had been assimilated, the doubling period lengthened for a while, then began falling again.

The low point for the doubling period was reached in the decade from 1950 to 1960—33 years, corresponding to a worldwide growth rate of 2.14 percent per year. *This was undoubtedly the fastest growth rate the world population will ever experience.* From here on out, population growth will diminish—not steadily, perhaps, but inexorably—until it reaches *zero.* It is even probable that it will swing below zero for some time until the total population reaches a lower level, more commensurate with Spaceship Earth's ability to sustain life in dignity. Or, if the worst happens, *population* may reach zero, at which point all talk of growth rates and doubling times stops.

From the figures given in the table we can safely infer that, during most of his existence on earth, man can have had no realization that the population was increasing in numbers. During the period from 4026 B.C. (6000 years ago) to 1650 A.D.—i.e., from about the time of the invention of writing and record-keeping to just shortly after the birth of Isaac Newton—the world population increased at an average rate of just slightly in excess of 0.032 percent per year, with a doubling time of 2139 years. When change takes place that slowly, how can anyone know there's any change at all?

Suppose you were born into an "average village" during that period, a village of just 100 people; and that you lived your allotted Biblical three score and ten years. (Lucky you! Three-quarters of your siblings, in those days, died before they could walk.) In the last year of your life you looked around and noted (if you were *very* observant) that your village had grown—to a grand total of 102 people. From 100 to 102, in 70 years. Talk about runaway population growth! That was the average rate of change during all the time man was writing histories—until the modern era.

But the average is a dangerous abstraction. The "average village" may have increased from 100 to 102 in a man's lifetime, but it was probably ravaged down to 70 or so several times by disease; and it may have burgeoned to 150 a time or two and been cut back 50 percent within a short time by war and pillage. Fluctuations were the order of the day: a 2 percent *per lifetime* over-all rate of change would be imperceptible. No wonder that the cyclical theory of history was the predominant view of most men; and that no one conceived of the idea of Progress.

There were great variations from region to region. Significant population growth in one area would be offset by depopulation in another. Looking at evidences of depopulation, an intelligent man could quite understandably generalize from a particular region to the entire world, ending up with a mistaken conclusion. In 1721 the great political philosopher the Baron de Montesquieu wrote in his *Persian Letters:*

> How is the world so thinly peopled in comparison with what it was once? How has nature lost the wonderful fruitfulness of the first ages? Can it be that she is already old and fallen into decline?
>
> I dwelt for more than a year in Italy, where I saw nothing but the ruins of that ancient Italy, so famous in former times. Although all the people live in the towns, they are quite deserted and empty. . . .
>
> In short, I have reviewed the whole world, and found nothing but decay. . . .

This was written only 77 years before Malthus was to conclude that the gravest danger for the world was not the shrinkage of population but the growth of it.

Today our mythical average village would increase from 100 people to 407 in a man's lifetime. Anyone can notice a change that great.

So much for the past: What about the future? What would happen if the world population continued to increase at the rate that characterized the decade 1960–1970, beginning with the 1970 population?

Table 10 shows what would happen if the world were to continue its present 2-percent growth rate indefinitely. In only 615 years there would be literally "standing room only" on all the land areas of the world. Or, if you wish to assume we could pave over the oceans, it would be SRO over the entire world in only 677 years.

TABLE 10

Hypothetical Future Population of the World
ASSUMED: *indefinite continuation of 1960–1970 rate of population growth, starting with 1970 base.*

TERMINAL CONDITION ASSUMED	POPULATION	TIME TAKEN TO REACH CONDITION	DATE REACHED	BACKWARD TIME, EQUIVALENT DATE
Standing room only, land areas only	8.27×10^{14}	615 years	2585 A.D.	1355 A.D.
Standing room only, total earth surface	28.34×10^{14}	677 years	2647 A.D.	1293 A.D.
All earth converted to human flesh	1.33×10^{23}	1557 years	3527 A.D.	413 A.D.

It is hard to think of dates in the future, so suppose we imagine this population growth taking place with a reversal of time. By the time we reached SRO conditions on the land areas we would be back to the seventh year of the Black Plague, the year 1355 A.D. Only a little later, in 1293 A.D., the oceans also would be covered with people (and Dante would be enjoying his second year of married life—but not with Beatrice).

But let us not be niggardly in our imagination. We don't all have to stand up on the same plane. We can build buildings, up into the sky. We can burrow into the earth. How far can we go? Who knows? In the limit, we could convert all the materials of the earth into human flesh. (There are serious chemical problems in converting iron, for instance, into glycogen—but let us be generous in our assumptions.)

(And don't ask about the comfort of the people in the center of this squirming, writhing ball of human flesh, with four thousand miles of bodies piled above them. People adjust, you know; or so the infinitely flexible apologists for the status quo tell us.)

If we assume an average weight of 45 kilograms for each human being (men, women, and children), the 5.983×10^{24} kilogram mass of the earth could (hypothetically) be converted to 1.33×10^{23} people. At the present rate of growth this would be achieved in only 1557 years. Measuring it in backward time, the Goths and the Vandals would be happily sacking Rome. We wouldn't even be back to the birth of Christ.

On the *day* when the entire earth was finally converted to human flesh more than
$$7,300,000,000,000,000,000 \text{ people}$$
would be born. (Just how many more depends on the death rate assumed.)

On the *next* day, there could be a net increase of only
$$2,200,000 \text{ people.}$$
This would be "financed" by the daily rain of some 10,000,000 kilograms of meteoritic dust on the earth. On that "next" day the rate of increase of the human population would abruptly drop from 2 percent per year to 0.0000000000006 percent. Such a sudden adjustment just might be a bit difficult to make.

Ridiculous? Of course. So what's the point of this mathematical caper? If the point is not understood, irrelevant conclusions will be extracted from the exercise.

Every once in a while the editor of a magazine that has not previously concerned itself with population problems decides he really should do a "special" on the subject. Typically, he calls in a sports reporter, art reporter, drama reporter, or civil rights reporter and tells him to find out what it's all about and write the lead article. Just as typically, the twenty-one-day specialist blows his top when he runs across calculations of the sort given here. If he is a witty fellow he then has a field day with the forebodings of the population kooks. Divested of wit and rhetoric, his treatment boils down to the following set of propositions:

1. The kooks are trying to scare the bejesus out of us so that we will abandon our tried-and-true policy of perpetual growth.

2. They say that the population will ultimately be so dense that we will . . . (then follows one of the abhorrent mathematical conclusions).

3. They've apparently never heard of Scientific Progress . . .

4. . . . or Space.

5. Since it is ridiculous to say that people would ever allow themselves to be packed together like sardines, everything the population kooks say is false.

6. *Ergo* there is no population problem.

The real point of the mathematical exercise (so often missed) is to compel choice. People adopt a *laissez-faire* attitude toward population because they refuse to face the hard choices of population-control.

What is the optimum level of population?

What standard of living is that decision based on?

How do we choose from among alternate standards?

How do we deal with differences of opinion?

How can we control breeding?

How can we justify coercion?

Who decides?

And so on.

If there is no population problem, there is no need to face these fearful questions.

Population kooks cite their curious mathematical conclusions in the hope that they can convince the complacent that choice is necessary, either now or in the *very* near future. The hypothetical conclusions are intended as a *reductio ad absurdum,* which has the following implicit form:

1. Let us assume that there is no need for decision, no need for change, and no reason to think that change will be forced upon us.

2. Let us calculate the consequences of continuing present trends into the indefinite future. (And let us grant the most unbelievable technological possibilities, e.g., turning granite into food.)

3. When we do this we discover that at some time in the future, perhaps as early as six hundred years and certainly no later than sixteen hundred years, an abrupt change of a very nasty sort will be forced upon us.

4. *Ergo* refusing to change voluntarily will result in change being forced upon us.

Lemma: a change of our own choosing *can* be pleasanter than the unavoidable change that will be forced upon us if we refuse to make a choice. Loss of freedom to breed is less horrible than massive death by starvation, epidemics, social chaos, and insanity.

Though rigorous proof is far from possible, the all but universal belief of those who have studied population deeply is that the time for revolutionary change in human behavior is much closer than six hundred years in the future. It may be tomorrow.

In fact, when the smoke has cleared, we will likely discover that we really should have changed yesterday.

It's later than you think.

From here on out no intelligent broad-gauge decisions can be made in economics, politics, or anything else that touches on human welfare, unless the decision-makers feel deeply in their bones the following truths:

1. We live on a spaceship. *Men* may escape from it, but *mankind* cannot.

2. The past two hundred years have been an absolutely exceptional period in the million-year history of *Homo sapiens*. It has been an orgy of expansion and exploitation of irreplaceable environmental riches.

3. We are only a few moments away from the end of the orgy . . .

4. . . . which will never be repeated. The rich mineral deposits lying near the surface, the apparently boundless virgin forests, the incredible concentration of marine fishes—all, all will be gone, never to return. The *openness* of the world will be gone.

The loss of openness that will be experienced in changing to a steady-state economy is no small loss and was foreseen by Adam Smith in 1776. In his *Wealth of Nations* he spoke movingly of his fears:

> It is in the progressive state, while the society is advancing to the further acquisition, rather than when it has acquired its full complement of riches, that the condition of the labouring poor, of the great body of people, seems to be the happiest and the most comfortable. It is hard in the stationary, and miserable in the declining state. The progressive state is in reality the cheerful and the hearty state to all the different orders of the society. The stationary is dull; the declining melancholy.

Much more can be, and indeed has been, said in the last two centuries about the disadvantages of living in a steady-state world. To what extent are these disadvantages "of the essence" of the steady-state (to use Aristotelian language), and to what extent are they merely "accidental"? That is for us to find out, perhaps to *determine*. But there is no escape for us, on this our spaceship.

The orgy is nearly over.

CHAPTER 21

Parenthood: Right or Privilege?

"I fear," said Carl Linnaeus, "that I shall not have any undergardeners this summer to do daily work, for they say they cannot work without food, and for many days they have not tasted a crust of bread. One or two widows here are said not to have had any bread for themselves or their children for 8 days, and are ashamed to beg. Today a wife was sent to the castle [i.e., to the dungeon] for having cut her own child's throat, having had no food to give it, that it might not pine away in hunger and tears."

We learn as much about history from what is not said in contemporary documents as from what is. Reading between the lines of this letter written by the great biologist (who perfected the basic system still used for classifying plants and animals), we learn much about the attitudes and social system of the eighteenth century.

Welfare payments are not mentioned in this letter, written March 17, 1772. Not only did they not exist—it never occurred to the writer that such things should exist. If poor people didn't have money to buy food, they would just have to starve. The fact that it was not their fault was irrelevant and was not mentioned. It is obvious that Linneaus himself, and all his wealthy associates, would have plenty of food. This also was assumed without mention. That the wealthy might help the poor *a little* is indicated by the reference to begging: but only a little. Of course, only a small proportion of the all too numerous poor could be helped because the fundamental shortage was of food, not money.

177

That a mother might kill her child to prevent its suffering was regarded as natural (or almost natural), but law and order had to be upheld, and so such a mother had to be put in jail. Periodic famines like that of 1772 were part of the "natural order," and poor people would just have to take account of them in their decisions. They would have to save for a rainy day; they would have to avoid having too many children to feed. No state welfare would save them; and private philanthropy was a marginal thing.

To some extent poor people did take account of the fact that there would be little help for them when times got tough. Their planning was not perfect simply because they were fallible human beings; but they did prepare for hard times. The family was the unit of responsibility and power—power to determine the number of children produced, and responsibility for taking care of them, disposing of them, or helplessly watching them die if there were too many. The large family of eight to sixteen children that most people think was typical before Margaret Sanger's time was, in fact, common only in America, where an ever-expanding frontier made it possible, and in Europe during Victorian times only, i.e., in the nineteenth century. Before that, European families were much smaller. Four children in the family was commoner than twelve.

It may be a mistake to speak of "population control" in such a society: there was no conscious control by the whole community. There was, however, something that might be called family population control. Knowing that it could obtain little help from the community, the family assumed the responsibility of keeping its numbers down to a level near the "carrying capacity" of that portion of the environment to which it had access. Many such individual family decisions produced a sort of aggregate population control for the whole community.

How did the family implement its decisions? In many ways. To begin with, no one ever spoke of a "right" to marry. If there were many children in the family, it was expected that quite a few of them would remain single. To marry without the tacit consent of the elders of the family (principally the father) was to court economic and social disaster. Romantic love was for the well-to-do only, and even among that tiny minority it was regarded as a dangerous aberration. Among the poor, celibacy was common. Some of the celibates went into the Church as priests or nuns; others went into domestic service, where a lack of personal family obligations and distractions was a great advantage—to the master.

Celibacy and chastity were not synonymous. For the males, prostitutes gave an escape from parenthood. The extent of prostitution was sometimes astonishing. In Rome, in 1527, it was conservatively estimated that there were at least 1500 prostitutes out of a total population of only 55,000 people. LaMont Cole's empirical rule tells us that about one-half of any population is between the ages of 15 and 50; and about one-half of these are ordinarily females. So the population of females from which the prostitutes were drawn should have been 13,750. That would mean that 11 percent of the eligible women (1 in 9) were prostitutes. This is surely an underestimate. The holy city had a large population of priests, thus diminishing the proportion of women in the total population, which means that considerably more than 11 percent of the adult female population followed the "world's oldest profession."

Even if not intended as such, prostitution serves as a means of population control. There is a limit to prolificness, and one prostitute serves many men, whose fecund attentions are thereby diverted from legitimate wives. In addition, for a variety of reasons (not all understood), prostitutes as a class are less fertile than wives. Sooner or later gonorrhea seals their Fallopian tubes shut, putting an end to the threat of pregnancy. Sterility is, of course, a professional asset.

For females other than prostitutes, celibacy used to mean almost complete chastity. The abstraction called "virginity" was quite literally a valuable *property*, not alone of the woman "possessing" it, but even more of her father, who had a daughter to sell in marriage. The higher the economic status of the family, the more valuable virginity was. When a young woman "fell" and produced a child—irrefutable evidence of her spoiled condition—the most barbaric sanctions were imposed upon her.

Delayed marriage, lifetime celibacy, prostitution, venereal disease, and sanctions against bastards and the mothers of bastards constituted a powerful system of population control operating at the family level. To mitigate any one of the elements in such a system was to diminish its effectiveness in keeping population under control. The importance of these factors in controlling population was seldom recognized; but thoughtful men did realize that the officially abhorred institution of prostitution played an essential role in the *system of virtue* (as it was called). Such an insight is halfway to more important demographic knowledge. Napoleon, for example, remarked that "prostitutes are a necessity. Without them, men would attack respectable women in the streets." The Victorian scholar W. E. H. Lecky, in a famous passage in his *History of European Morals* (1869), justified the apparently ineradicable profession by systems analysis:

> Herself the supreme type of vice, she is ultimately the most efficient guardian of virtue. But for her, the unchallenged purity of countless happy homes would be polluted, and not a few who, in the pride of their untempted chastity, think of her with an indignant shudder, would have known the agony of remorse and despair. In that one degraded and ignoble form are concentrated the passions that might have filled the world with shame. She remains, while creeds and civilizations rise and fall, the eternal priestess of humanity, blasted for the sins of the people.

One of my happier fantasies is that I may someday have the pleasure in Heaven (or Hell) of introducing Mr. Lecky to Kate Millett, Betty Friedan, and Simone de Beauvoir and then standing back to enjoy the fireworks.

For those who did not remain celibate there were still defenses against a personal population explosion. Mere delay of marriage has considerable effect; the older a woman is at the time of marriage, the fewer children she will produce, statistically speaking. After she is married (even if not before), her fertility can be diminished by contraceptive measures. Until modern times methods of contraception may not have been very effective, but they were better than nothing. Contraceptive recipes are to be found in Egyptian papyruses dating from about 1550 B.C. During the past few centuries in Europe *coitus interruptus* ("withdrawal") has been the most common method of birth control in daily use.

Many demographers estimate that the most widely used single method of birth control throughout the world now, and for centuries, has been abortion.* Laws made by men have forbidden the practice of abortion in recent times in Europe, sometimes specifying the direst of punishments. The practice was, until the nineteenth century, hardly affected by harsh laws and theological thunderings. Practice was confined to the female subculture: only women could be aborted, and the operation was carried out by women: the pregnant woman herself, a woman friend, or (more often) a midwife. In the nineteenth century the two subcultures began to grow together, and male physicians took over much of the practice of midwifery. Thus began the conflict over the legalization of abortion that continues to our day. The illegality of the operation has not altogether prevented it: France and Italy, both nominally Catholic countries, have long had a rate of illegal abortion undeniably greater than the birth rate.

Before the development of modern medicine, abortion was somewhat dangerous. A woman finding herself unwillingly pregnant might rationally conclude that she would rather let the pregnancy proceed to term and then solve the problem. There was one more method of family population control: infanticide.

Most people think of infanticide as a practice of "savages" only, but the studies of the eminent historian William L. Langer abundantly demonstrate that it was quite common in Europe as a method of family population control clear down to the end of the nineteenth century. Infanticide in Europe was not overt and frank, as it often is among "savages"; it was disguised, and the discussion of it was under a taboo—the "civilized" way of doing such things. Parents did not usually kill their own children but turned the job over to a specialist, who nominally ran an infant nursery or "baby-farm." As Langer says:

> The least offense of these "Angelmakers," as they were called in Berlin, was to give the children gin to keep them quiet. For the rest we have the following testimony from Benjamin Disraeli's novel *Sybil* (1845), for which he drew on a large fund of sociological data: "Laudanum and treacle, administered in the shape of some popular elixir, affords these innocents a brief taste of the

* Commonly, people contrast "birth control" with "abortion"; but strictly speaking this is wrong, as the theologian Joseph Fletcher has pointed out. Abortion is the *only* method of birth control; all other methods are ones of conception control.

sweets of existence and, keeping them quiet, prepares them for the silence of their impending grave." "Infanticide," he adds, "is practised as extensively and as legally in England as it is on the banks of the Ganges; a circumstance which apparently has not yet engaged the attention of the Society for the Propagation of the Gospel in Foreign Parts."

It was also customary in these years to send babies into the country to be nursed by peasant women. The well-to-do made their own arrangements, while the lower classes turned their off-spring over to charitable nursing bureaus or left them at the foundling hospitals or orphanages that existed in all large cities. Of the operation of these foundling hospitals a good deal is known, and from this knowledge it is possible to infer the fate of thousands of babies that were sent to the provinces for care.

The middle and late eighteenth century was marked by a startling rise in the rate of illegitimacy, the reasons for which have little bearing on the present argument. But so many of the un-wanted babies were being abandoned, smothered, or otherwise disposed of that Napoleon in 1811 decreed that the foundling hos-pitals should be provided with a turntable device, so that babies could be left at these institutions without the parent being recog-nized or subjected to embarrassing questions. This convenient ar-rangement was imitated in many countries and was taken full advantage of by the mothers in question. In many cities the au-thorities complained that unmarried mothers from far and wide were coming to town to deposit their unwanted babies in the accommodating foundling hospitals. The statistics show that of the thousands of children thus abandoned, a significant proportion was the offspring of married couples.

There is good reason to suppose that those in charge of these institutions did the best they could with what soon became an unmanageable problem. Very few of the children could be cared for in the hospitals themselves. The great majority was sent to peasant nurses in the provinces. In any case, most of these chil-dren died within a short time, either of malnutrition or neglect or from the long, rough journey to the country.

The figures for this traffic, available for many cities, are truly shocking. In all of France fully 127,507 children were abandoned in the year 1833. Anywhere from 20 to 30 percent of all children born were left to their fate. The figures for Paris suggest that in the years 1817–1820 the "foundlings" equalled fully 36 percent of all births. In some of the Italian hospitals the mortality (under one year of age) ran to 80 or 90 percent. In Paris the *Hospice des Enfants Trouvés* reported that of 4,779 babies admitted in 1818, 2,370 died in the first three months and another 956 within the first year.

Disraeli was an important political figure and a well-known writer: one might expect his acid remarks to provoke a storm of protest and a flurry of action. But they did not, probably because most practical men recognized the necessity of infanticide if the family was to continue to act *responsibly*.

The word is used advisedly, in the best Frankelian sense. The family, and not the state, used to be responsible for the care of the children produced. For the state to have prevented the family from doing away with a redundant child—redundant because in excess of what the family could probably take care of in hard times—without at the same time taking over the care and feeding of the child would have been an irresponsible act on the part of the state, since it would be the parents who would have to suffer the agony (in Linnaeus's words) of seeing the child "pine away in hunger and tears" at some unknown future time of general want.

The need for population control gets tangled up with the desire to prevent pain and suffering, for which philanthropy is a response. Actions need to be analyzed in terms of Frankelian responsibility. The matrix for displaying the characteristics of the various systems of environmental utilization becomes relevant, and needs to be displayed once more (Table 11), this time with the inclusion of Case IV, which was not needed in discussing pollution problems since the philanthropic approach it describes does not constitute a political system. Philanthropy is, however, of importance in taking care of the destitute, the care of which has evolved through a succession of stages in the matrix that is worth describing before we take up the evolution of population control.

During the eighteenth and nineteenth centuries there was a remarkable growth of the belief that each of us is, or should be, his brother's keeper. The historical reasons for this are far from completely understood. Is it too cynical to say that the increase in percapita wealth made it possible for men to afford the luxury of Christian ideals? Be that as it may, the attitude of *other-concernedness*

TABLE 11

The Four Possible Systems of Environmental Utilization

| | RULES OF THE GAME | | | | | RESULTS OF THE GAME | | | |
| | UTILIZATION OF ENVIRONMENT BY: | | PROCEEDS GO TO: | | | GAIN FROM STRESSING THE SYSTEM: | | | |
CASE	INDIVIDUAL (1)	GROUP (2)	INDIVIDUAL (3)	GROUP (4)	Name of the game	OVER-ALL GAIN (5)	GAIN TO THE DECISION-MAKER (6)	INTRINSIC RESPON-SIBILITY (7)	TEMPTATION TO SABOTAGE INFORMATION (8)
I	✓		✓		*Private Enterprise*	−	−	+	0
II		✓		✓	*Socialism*	−	0	0	+
III		✓	✓		*System of the Commons*	−	+	−	(0)
IV	✓			✓	*Philanthropy*	−	0	0	0

grew and led to the foundation of societies for the prevention of cruelty to animals, for the abolition of slavery, for the protection of children, and for the liberation of women (in that historical order!).

In the nineteenth century more and more people thought it a shame that innocent children should suffer for errors in procreative judgment made by their parents: couldn't the children be somehow taken care of? In response to this need, philanthropy developed on an increasingly larger scale and with ever more organization.

In a matrix of the possible systems of environmental utilization, philanthropy fits in as Case IV. An individual man who is more successful than most in utilizing the environment may accumulate a personal fortune. But then he gives it to others, to the group, perhaps through a philanthropic foundation. If the philanthropist-to-be foresaw the eventual disposition of his wealth, the way in which he used the environment would be as indicated for Case IV in the table. Certainly he would have nothing to gain by mistreating the environment. However, philanthropists generally do not foresee their eventual avocation at the time they are accumulating their fortunes, so the zeros in the last three columns for Case IV are of little significance. It is surely seldom that a poor young man adopts a lifelong goal of becoming a wealthy philanthropist.

Philanthropy is an uncommon avocation; it certainly is not a political system. Yet it may play an important role in the evolution of political systems. Large-scale philanthropy is, in principle, an unstable intermediate stage in this evolution. The instability has its roots in human nature—in the competitive urge, and in envy. A philanthropic arrangement can destabilize in either of two contradictory ways.

Anyone who has much to do with fund-raising (for a museum, say) sooner or later runs into a "competitive exclusion principle" in philanthropy. If all the gifts are much the same size, donors may stimulate each other in a game of one-upmanship, which is fine for the organization. But if one donation is orders of magnitude greater than others, the result can be chilling. The big donor, in effect, wins the potlatch and puts an end to the game of one-upmanship. Given the ego of man, philanthropy is a delicate flower.

Philanthropy can come to an end in another way. Donors may tire of the game of one-upmanship, feeling that they are being played for suckers by appeals to their consciences. Dealing with a widespread social problem by voluntary philanthropy introduces the fatal weakness that afflicts the system of commons: it rewards those with poor consciences. To try to prevent this, big donors may employ "jawbone responsibility." If this is effective, the system is as coercive as arbitrary law. If it is not effective, it is labor lost. Sooner or later, on a large scale or small, it becomes ineffective, and then (if the function supported by philanthropy is needed) the commons-related system of voluntary philanthropy is replaced by a system of taxing everyone —*mutual coercion, mutually agreed upon*. In American history, with the people's widespread distrust of socialism, this evolution has taken place in two stages.

In the first stage, nongovernmental agencies like the Community Chest persuaded business firms to levy uniform taxes on all their employees: "voluntary donations" at "suggested" percentages of the wages. This *almost* puts an end to the evil of an appeal to individual conscience, since the "suggested" donation has the coercive power of a royal "request." But there is still some variability as between members of different business concerns. With the passage of time the donors come to recognize that there is little psychological difference between a deduction from the paycheck made by the business concern and passed on to a large, impersonal private philanthropic organization and a deduction made by the business concern and passed on to a large, impersonal governmental agency. The latter may (or may not) be less efficient; but supporting it on a nonvoluntary basis is certainly "fairer." It is also socialistic. But eventually it is preferred.

This, then, is the typical evolutionary path of our attempts to deal with the heartrending problems of poverty:

1. The first stage is one of isolated acts of individual philanthropy, which cannot be converted into a stable political system;

2. In the second stage the need is handled by a system of the commons, the voluntary nature of which penalizes people with consciences and subjects everyone to a pathogenic "double bind"; the resulting instability leads to the third stage.

3. In this stage the ideal of law is adopted: "mutual coercion, mutually agreed upon." The voluntary feature of giving is abandoned,

and people are freed from the destructive "double bind" of an appeal to conscience.

Taking care of the unfortunate has evolved, then, from Case IV to Case III to Case II. Population control, as we shall see, evolves from Case I to Case III to Case II—though the evolution is not yet complete.

In the first stage—which held sway in Europe for many centuries —population was controlled by a private-enterprise system, the family. The family had the power to produce children; and it had the responsibility of taking care of them.

Then the growth of "humanitarianism"—of concern for others— led to the evolution of the welfare state in the nineteenth and twentieth centuries. Whatever one may say about its virtues (and it has many) the welfare state (as it has evolved so far) has a fatal flaw as concerns population control in that it separates power and responsibility:

Power to produce children resides in the family.

Responsibility for taking care of children resides in the state.

In the words of a pronunciamento of the United Nations, signed by some thirty nations in 1967:

The Universal Declaration of Human Rights describes the family as the natural and fundamental unit of society. It follows that any choice and decision with regard to the size of the family must irrevocably rest with the family itself, and cannot be made by anyone else.

Notice that this gives the family a right without any corresponding responsibility. *So long as power and responsibility are thus separated, population control is impossible.* Not a single nation in the world has its population under control: everywhere there is continued growth. Evolution is incomplete.

In matters of reproduction the system we are now operating under is the system of the commons. Every family can now take from the common store to keep its children alive, but the benefits of having children accrue to the family.

It may be questioned whether there are benefits in having children in the modern world, particularly in a nonfarm economy. What are the benefits?

This question is not very relevant. Families act *as if* something is to be gained by having children. It doesn't matter whether their judgment is right or wrong. Breeding couples who resist an appeal to voluntarily restrict their fertility will produce more children than will those who respond to the appeal. Nonconscience has a selective advantage over conscience. The welfare state creates a commons for the children to draw upon. The children of the conscienceless will be a larger proportion of the population in the next generation than their parents were in this. To produce a runaway process ("positive feedback") it is necessary only that the transmission of conscience be hereditary *in the most general sense*—that children resemble their parents more than they do the population at large. It does not matter whether the "heredity" is *genetic*—through chromosomes, genes, and DNA—or *social*—through custom and education. Studies show that the daughters of women who have more than the average number of children for their generation do in fact have more children than the average in *theirs*—which is all that is required to produce destructive runaway feedback. As Charles Galton Darwin, the grandson of Charles, put the matter in 1959, on the centenary of the publication of the *Origin of Species:* a purely voluntary system of population control selects for "philoprogenitiveness" and results in certain failure of the control system.

In this, as in all matters, on a spaceship, the system of the commons ends in tragedy.

What shall we do? Since we will always live on a spaceship, we must abandon the system of the commons. We must bring power and responsibility together again in the same locus.

We *could* go back—to the private-enterprise system of population control we used to live under. But do we have the toughness to do so? Can we stand idly by and see innocent children starve to death in hard times? I doubt it.

We got rid of that cruel but effective system of population control for what seemed, and seem, good humanitarian reasons. In adding the idea of the welfare state to the social system, we failed to remember that "we can never do merely one thing." When welfare was added to the political system without changing the right to breed, a system of the commons was brought into being. The combination made population control impossible—save by the ultimate cruel measures of Nature: starvation, mass disease, and social chaos.

The system of the commons we now live under separates power and responsibility. It is an unstable state. If we want civilization to survive, and if we are unwilling to go back, then we must go forward. We must take the next step in evolution and bring power and responsibility together once more, this time in the community. The community, which guarantees the survival of children, must have the power to decide how many children shall be born.

The conclusion is frightening to people reared in the Western tradition. But there is no escaping it. The dangers of state control are immense. How can we circumvent them? This will surely be one of our major concerns for the rest of our lives, for as far into the future as we can see.

CHAPTER 22

Three Phases of Population Control

Population control is inevitable; population control is impossible.

On a spaceship, population will inevitably be controlled someday by "Nature"—by epidemics, starvation, social disorder, psychological breakdown, or some other "natural" abomination we have not yet become aware of. However, that is usually not the sort of control we have in mind when we speak of "population control"; we usually mean control by man, by human decisions. This second kind of control seems, at the moment, to be impossible—impossible because we are afraid to initiate radical change in society. We know at the outset that change will be opposed for religious, ethical, legal, political, and emotional reasons.

Population control is impossible: but we must somehow accomplish the impossible.

Who's *we?* Since we are on a spaceship, obviously "we" is everyone—all three and a half billion of us. How do you get agreement among three and a half billion people? By democratic means? How long does it take? Six hundred years? Sixteen hundred? Six thousand? We don't have that long before Nature takes over.

On a spaceship, population control will ultimately have to encompass all peoples—but not in the beginning. How could we Americans (for example) force population control on all the rest of the people in the world? By conquering them? There are seventeen times as many of them as of us. Or we might see the conflict as one of rich, industrialized countries (with a rate of increase of about 1 percent per year) versus poor and poorly industrialized countries (increasing at about 3 percent per year). Should the rich countries, in concert, make colonies of the poor, readopting the nineteenth-century philosophy of "the white man's burden," and forcing population control on them?

Putting aside all moral questions for the moment, who—as a purely and narrowly practical matter—would at this moment recommend such a course of action? No one, I think. Whatever our periodic lapses, we do honor the idea of national sovereignty in principle; we are not about to violate this principle and directly force population control on others. For the foreseeable future, in spite of the undeniable fact that we are all confined together in the same spaceship, the only thing a slow-breeding rich country can do is try to persuade the more populous and more rapidly breeding poor countries to slow down their breeding in order that they may increase their own rates of economic progress.

Honoring national sovereignty, we Americans can preach to the poor countries—and we no doubt shall. We will be much more effective, however, if we set an example and bring our own rate of population growth down to zero or less. How shall we do this?

Population control must be focused on women. So blunt a statement evokes cries of "Male chauvinism!" but any other approach is worse. I cannot pretend to be objective, because I am a man; but I can try to imagine myself a woman. . . . If I were a woman I would be continually running the risk of pregnancy. As a woman, I ask myself if I would trust men to take the measures required to keep *me* from getting pregnant? I answer with a resounding *No!* . . . Is that male chauvinism?

Although it takes both sexes to "create" a child, only the female can become pregnant. Biology, in effect, has made women responsible. Saddled with this inequity, women had better demand power to match their responsibility.

As the community takes over the control of population, it may be tempted to enunciate a doctrine of "joint parental responsibility" for the births that occur. The moment it enunciates a policy based on such a doctrine it will discover that it has "opened up a can of worms."

Suppose the community-decreed limit is two children per couple. How would the law respond to the problems presented by the following not unlikely cases?

1. Mary and John get divorced, after having two children. Mary takes the children. Both remarry, their new partners having had no children previously. Suppose Mary's new husband wants a child "of his own"—can he have one? If so, Mary must exceed *her* quota. What if John's new wife wants to be a mother—is she forbidden to do so because John has twice fathered children? . . . If she promised to conceive extramaritally, would that make it all right?

2. A young woman has intercourse with several men in one month and becomes pregnant. She doesn't know who the father is, and "paternity tests," which can only *exclude* some of the candidates, do not tell us. Should each of the nonexcluded men be charged with one child? Or only a fraction of a child?

3. Five men and three women join in a group marriage. If a quota is to be assigned to the group, what should it be? $3 \times 2 = 6$? $5 \times 2 = 10$? $[(5 + 3) \div 2] \times 2 = 8$?

We haven't even considered the complications introduced by extramarital affairs, and the legal consequences of condonation. I'm afraid there are more patterns of marriage and sex than are dreamt of in Doris Day's philosophy. The law ignores this variety to its peril.

The chain of legal evidence that establishes maternity is really quite good. The evidence for paternity is always shaky, and putting a policeman under every bed really wouldn't help. "It's a wise father that knows his own child," said Shakespeare, and the science of serology hasn't changed the situation much yet.

To say that the two sexes should be equally responsible is to forget that we are not a perfectly monogamous people. Extramarital intercourse is not rare; and divorce and remarriage create what has been called "serial polygamy." If coercion is ever used in population control it will likely involve the use of sterilization. The sterilization of x men would be much less effective in reducing births than the sterilization of x women. Given a reservoir of political resistance to community control of population, one could realistically expect that even the tiniest minority of fertile men in this reservoir would be adequate to impregnate all the impregnable women in it. Many children can be produced by only a few fertile men, if fertile women seek to subvert population control.

By contrast, if women are made the target of population control, the number of children produced by the small number of women who escape the control net will, in fact, be only a small number.

I suggest that progress in controlling population within the nation will occur in three phases, which will overlap in time. These are:

1. *Voluntary phase:* the system of birth control is perfected.

2. *Educational phase:* people are persuaded to want fewer children.

3. *Coercive phase:* breeding by noncooperators (no more than a small minority of the population) is legally restricted.

To those who say the coercive phase is "unthinkable" I say *fine:* if the job can be done using only the first two approaches, there is no need to call for a third. But if the third phase is ultimately required, we had better think about it a bit beforehand.

1. Voluntary Phase

The goal of this phase is simply one of *no unwanted children.* No single *method* of birth control is foolproof, but there can be a perfect *system* of birth control. All that is necessary is that elective abortion be included in the set of methods used—as a back-up method, when other methods fail (for whatever reason). Abortion on the request of the woman can be justified as a necessity for the emancipation of women. A century ago we got rid of compulsory servitude; now we must get rid of compulsory pregnancy, and for much the same reasons.

Society has a real stake in putting an end to the birth of unwanted children. The social cost of unwanted children has been revealed by a Swedish study. For a generation Sweden has had a very slightly permissive abortion law. Most women have been denied the abortions they wanted. After more than two decades of the operation of this law, two investigators sought out children born twenty-one years earlier to mothers who had sought, but had been denied, abortions. In other words, these children were unwanted by their mothers. As young adults they were compared with others of the same age, matched carefully for area and socio-economic status, who had presumably been wanted at the time of birth, since their mothers had not requested abortions. As compared with the controls, the unwanted children were not as healthy; they had received more psychiatric attention (presumably because it was needed); they used alcohol more; the boys had a higher rejection rate by the army; and the girls became pregnant at an earlier age.

In a welfare state everybody pays part of the cost of unwanted children. Even if society were completely indifferent to the happiness and welfare of women, it still would have ample reason to exert itself to make the system of birth control perfect. We need research to find better methods of birth control. We need to make the methods we have as available as tap water to everyone everywhere, without shame. (Attempts to restrict birth control to certain ages and to the married only are sure to increase the tax burden without bringing any perceptible improvement in morality.) We still have a long way to go in the delivery of this kind of medical service (as well as others); but we are making progress.

It is unlikely that we will make a significant move into the educational phase until we recognize this hard truth:

Birth control is not population control.

Almost everybody regards the two terms as synonymous. People are encouraged in this belief by organizations that collect money for the second purpose and then use it for the first—which fails to produce the second. In India, for example, there was a gratifying increase in the use of birth control beginning in the middle of the present century; but the rate of population increase rose steadily from 1.3 percent per year in 1951 to 2.5 percent in 1968.

Why does a woman have babies? The *system* that causes women to produce babies can be analyzed into three components:

message——reception——performance

Sometimes consciously, but more often unconsciously, society exposes a woman to one message or another having to do with the desirability of her having babies, e.g., "Stop at two," or "They're cheaper by the dozen." Many different messages are bandied about.

Because "society" is an abstraction, there is some ambiguity and unclarity in the message "society" sends; or to put it another way, the reception of a message by the woman is more or less imperfect (partly because it may conflict with her pre-existing desires).

After she's received the message, her performance may not be perfectly congruent with the altered message she hears. She may decide: "no baby," but if she is using only the rhythm method to achieve this goal, assuming she has a rhythm, her performance will be only about 84 percent effective each year, on the average.

In the light of this threefold analysis of the system of population control we see why birth control is not population control. Table 12 is constructed on the assumption that a woman's reception of society's message and the performance of birth control are both perfect. Given this hypothetical perfection, population growth will be determined by the message. Let us examine some possible messages, one at a time, to see their effect. For simplicity, we assume all women marry and all women are fertile, and we ignore such complications as multiple births, infant mortality, and maternal mortality. Plugging in these variables would modify the conclusions only slightly, because they partly cancel each other out.

"Stop at two" ultimately produces a Zero Population Growth society, of course. Assuming, to begin with, that the population hasn't risen beyond a level compatible with human dignity in a spaceship, society can exist indefinitely, guided by this message.

The ZPG condition is also produced if the only message each woman receives from society is "I must have an heir," i.e., a boy. Half the women would stop breeding after having only one child, a boy. A fourth of the women would stop after having a girl, then a boy; one-eighth after having girl-girl-boy; and so on. This *averages* two children per family (actually, slightly less, because a woman who had had, say, sixteen girls in a row might well refuse to listen to the message any longer).

Consider the catchy refrain from "Tea for Two" in the musical comedy *No, No, Nanette*, ". . . a boy for you, a girl for me. . . ." If this were the sole message women heard, they would (under our assumptions) produce families with an average of three children. This is not ZPG. Of course, not many of the world's 3.6 billion people have ever attended a performance of *No, No, Nanette*. But hundreds

TABLE 12

A Systems Analysis of Population Growth

Demonstrating that birth control is not synonymous with population control.

MESSAGE. SOCIETY'S DIRECTIVES, IMPLICIT OR EXPLICIT	RECEPTION PRECISION ASSUMED	PERFORMANCE EFFECTIVENESS OF BIRTH CONTROL ASSUMED	FERTILITY APPROXIMATE AVERAGE NUMBER OF CHILDREN PER FAMILY	INCREASE FACTOR OF INCREASE PER GENERATION	CONSEQUENCES LONG-RUN EFFECTS, IN A SPACESHIP
"One's enough"	Perfect	Perfect	1	0.5	Depopulation; then extinction
"I must have an heir"	Perfect	Perfect	2	1 (ZPG)	Dignity possible
"Stop at two"	Perfect	Perfect	2	1 (ZPG)	Dignity possible
"A boy for you, a girl for me"	Perfect	Perfect	3	1.5	Ruin
"An heir and a spare"	Perfect	Perfect	4	2	Ruin
"Cheaper by the dozen"	Perfect	Perfect	12	6	Ruin

of millions of them have been exposed to the messages of Planned Parenthood. Multitudes of the illiterate people of the world have seen P-P billboards showing a happy mother and father with just two children—a boy and a girl. The message is unfortunately ambiguous. "Just two," is fine; but "a boy for you, a girl for me" is not. Which of these two messages comes across to poor and illiterate women? If the latter, as I suspect, they will not stop until they have produced three children (on the average), which is ruinous on a spaceship.

In India, the leading indigenous message is "an heir and a spare." For a complex of social reasons an Indian woman will be uneasy until she has at least two sons. Two sons means, on the average, four children. The result: a doubling of the population every generation. This is approximately what is happening in India. Her growth rate is 2.5 percent per year, yielding a doubling time of only 28 years. Ruin comes on like a hurricane, and dignity goes out the window.

Birth control is not population control: perfect birth control merely permits women to have the number of children they want. There will be population control only if women want the right number of children. In every country in the world in which an attitude survey has been made with respect to family size, women want too many children to produce ZPG. Population growth will be achieved only when women's attitudes are changed; changing these is the goal of the second phase in population control.

2. Educational Phase

How do we change people's attitudes? By education, we say—but the word "education" hides a world of complexity. To be effective, education has to be tied to the culture; that means that education must vary from country to country, and from culture to culture. Let us restrict the discussion to the United States, which will supply us with quite enough difficulties.

We must give careful attention to the messages young children hear, particularly young girls, for these messages powerfully form their attitudes toward marriage and the family in later years. Some of the messages children are subjected to in our elementary schools encourage recklessness on board the spaceship.

Recall the Dick-and-Jane books. What is their population message? Simply this: *there is only one normal way to live—*HAVE CHIL-DREN. Dick and Jane's parents have children, of course; but so also do the neighbors on the left, those on the right, the ones across the street—in fact, all God's chillun have chillun. In the literal sense, anything else is *unthinkable*. Exposed at a tender age to such a message, what is a little girl to conclude? Plainly that she just has to become a mommy when she grows up. Nothing else is normal. That's the message of the Dick-and-Jane books.

I think it's time to change the message. We shouldn't get rid of it entirely; but we should augment it with another message, a contradictory one. Let us introduce first-graders to delightful Aunt Debbie —thirty years old, pretty as a picture, and fond of children (but only in small doses). She is a working woman and likes her job. She likes her freedom. She also likes men. The children just love her and look forward to her visits.

Jane, in the depths of her subconscious, wonders whether she wants to be like Mommy when she grows up, or like Aunt Debbie. She doesn't know. She just doesn't know.

And she shouldn't, not at her age. Let Jane grow up hearing two messages: being a mommy is nice—but so also is being a Debbie. Let her find her own identity. Later. And let society make it possible for her to live a psychologically rich and respected life if she decides that parenthood is not for her. We will all benefit if women are freed to find their own identities and not pressured into having children they do not want.

In the elementary grades we must keep the option of childlessness alive in the child's mind. At the secondary level we need to display a wide spectrum of enticing vocations available to nonparents. A significant part of our success in population control will come as a "fall-out" from making it possible for more women to become scientists, artists, machinists, businesswomen—the list is endless. It even includes work in the nursery—the community nursery, that is—as professionals in child care. We not only have too many children, we have too many poorly taken care of. We need to pay women to fulfill this role, so important to the nation, instead of expecting them to be unpaid slaves. Paradoxical as it may seem, if we pay them well for taking care of children, they will probably breed less.

3. Coercive Phase

Some think this phase will never be needed. They may be right—but I think not, for the purely Darwinian reason that *voluntary population control selects for its own failure.* Noncooperators outbreed cooperators. It is inconceivable that a nation of hundreds of millions could be without its noncooperators, so we had better begin to think about a third phase of population control, a coercive phase.

I said *think about*—no more. Not yet. The dangers of coercion are grave. We would not run such dangers, ever, except that we live on a spaceship and know that purely voluntary population control is self-defeating. We must do a great deal of thinking about ways to keep coercion under control before we can safely act decisively. We need imaginative social engineering. We can see farther than we can act.

Coercion is a spectrum, ranging from tax incentives to detention camps. Even government-financed persuasion—education—can be considered a form of coercion. It is tempting to opt for tax incentives as being a gentler form of coercion, one that is compatible with conventional ideas of freedom; but even these have dangers. If we tax parents for having too many children, some of the punishment is passed from the parents to the children, who are not, in any sense, responsible for the sins of their parents.

It has been suggested that the amount of a person's retirement annuity be inversely related to the number of children he or she has produced. This scheme would not harm the children, who should be on their own by the time their parents retire. There are, however, two substantial criticisms to be made of the proposal. First, it may be questioned whether the bait would in fact be effective. How many people, at the fertile age of twenty-five or thirty, believe *in their bones* that they will someday be old? How many will sacrifice the present pleasure (whatever it is) of having children for a problematical future pleasure of more money to spend in their dotage when (they rightly suspect) the edge of all pleasure is dulled? Besides, they may not live that long. (True.) Or the social system may collapse, wiping out their retirement fund. (This also is true, but it cannot even be discussed, without prejudice, by the Establishment that proposes a delayed reward for nonproductivity.)

The second objection to the proposal is more fundamental: this is but one more system that selects for its own failure. Those adults who respond to the incentive, and are rewarded, have fewer children than those who ignore it. If the difference between the two groups of parents depends on temperamental characteristics that are even in the slightest degree hereditary—foolhardiness? courage? prudence? philoprogenitiveness?—then the relative frequency of the genes that make for the desired response to the incentive will decrease with the succession of generations. It is hard to be enthusiastic about a scheme that is deficient on this most fundamental of grounds.

The economist Kenneth Boulding has proposed what he calls his "green stamp plan" to lower the birth rate by using the market mechanism long employed to allocate scarce material resources.

> I have only one positive suggestion to make, a proposal which now seems so farfetched that I find it creates only amusement when I propose it. I think in all seriousness, however, that a system of marketable licenses to have children is the only one which will combine the minimum of social control necessary to the solution to this problem with a maximum of individual liberty and ethical choice. Each girl on approaching maturity would be presented with a certificate which will entitle its owner to have, say, 2.2 children, or whatever number would ensure a reproductive rate of one. The unit of these certificates might be the "deci-child," and accumulation of ten of these units by purchase, inheritance, or gift would permit a woman in maturity to have one legal child. We would then set up a market in these units in which the rich and the philoprogenitive would purchase them from the poor, the nuns, the maiden aunts, and so on. The men perhaps could be left out of these arrangements, as it is only the fertility of women which is strictly relevant to population control. However, it may be found socially desirable to have them in the plan, in which case all children both male and female would receive, say, eleven or twelve deci-child certificates at birth or at maturity, and a woman could then accumulate these through marriage.
>
> This plan would have the additional advantage of developing a long-run tendency toward equality in income, for the rich would have many children and become poor and the poor would have few children and become rich. The price of the certificate would of course reflect the general desire in a society to have children.

Where the desire is very high the price would be bid up; where it was low the price would also be low. Perhaps the ideal situation would be found when the price was naturally zero, in which case those who wanted children would have them without extra cost. If the price were very high the system would probably have to be supplemented by some sort of grants to enable the deserving but impecunious to have children, while cutting off the desires of less deserving through taxation. The sheer unfamiliarity of a scheme of this kind makes it seem absurd at the moment. The fact that it seems absurd, however, is merely a reflection of the total unwillingness of mankind to face up to what is perhaps its most serious long-run problem.

The general effect would be to allocate child-permits as we now allocate Cadillacs—to the richest. The scheme would fail to do this to the degree that there is a "philoprogenitive instinct," inheritable in the most general sense; to this degree the scheme would select for its own failure. But the scheme might be a useful interim measure in getting people used to the idea of parenthood as a licenseable privilege instead of a right.

We make people take driving tests before allowing them to drive cars, but any idiot can become a parent, which is an immensely more demanding activity.

There is only one way to eliminate the counterproductive effect of choice in population control, and that is to get rid of the choice itself. The logic of choice-exclusion is not new, merely the application of it to parenthood. We *might* allow freedom of choice in the robbing of banks; but we don't, because freedom of choice would favor robbers and select against conscience. Freedom would be counterproductive, with respect to widely accepted goals of society that we treasure even more than freedom. It is hardly necessary to spell these out.

Freedom to breed is also counterproductive in the same sense, but with this difference: it is only counterproductive beyond a certain level of population or population-growth rate. The morality of breeding is situation-sensitive. If we want to be equitable in the allocation of the right to breed, we must say that an individual has such a right until she has n children, but not beyond. Beyond n she has broken the law.

Laws that take account of situations present serious problems of enforcement. An absolute proscription is comparatively easy to enforce because it facilitates the linkage of emotion to law. Emotional reactions legitimate law. When a bank robber is caught, we are unhesitatingly against him. But what is our reaction to a killer of bears, if anyone with a license is allowed one bear per season? Before we know how to react to the killer, we have to know whether he has a license, what sort of gun he used, and whether this is in fact his first kill of the year. Such nit-picking tends to drain emotion from our reaction and endangers the legitimation of the law. This is one of the reasons why poaching is harder to control than murder.

Coercive control of population will be difficult. Even if we avoid the administrative rulings as to the limits, writing all limits into law, we still will need bureaus to ferret out the facts. This is unfortunate, doubly so at the present time because of the low esteem in which bureaus are held. "Bureaucratic" is a pejorative, almost solely so. But population control will never work without good bureaucratic implementation. This is one more reason why we will not soon achieve population control. In the meantime, pollution and the ills of overcrowding will get worse. We will have to stew in our own juices for a while longer.

As always in our society, worshipers of Progress have hoped that a technological "breakthrough" might relieve us of the necessity of making hard decisions in the ethical, social, and political realms. They have dreamed of a contraceptive that could be added to the water, thus making everyone automatically and safely sterile. The hypothetical contraceptive could be countered with an antidote available only on prescription from the population-control bureau. In the reverse of the present situation, sterility would be easy and automatic, fertility difficult.

The dream is seductive, but it does not really bypass the ethical, social, and political problems. We would still have to get community agreement to use the sterilizing agent.

In addition, the proposal is even technologically suspect. The chemist Carl Djerassi, one of the principals in the "pill" technology, has given a more than sufficient number of reasons for believing that a drinking-water contraceptive will never be found.

The pharmacological standards for an acceptable agent are extremely severe. It would have to be effective and not harmful over an extremely wide range of water intake. It would have to be stable in solution in contact with all the substances that make up pipes, valves, and water containers. It should have no adverse effects on children and old people, who don't need it. It should have no detectable side effects.

How would one control the problem of bootlegging untreated water? Or bootlegging antidotes?

How would one even *find* such a substance? The usual way of looking for a new substance is by *animal tests first,* then human tests. But the ideal substance would be one that sterilized humans only, and not our cats, dogs, horses, cows, and other domestic animals. Of course we might settle for less than the ideal, but in testing substances there would always be a chance that the perfect substance, as determined by animal tests, would be ineffective in humans. Contrariwise, a poor substance (according to animal tests) *might* be perfect for humans—but how would we ever find that out, following the "animals first" rule for testing new drugs?

Not in new technology will the answer be found to population control, but in new approaches to social and political change. We have no proven techniques for converting from one set of ethical standards to another—not painlessly.

How can the transition from a voluntary to a coercive system be made? Must it be by an intermediate stage that combines legal freedom with *de facto* guilt assignment to parents who have more than two children? Older citizens who had their four or six children long before they were aware of the population problem do not take kindly to being lectured at by nulliparous young females from Zero Population Growth, Incorporated. Nor do younger parents who are still weighing the merits of population control like to be subjected to "jawbone responsibility," in the absence of genuinely operational responsibility.

"Guilt-pushing" is an old and honored tradition in liberal reform movements. Whether guilt feelings are less painful than legal restraint may at least be doubted. Whether the cultivation of guilt makes for a healthy society may also be doubted. But anyone reading the left-wing press (of which the *New York Review of Books* is an example of quality) is left with no doubt that many individuals in that segment of our society denoted by the term "intellectuals" are quite literally addicted to guilt. (Or is guilt-pushing merely the last and despairing bludgeon of the reformer when he becomes convinced that he is impotent if restricted to cleaner weapons?)

We could certainly benefit by finding a healthier way to effect the transition from the present voluntary system of family population control to the coercive system we must ultimately accept. Is there a better way? . . . Social inventors will please step forward!

CHAPTER 23

Beyond Lysistrata?

Briefly, where do we stand now, vis-à-vis the question of population control?

Population control is inevitable; the question we ask is: by what agency—Nature or man? What we call—for want of a better term—"human dignity" can be preserved only if man takes charge of population control. Technology and education can help in the task but, since we are not willing to forgo the humane arrangements of the welfare state, coercion also must ultimately be used—"mutual coercion, mutually agreed upon," by a large majority of the population. Though each new area of application is resisted at first, coercion ultimately is accepted as we clearly see the necessity of it. When our understanding reaches this point, we experience an inward feeling of freedom again because "freedom is the recognition of necessity." It is the transition that is painful and dangerous.

The choice facing us is not freedom versus restraint, but restraint in breeding versus all other restraints. Every increase in population requires additional restraints in our access to, and use of, the environment. If mankind could, for example, reduce world population to only a small fraction of its present size, and restrain breeding to keep it there, most of the present (and coming) environmental restraints that we regard as onerous could be eliminated.

Whether population is stabilized at the optimum level or (as seems far more likely) at a level far above the optimum, stabilization requires (to put the matter simply) that the average number of chil-

205

dren per woman be but two. The pain of stabilization is no less at overpopulated levels than it is at the optimum.

Such appear to be the necessities, according to the best information we have now. Is there no escape from these conclusions?

A good chess-player, before putting into play a clever sequence he has just thought of, moves around to the other side of the board (mentally) and asks: As my opponent, what defense should I use? If he cannot succeed in thus mentally *changing places*, his strategy will likely prove defective.

A good militarist follows the same discipline. In his mind he changes places with the enemy in order to test the soundness of his strategy. This is not easy; but it is essential.

So also in theoretical matters—in science and in the application of knowledge to human affairs. After reaching what seems to be an unavoidable conclusion, one must endeavor to shuck off one's commitment and examine the conclusion as an unfriendly opponent would. Changing places, can one see another possibility?

One of the practical conclusions of the analysis given in this book is this: population control and freedom to breed are irreconcilable. To preserve a measure of human dignity women must give up their "right" to have as many children as they wish.

Changing places, I have looked for an escape from this conclusion (which many people regard with horror). Looking for an escape, I have found one. Whether it is an "acceptable" one I don't know. But let me describe it, as an advocate might; then let the reader decide.

One of the possible technological developments looming on the horizon is that of "sex determination"—being able to choose the sex of a child before birth with 100 percent success. Never mind how this might be done—there are several possibilities—just imagine that the day has arrived when we can do it. (Technically, the problem seems not intractable.)

If perfect sex determination is achieved, women can then be freed of *all* restrictions on the *number* of children they produced, PROVIDED: they submit to the single restriction of having *only one girl child* per woman. Population size might fluctuate considerably from generation to generation, as the average completed family size varied from (say) two children to eight, but there would be fluctuations only, and no long-term growth trend so long as each breeding woman left only one breeding daughter among her descendants. If the mean about which fluctuations occurred was the optimum, the fluctuations would be compatible with human dignity.

Easily said: but would the consequences of accepting this new restriction be acceptable? We can never do merely one thing: what else would—or might—happen if we altered the sex ratio drastically? What other alterations would be called for to make a stable, acceptable system? ("Acceptable," if ever, only after the first shock and reflexive rejection have passed.)

At this point, I suspect, many members of the Women's Liberation Movement will rise up in arms. They may view diminution of the relative numbers of their sex as a threat to the power of women. If so, they are wrong: they overlook the power that comes with scarcity. The medical profession, ever jealous of its not inconsiderable prerogatives, understands this and continually works to restrict the number of doctors trained. Women should consider its example.

Aristophanes' Lysistrata understood this principle. She knew there was something men wanted that only women could give, even in Greece. Seeking an end to a war, she set up an Attic Women's Lib with NO SEX on its escutcheon. Her strategy was sound.

If women can control the sex of their children and if they wish to improve the bargaining power of women in future generations, they should produce an excess of male children. But with a large male-to-female ratio, monogamy would leave many men "out in the cold" and dangerously dissatisfied. It would be hard to create a stable state from such explosive material, so a shift to polygamy would be required.

"But is polygamy natural?" some might ask. With as much justice one might ask, "Is monogamy natural?" Many artists have asked the second question. The poet Shelley, for example, took issue with custom in these words:

> I never was attached to that great sect,
> Whose doctrine is, that each one should select
> Out of the crowd a mistress or a friend,

And all the rest, though fair and wise, commend
To cold oblivion, though it is in the code
Of modern morals, and the beaten road
Which those poor slaves with weary footsteps tread,
Who travel to their home among the dead
By the broad highway of the world, and so
With one chained friend, perhaps a jealous foe,
The dreariest and the longest journey go.

True Love in this differs from gold and clay,
That to divide is not to take away. . . .
                                    . . . Narrow
The heart that loves, the brain that contemplates,
The life that wears, the spirit that creates
One object, and one form, and builds thereby
A sepulchre for its eternity.

Mind from its object differs most in this:
Evil from good; misery from happiness;
The baser from the nobler; the impure
And frail, from what is clear and must endure.
If you divide suffering and dross, you may
Diminish till it is consumed away;
If you divide pleasure and love and thought,
Each part exceeds the whole. . . .

If, not bound by tradition, we seriously ask what is "natural," we undoubtedly have in mind some question about the best proportion of men to women in the relationships between them that are broadly characterized as "marriage." Which would be best: monogamy, or a form of polygamy—either polygyny (several women per man), or polyandry (several men per woman)? Or a more fluid arrangement that might be called "promiscuous"? (Unfortunately this adjective is pejorative and interferes with objectivity.) Which arrangement fits "human nature" best?

I don't think that anybody knows the answer. The true answer must take account of human variability, which the writings of most moralists do not. It also must allow for the reality of selection: an enduring social arrangement selects for those who can be happy under it, thus in the end altering "human nature" to fit. *Man makes himself*, as Sartre said. The question is: What do we want to become? And why?

Whatever marriage-like ties there be, they must satisfy criteria roughly classifiable under the headings of physiological, emotional, social, and economic. The last is perhaps the least important in a welfare state, particularly in an aggressively equalitarian one. The middle two cover deep waters indeed; I will pass them by. The first, the physiological criterion, is perhaps the easiest to make something of.

What can we say about the relative sexual prowess of men and women? It is next to impossible to be objective about such a question. The pride of the speaker is involved: whatever he (she) says will be held against him (her). He (she) fears unintended self-revelation. And anyway, since the issue of pleasure is involved, how can *ego* compare his (her) pleasure with that of *alter*?

The Greeks conceived an ingenious "thought experiment" to settle this question. If the myth be true, it gives the answer.

The infidelities of Zeus were known to all—including Hera, his wife. When she was reproaching him one day for his behavior, he defended himself on grounds of equity, arguing that though he slept with many partners and she (quite properly) with only one, their pleasures were equal because "women, of course, derive infinitely greater pleasure from the sexual act than men."

"What nonsense," cried Hera. "The exact contrary is the case, and well you know it."

Fortunately the Greeks had a truly objective way of approaching this question. Teiresias, when a young man, had witnessed two serpents coupling. When both attacked him, he struck at them and killed the female. For this, he was turned into a harlot who became celebrated in her profession, which she practiced for seven years. At the end of this time she again witnessed an act of serpentine sex and again killed one of the snakes, this time the male. The hetaira was transformed into Teiresias again, complete with his memory of her past. Having experienced sex in both forms, Teiresias was in the perfect position to compare the pleasures of the two.

The gods appealed to him to settle their dispute. He answered:

> If the parts of love-pleasure be counted as ten,
> Thrice three go to women, only one to men.

With the pique so common among Greek gods, Hera struck Teiresias blind for giving such an answer. (Had she been a better logician she would have attacked Zeus's reasoning instead.) Zeus, in gratitude, gave Teiresias the inward sight for which he became famous during the remainder of his life.

Making due allowance for the variability of people and the uncertainty of the evidence, it seems probable that a ratio of several men to one woman satisfies physiological criteria better than does the reverse ratio. It may also be better socially: at least, one can make a plausible argument for it. There are reasons for thinking that many children in a family are better than two. The multichild family can be produced without violating the conditions needed for ZPG if polyandry is instituted and every woman is restricted to one daughter. The woman would have both sexual and maternal needs satisfied, and (if our physiological assumptions are correct) the men should have no complaints.

In addition one might argue that since the more complex society becomes, the more attention should be given to the education of the young, many fathers should be better than one. Divorce could be expected to continue, but its harmful effects on the young would be lessened if the children always stayed with the mother, with only a fraction of the "fathers" being lost to the children at the time of a divorce.

The full consequences of such a polyandrous system are hardly predictable, but it would undoubtedly make forever impossible the equality of the sexes: women would clearly be the superior sex.

Would this be bad? A remark made in another context by the poet Robert Graves would argue otherwise: "In my view the political and social confusion of these last 3000 years has been entirely due to man's revolt against woman as a priestess of natural magic and his defeat of her wisdom by the use of intellect. He has given her the choice of becoming either a housewife, a plaything, or a careerist." Spokesmen for the Women's Liberation Movement assume that women must reject the first two and embrace the third. Perhaps there are richer possibilities to be explored.

That the dominance of the male can be perilous for the species has long been known to biologists. Whatever may be the origin of polygyny, once it arises it poses serious threats to the continued existence of the species. Polygynous species usually show marked sexual dimorphism, with the male being much larger and better armed than the female. A male walrus weighs three times as much as the female. The armament of male elks, moose, and other ungulates is well known. The size and armament of the female shows what the environment (outside the species) is selecting for. The additional weight and weapons of the male are due entirely to *intra*specific competition among males fighting for females, and are otherwise grossly maladaptive. Selection for extraspecific maladaptation is inevitable in a polygynous species.

It is quite possible that the maladaptive human characteristics decried by Graves are the result of the same destructive type of selection in humans. Polygyny has been much commoner than polyandry among humans during the past six thousand years; and even monogamy has usually amounted to the same thing because it has been coupled with the "double standard." Pure monogamy has been as rare as pure water.

Polygyny selects for a bellicosity that is increasingly less compatible with the survival of the species. Diminishing the bellicosity will be a complicated and prolonged process, but one that should be encouraged. We should not lightly dismiss any measure that shows promise of furthering such a change. That includes polyandry.

CHAPTER 24

Beyond Fatalism

How seriously should the reader take my proposal that we achieve
ZPG conditions not by a rigid control of the total number of children
a woman might have but by adopting polyandry coupled with sex
control and a rigid limit of one girl child to each woman? I don't
know. I have presented the proposal in the intemperate language of
an advocate, but let me now admit that I don't know whether the
polyandrous system would be better or not. The "secondary" alterations such a change would require would touch every significant
facet of our existence.

Think, to begin with, of the architectural changes that would follow the change from the one-man-one-woman family to a one-
woman-many-men group. Cities would have to be rebuilt. (They will
have to be anyway, for other reasons, so too much should not be
made of this.) Other changes would be even greater. It is hard to
believe that any single person has the wisdom to predict all the significant changes that would be required to realize the best potential
of a system of polyandry. Many men and women will have to apply
their minds to such a problem before we can have any confidence in
the predictions and hence be in a position to judge wisely. Cautious
experiments would be desirable.

Our automatic reaction to all such proposals is to reject them out
of hand. Why? Because (we believe) we dare not bring about
planned social change of a profound order.

This is very curious. As regards technology, our attitude has long been that ascribed to good engineers: "The difficult we do immediately; the impossible takes a little longer." The euphoria this bespeaks has been no small part of the secret of the Western world's phenomenal growth in power in the last two centuries.

Westerners who have tried to graft the scientific-industrial scion onto the stock of traditional societies in the less "advanced" parts of the world have discovered that the graft often fails because of a sort of immune reaction. Change in a traditional society is frequently inhibited by an attitude of "whatever will be, will be." We outsiders call it fatalism. We think that only *they* suffer from it—not *we*.

But we do. *Our* fatalism manifests itself in two ways. The first is in our worship of the Technological Imperative: "Whatever we can invent we are required to use." This is as fatalistic, and as primitive, as anything the most backward country in the world exhibits. Happily, with the defeat of the SST, we may have begun to escape this kind of fatalism.

The second manifestation of our fatalism is in our almost total refusal to make *planned* social changes. Unplanned ones we make constantly, and the magnitude of many of them is monumental. Think of what the mechanized cotton-picker did to the social equilibrium of this country, not alone in the South, where it displaced black workers, but perhaps even more in the North, where unemployed Southerners moved into the city centers without anyone's having done an iota of planning for their accommodation. The unplanned changes that resulted still have not run their course.* What we call "the urban problem" could almost as accurately be called "the cotton-picker problem." That's not overly accurate, but neither is the usual name.

Then there is the automobile, which for decades we saw only as a toy and a convenience. Of this, E. J. Mishan has said:

I once wrote that the invention of the automobile was one of the greatest disasters to have befallen mankind. I have had time since

---

* The first persons to invent an almost-satisfactory cotton-picker, the Rust brothers in the 1930s, foresaw that their invention would cause vast social changes and, forgoing easy profits, tried to control the introduction of their machine. For various reasons, both financial and political, they were unsuccessful. The sense of social responsibility they exhibited is, so far as I know, completely without parallel among inventors.

to reflect on this statement and to revise my judgment to the effect that the automobile is *the* greatest disaster to have befallen mankind. For sheer, massive, irresistible destructive power, nothing—except perhaps the airlines—can compete with it. Almost every principle of architectural harmony has been perverted in the vain struggle to keep the mounting volume of motorized traffic moving through our cities, towns, resorts, hamlets and, of course, through our rapidly expanding suburbs. Clamour, dust, fumes, congestion and visual distraction are the predominant features in all our built-up areas. Even where styles of architecture differ between cities—and they differ less from year to year—these traffic features impinge so blatantly and so persistently on the senses that they submerge any other impressions. Whether we are in Paris, Chicago, Tokyo, Düsseldorf, or Milan, it is the choking din and the endless movement of motorized traffic that dominate the scene.

Strong as the economist's statement is, he has no more than hinted at the social destruction the automobile has caused.

Clearly, the options facing us are not whether we shall have social change or not, but whether we shall or shall not try to plan change. To put the matter another way: shall we, like any primitive people, be totally fatalistic in our attitude toward social change—"whatever will be, will be"—or shall we attempt the impossible and seek to mold ourselves? Though the difficulties are formidable, I rather think that we shall slowly move toward controlling our own destiny. If so, the question we will ask of each new invention will be not "Can it make a profit?" but "Can we use it to further social change we regard as desirable?"

If this be true we will create a world that is utterly different from the one we have lived in for nearly two centuries. It is customary to regard the publication of Condorcet's *Historical Picture of the Progress of the Human Mind* as marking the beginning of the age of "Progress." Progress has come to be identified almost wholly with technological progress—a progress in "hardware," as computer men would call it. But whatever changes may have been wrought in his dreams by his spiritual descendants, Condorcet himself, as is evident from the very title of his book, was concerned primarily with "software," with the furnishings of men's minds, with their habits, laws, customs, and ethics. "Nature," said Condorcet, "has assigned no limit to the perfecting of the human faculties . . . the perfectibility of man is truly indefinite." It is time we turn our attention from the things of mankind to man himself.

CHAPTER 25

The Return of the *Beagle*

Once more we see the observation deck inside the mountain, but it has been transformed. At the edges of our vision there are still half-seen traces of technology—dials, meters, lights, and shiny surfaces. In the center, and dominating, is what appears to be a stage set of the porch of a river restaurant. The scalloped edge of a crimson-striped awning, hanging down, moves indolently in the gentle breeze (thanks to a small hidden fan). Surrounding the porch is a tangle of artificial reeds hiding a speaker that emits the recorded sounds of crickets and katydids. Beyond the reeds, where a placid river should be (furrowed by canoes and sailboats), lies the plain of Quo, partially obscured and swarming again with bodies.

The people on the porch are now both men and women, and inexpressibly younger and gayer than the complement of Argotes with which the voyage began. Two of the men wear T-shirts; the others are more elegantly dressed, mostly in sport clothes. Lace, frills, bonnets, and ribbons bedeck the women, equaling in color the still-life of wineglasses, bottles, and artificial fruit on the white table-cloths.

The scene, in fact, is Renoir's "Boating Party," lovingly reconstructed. The people show a surprising resemblance to Renoir's, though their range of color is greater. Fairest by far is Alphonsine, with the blue-ribboned straw hat. Darkest is the farthest figure, a boy; or perhaps Sinjon, in the brown bowler hat, with his back to us as the scene opens. The nearest girl, Aline, puckers her lips as she talks to a dog made of yarn scraps. Pink-cheeked Lester, with his wispy red beard, leans over Ellen and Gus, seated at the near

216

table. He is teasing the frowzy-looking Ellen: "If only your great-grandmother hadn't been so dumb you wouldn't be having so much trouble understanding how we're going to get off this tub."

Ellen's whisky voice explodes: "What do you mean, *my* great-grandmother? She was yours as much as mine. The Three Graces were great-grandmothers to us all. If I'm slower than you it's just because no one educated me properly. I'm as good as you are."

"Not necessarily, Ellen." It was Gus who spoke, pushing his straw boating hat a bit farther back on his sweaty head. "Not necessarily —yet. Eventually all our genes will be mixed around together, but linkage is like friction: it slows down the reshuffling. I suspect all you women are *really* different from us. For this generation, anyway. Have patience: it isn't permanent. You'll outgrow it in a few generations."

"What do you mean, *I* will outgrow it? I won't be here in a few generations. That'll be my granddaughter. Don't be so snotty. If the Three Graces hadn't introduced sex into this benighted *Flying Dutchman,* you wouldn't even be here."

"Ah," responded Gus, his eyes twinkling, "but the *I* that *would* be here would be immortal."

Aline brusquely put the dog down on the table, shoving it and the grapes away from her.

"Oh, crap! Who wants to live forever if there's no sex? The Immortals lived for five thousand years, and what did they have to show for it? A lot of high thought and low cocks. Until my great-grandmother turned off the Anti-Sex valve they didn't have anything to live for."

"Then they must have had something to die for. And did," taunted Lester. "The price of sex turned out to be mortality. Was it worth it?"

"What do you think, Alphonsine?" Gus raised his voice to catch the attention of the girl at the rail. Alphonsine arched her brows, rolled her eyes, smiled broadly, turned red—and said nothing.

" 'Better fifty years of Europe than a cycle of Cathay,' " murmured the deep voice of the Baron, standing at the rail behind Aline; built like an ox, he had an air of power and authority.

Others, attracted by the dispute, turned and joined in.

"What's Cathay?" Henrietta asked sharply, putting down her glass. "And how much is a cycle? I'm not buying until I know the price."

"How can you know the price?" The man in the brown hat turned his chair so he could lean back against the railing. His eyes were brown too, and as moist as a deer's; his nose long and flat on his face, but not broad; mouth firm and serious. "How can anyone know the price? Those who are immortal are spared the fires of concupiscence that disturb the even tenor of most men's lives; they know nothing of the blessed relief of concupiscence. But those who enjoy sex—or say they do—will never know the calm of wise old age without senility. Insofar as my imagination permits me to compare the two incomparables, I think I would opt for immortality, had I the opportunity."

Ellen, out of the side of her mouth, leaning over to Gus: "He *would*. God, what a frost he is inside!"

The general hubbub was interrupted by the youngest of the males, a beardless, small-faced youth with a sharp nose and quick movements. He rose, calling for attention with a slide-rule.

"Hey, look, gang. There's something we've got to do right away, and it's going to be rather pretty, if I've calculated right. Before we can go home safely we've got to cast off the Dyson Pack that's kept us going for five thousand years. This is your last chance to see it. I don't think any of you have seen it before—"

"I have." It was the bearded man in the blue hat speaking.

"Oh, yes; you, Pierre. You see everything. Well, it's worth seeing, don't you think? Its activity is low enough now so that we can safely look at it for an hour or more. For thousands of years the safe limit was ten seconds. None of the Immortals ever saw it. . . . Come on, I'll show you the way. Let's go down and cast off."

"My, this is wonderful!" The woman in the brown feathered hat ran her gloves over the glass wall.

"It's leaded glass, Jeannie," said the young engineer. "Two feet thick, and still not enough protection against radiation from the Dyson Pack in its prime. Eight feet high, twelve feet wide. Quite a view window out onto the universe, don't you think?"

The group was looking out at the profusion of stars glistening against a black matrix.

"They never look so lovely where we live," said Henrietta.

"That's because the first generation of Quotions really smoked up the bubble, but good," said Lester. "The smoke came off, but the plastic was permanently corroded. Where's the Dyson, Linus?"

"Outa sight, over t' the left. I'm going to bring it around now so you can see it before we cast off." He threw several switches on the left wall and turned a knob. "Or rather, what I'm really doing is turning our tub on its axis until we can see it. It'll take a few moments."

There was a distant hum and a slight feeling of angular acceleration as the field of stars moved around. A glow grew at the left side, followed by the sight of what appeared to be a sun in full eclipse, with dancing streamers of flame projecting outward from the occluded disk. Out of the black center a tenuous, luminous rope stretched toward the *Beagle;* a fluctuating stream of light, moving slowly in sinusoidal waves. Spontaneous *ah-h-hs* came from the viewers, their eyes transfixed by this all-but-living entity.

"The plasma wave-guide," said Linus. "Our umbilical cord. All our energy has come through that for five thousand years. Only energy; but in effect, all our food, all our recycled materials; our light, our heat, our life. Negative entropy; life itself. Now it's near the end of its useful life and we've got to cast it off. Once we do that, all we've got to go on is the energy stored up inside the *Beagle.* That will last us only about two months with no extra activity; or about a week if we make a landing. So we will have just a week's leeway. No room for mistakes. Our plans had better be right. Once we've cast off we're on our own."

The last remark cast a spell over the spectators. *The irrevocable:* a solemn thought on any occasion—but now, the irrevocable standing between five thousand years and one week's grace.

"Do we have to cast it away?" asked the woman with the gloves, who seemed the least burdened with heavy thoughts. "It's so pretty!"

"And dangerous, Jeannie. The shuttle ship doesn't have enough shielding. Fine thing if we land on Earth with a full-blown case of radiation sickness. Besides, the flux would play havoc with the computers on the shuttle."

A long, thoughtful silence.

"How far away is the pack?"

"It's about . . . no, I don't know. Maybe a thousand kilometers. We'll know when we cast off, by the number of seconds it takes to roll the visible plasma back to the Pack. . . . We might as well do it now. Everybody ready?"

Linus took a key out of his pocket, opened a large safe with it, then an inner door with a combination, uncovering a single switch. With great deliberation and with all eyes upon him he threw the switch and the light went out from the nearest portion of the waveguide, the darkness traveling away from them like the sputtering fuse of an explosive charge. Immediately after throwing the switch, Linus turned a knob, setting off an electric metronome that counted out the seconds.

After twelve seconds someone said, "I can't tell where it is now because of the light from the pack."

"You'll know when it gets there," said Linus. "The center of the Dyson will light up like a skyrocket, and it'll be off to Andromeda. After that you have no more than five seconds to watch, and then everybody scoots up the stairs."

"Twenty-eight," said Pierre.

Twenty-nine.

Thirty.

Thirty-one.

The center of the disk slowly burst into a flower of flames.

"Farther than I thought," said Linus. "Thirteen hundred and fifty kilometers. . . . Now, git! Up the stairs, all of you, before we get our tails burned."

With a rush they headed for the rear of the room, women first, and disappeared up the stairs.

Topside, on the porch once more, the tables were pushed together and they all took chairs—all but Alphonsine, who perched on the railing, facing inward, her cheek pressed against one of the iron uprights that supported the awning. The Baron sat at one end of the table, his grizzled face examining the group expectantly. At the other end, Lester. The Baron leaned on the table with his brawny arms and began.

"We've got some time now and we had better use it to make sure everybody understands what we've got to do and why. We don't want anybody to feel rushed or pushed. Everybody has to understand. We've got plenty of time to talk about it."

"Plenty of time?" asked the man in the red-ribboned straw hat. "Plenty of time? Cut off from the Dyson, we're like a prisoner with a sentence of death hanging over us. It's like a pendulum ticking off the seconds. Plenty of time? Huh!"

"Plenty for what we need, Rivers," said the Baron imperturbably. "We don't need much time for the actual operations, and it'll be a good twenty hours before we can shove off. I think we can well spend our afternoon in a leisurely examination of where we are, how we got here, and what—probably—lies ahead."

Gus stood up with a wine bottle and set about filling the glasses. There was a long silence.

"What *does* lie ahead?" asked Pierre. "What do you think, Baron?"

"That's a good one. That's the million-kilogram question. What do we know? . . . For one thing, we know the last message our ancestors got from Earth, and when they got it."

He reached under the table and pulled up a folder of papers, shuffling and examining them as he spoke.

"Twenty years, three months, and thirteen days after the *Beagle* left Earth, this message was received. I will read you only the last few paragraphs.

"All in all I'd say we've weathered the worst storms, Jerry. The threat of a new epidemic of ecologists has been ruthlessly stamped out. Raymond B. Cowles the Third was burned on the Mall in Washington last Wednesday. A beautiful commemorative stamp of the event was issued and it is selling like hot cakes, to coin a phrase.

"The Gross National Product continues to rise, spurred on by the sale of pollution-control equipment, which makes up thirty percent of the GNP, which is now over eighty thousand billion. The price of food is high, of course. Bread, seven dollars and a half a loaf; eggs, three dollars apiece; and beef two hundred dollars a pound, if you can find any. Dieting is easy, which should be good for the health. This is fortunate because we have a tragic shortage of doctors: only one physician for every twenty-five people.

"The computerized security system at last has all the bugs ironed out of it. For the last five weeks the Crimeometer in the Rockies has registered zero every day. This news has been given a big play in the media and has done much to restore the people's faith in technology. In his Conditioner-side speech last week the President said: 'This brilliant technological victory over the human forces of chaos and disorder gives the lie to all who would doubt our steadfastness in the pursuit of progress. By hard work good men can do anything they set their minds to; for an American there are no limits. Now that the last great scourge of humanity is licked—Crime—we know that we stand at the beginning of a road that has no ending. For the first time in history, mankind has achieved complete and total stability. This means that the American future is measured not merely in hundreds or thousands of years, oh no! Our destiny is to last forever.We are the culmination of the dreams of mankind, the newly discovered country from whose bourn

"And that's it. That's the end. Jerry Wood immediately sent off a request for a repeat and everyone waited impatiently. The communication round trip then took two months. No reply. He tried again and again. Nothing. Finally he quit. Had the Earthlings blown themselves up completely? Or, after re-establishment of order, had they decided it was pointless to continue corresponding with a people whose very existence they must have increasingly come to doubt? Whatever the explanation on Earth, one thing was crystal clear here on the *Beagle:* we were alone."

"The umbilical cord had been cut," murmured Rivers.

There was a prolonged silence. Thoughtfully, several sipped their wine. Thoughtfully, Gus spoke.

"No idea what happened? No hint in earlier dispatches?"

"I don't know," the Baron replied. "I've read over the records of the preceding year and haven't found anything really solid. The name Raymond Cowles in that last communication caught my eye, and I did find a mention of him. Whether it has any significance or not, I don't know. But here it is. This came six months earlier.

" 'God himself couldn't please some people. When the Atomic Energy Commission issued its final report on reactor safety, all one hundred and forty-seven volumes of it, complete with the computer programs, amidst the general rejoicing a sour note was struck by an unknown scientist by the name of Raymond B. Cowles the Third. He is suspected of being an ecologist, but unfortunately our too lenient laws do not permit putting him to the torture to find out, so newspapers are allowed to print the trash he turns out. Here's the essential part of his statement.

" 'The AEC report has everything to recommend it except truth. The computer analyses are absolutely definitive—for computers. Computers handle more than ninety-nine percent of the decisions of the reactor systems, and for this aspect of safety computer analyses are both relevant and sufficient. But at the beginning of every action chain is a human link—and what can computers know of humanity?

" 'It is not merely the unintentional unreliability of human beings that is involved. We must fear intentional unreliability even more. Sabotage, to be blunt. This danger necessarily increases with size of population, though in a complex manner.

" 'Democracy is impossible with large numbers because the communication load goes up as the square of the population size. So we institute hierarchies. For a given type of hierarchy the number of levels increases only as the logarithm of population size. This is good. But unfortunately the feeling of alienation increases as a power function of the number of levels. The spontaneous response to alienation is the formation of tribes—groups within which communication is excellent and discipline is strong. It would be too much to expect the hidden goals of tribes to be congruent with the official goals of the nation. The work of the nation must be done by individuals, some of whom are tribesmen: herein lies the danger of sabotage.

" 'We hardly need to be reminded of the incredible devastation that can be wrought by a reactor's going critical. Sabotage can make this peril a reality. So consider the paradox we face.

" 'Because we regard the right to breed as an inalienable right, our population continues to grow without limit. Increased population means increased need for energy. This increase in need can be met only by atomic energy. But increased population size brings increased tribalism and increased danger of sabotage—ultimately a certainty.

" 'On the other hand, a nation that kept its population under control would not have to become tribalistic and could risk having the atomic reactors it does not need.

" 'The nation that needs atomic reactors dare not have them; the nation that can safely have them does not need them. This is the paradox the AEC computers never discovered—because they were programed for trivia. If this misleading report is made the basis of national policy, I see nothing but devastation ahead.'

"Did you ever read such arrant nonsense, Jerry? Why would any rational man blow up a reactor when he knew he would go up with it? Biting off his nose to spite his face. I'll bet this Doctor Cowles lives in so tight an ivory tower that he still believes the Japanese used Kamikaze pilots in the Second World War, though the latest historical research definitively shows that the Kamikaze were but the fevered figments of a propagandist's imagination."

Again a long silence. Aline tickled the recumbent yarn dog under the chin with a finger. The Baron put his papers away.

"I was wondering," said Gus, "if there *was* an atomic accident on Earth five thousand years ago, will it be safe to land on Earth yet, Linus?"

"No telling."

"Can't you pick up some readings when we get closer?"

"Not good enough. We'll just have to take our chances."

"We've burned our bridges behind us!" said Rivers angrily.

"You have any better ideas?" asked Lester.

Marcel, in top hat and with a full beard, spoke for the first time. He looked somewhat like Sigmund Freud. A nearsighted Freud, he blinked his eyes nervously as he made his points.

"It seems to me that what was most lacking on Earth all along was simple courage to face the truth. The reality principle. It wasn't that they hadn't been shown the truth. They had, time after time after time. But to no avail. They repressed it.

"I've made something of a collection of the best of these repressed truth-statements. I'd like to read you some of them, because there just may be something in them for us."

Like a visiting singer always prepared for a request, Marcel reached into the pocket of his frock coat and pulled out some pieces of paper, neatly written upon.

"The first one is from the man who began it all, Thomas Robert Malthus, writing at the beginning of the nineteenth century.

"A man who is born into a world already possessed, if he cannot get subsistence from his parents on whom he has a just demand, and if the society do not want his labour, has no claim of right to the smallest portion of food, and, in fact, has no business to be where he is. At nature's mighty feast there is no vacant cover for him. She tells him to be gone, and will quickly execute her own orders, if he does not work upon the compassion of some of her guests. If these guests get up and make room for him, other intruders immediately appear demanding the same favour. The report of a provision for all that come, fills the hall with numerous claimants. The order and harmony of the feast is disturbed, the plenty that before reigned is changed into scarcity; and the happiness of the guests is destroyed by the spectacle of misery and dependence in every part of the hall, and by the clamorous importunity of those, who are justly enraged at not finding the provision which they had been taught to expect. The guests learn too late their error, in counter-acting those strict orders to all intruders, issued by the great mistress of the feast, who, wishing that all guests should have plenty, and knowing she could not provide for unlimited numbers, humanely refused to admit fresh comers when her table was already full.

"That should be clear enough. But it was made even clearer a generation later by another Englishman, William Foster Lloyd, in a single sentence.

"To a plank in the sea, which cannot support all, all have not an equal right; the lucky individuals, who can first obtain possession, being justified in appropriating it to themselves, to the exclusion of the remainder.

"A few years later an economist, John Stuart Mill, approached the problem from a different angle:

"Society can feed the necessitous, if it takes their multiplication under its control; or (if destitute of all moral feeling for the wretched offspring) it can leave the last to their discretion, abandoning the first to their own care. But it cannot with impunity take the feeding upon itself, and leave the multiplying free.

"The thrust of these statements should have been clear: but they were ignored. Not answered; ignored. Finally this matter was taken up again in the twentieth century by the American poet William Wordsworth, who lived in California, I believe.

> "Malthus! Thou shouldst be living in this hour:
> The world hath need of thee: getting and begetting,
> We soil fair Nature's bounty. Sweating
> With 'dozer, spray, and plough we dissipate our dower
> In smart and thoughtless optimism, blocking the power
> Of reason to lay out a saner setting
> For reason's growth to change, adapt and flower,
> In reason's way, to weave that long-sought bower
> Of sweet consistency.—Great Soul! I'd rather be
> Like you, logic-driven to deny the feast
> To those who would, if saved, see misery increased
> Throughout this tender, trembling world.
> Confound ye those who set unfurled
> Soft flags of good intentions, deaf to obdurate honesty!"

"You call that clear?" asked Ellen. "Why do kooks feel they have to write poetry anyway, instead of just saying it out-and-out?"

"Ah! That's just the point," said Marcel, with an I'm-glad-you-asked eagerness. Eyes blinking, he turned on Ellen. "Men don't like to face the truth. That passage from Malthus occurs only in the second edition of his book. After that he repressed it. But he never renounced it. The public pretended he had never said anything. Lloyd and Mill were given the silent treatment, too.

"Truth is like the face of the Medusa: if you confront it directly, you may be petrified by fright. So, like Perseus, we must look at truth in the mirror of literature—the reflection of myth and poetry. By announcing that what is to come is a fiction we disarm the psyche and she opens her eyes—to the reflection. Denial is the door through which truth enters. Wordsworth, knowing the failure of Malthus, Lloyd, and Mill, opened that door."

The man in the brown hat, abstracted until Marcel was well into his discourse, had grown livid with anger as it continued. Brown eyes flashing, he spoke in a voice of controlled, cold fury.

"So that's how you sneak up on our moral problem—with filthy poetry! You know that no one here would agree to your obscene proposal if you made it directly—so you make it indirectly, prettying it up with fine verse. Well, I, for one, won't buy it. I trust that every decent man and woman here agrees with me."

Astonishment swept the room. Most of his listeners plainly had no inkling what it was that was bothering him. Lester bit his thumbnail for a moment, looked at it thoughtfully, rubbed it against a finger, and then raised his eyes to the speaker.

"Okay, Sinjon, let's look at it. No mirrors. For better or for worse, the shuttle ship can hold no more than twenty passengers and can make only one trip. There are fourteen of us. Fourteen of us here, in the mountain. Out there, on the plain, there are—how many? A million? Two million? So what shall we do?"

"I will not play God," said Sinjon. Probably unconscious of his gesture, he joined the tips of his long slender fingers in front of his chest as he gazed steadfastly at Lester.

"You mean you'll just sit here while the rest of us climb aboard?"

"What I mean, sir, is this. We are all congeners aboard this spaceship, elevated and lowly alike. Congeners pure and simple, and no man can save himself by killing another. In this setting the man who pays such a price has no moral individuality to save; in killing another (as he thinks) he in fact kills himself. Low and high alike, we are all derived from a single primal pair. Sharing one origin, we are identical in value and indistinguishable from one another in the eyes of God. Our thoughts must be on what happens to the entire human race. Whoever saves one moiety of it, saves the whole human race; he who kills one individual kills mankind itself."

There was an absolute silence for a long minute.

"Would you," said Lester quietly, "agree to drawing lots?"

"No! The human predicament sets stakes too high for gambling, responsibilities too deep for daring. No one can win in such a lottery. No soul can survive unscathed in a casting of the dice."

"I can only suppose, then, that you propose giving up your place to one of the lowly ones, as you call them?"

"Indeed I do."

"Alone?"

Lester, his breathing stopped, looked at Sinjon intently.

Sinjon waited a long moment before replying, in a very low voice, deliberately.

"No, God willing; not alone. . . . I shall take you with me."

Lester banged his fist on the table. "That, my friend, you shall not do! Oh, what nobility!" He sneered. "Volunteering others! Volunteer yourself, damn you! And good riddance; you will be helping natural selection along. We won't stop you."

In the general pandemonium Sinjon sat like a silent rock surrounded by an angry sea of opponents. The Baron called for order, speaking deliberately, capturing one after another with his eyes as he calmed the group.

Aline, craning her neck to look through the artificial reeds at the plain below, was the first to speak.

"You know," she said, "I've never thought of those bodies down there as *people*."

"Of course not," said Sinjon. "That attitude is at the very root of our moral imbecility. But those wretched creatures *are* our brothers. Only when we recognize our brotherhood with them can we ascend to a state of grace and make the one thinkable moral decision."

"That sounds nice, Sinjon," said Gus, "but I wonder if it's really true. After all, identical origin doesn't make identity. All of us get our negative entropy out of the same chowder pot, but we're not identical. Everything here goes back to the energy coming from the Dyson Pack, but we clearly aren't identical. . . . If we were, would we be arguing with each other?"

Gus waited for a reply from Sinjon. Hearing none, he went on.

"As for those Quotions down there, how can you possibly identify yourself with them? Look," he said, getting up and striding angrily to the control board on the left. "Look—or rather, listen. Just *listen* to what your 'brothers' sound like."

He pushed a button and turned a knob. On a screen appeared a replicate of the scene below, and out of the loudspeakers a sea of low and friendly moans drifted into the room, punctuated by melodious sighs.

"Now," he said, "I have here a tape made on the Serengeti plain in East Africa a generation before the *Beagle* left Earth." He manipulated the controls and, without taking away the picture of the Quotions, brought into focus on an adjacent screen a picture of thousands upon thousands of wildebeests interspersed with zebras and antelopes. From the speakers came a sound of soft mooing, punctuated with coughing snorts.

"Now," said Gus, "back to our friends on the plain of Quo for the sound again."

Moans seeped into the room once more.

"And what do you think will happen if we try to translate the Quotion 'language'?"

Gus struck the TRANSLATE panel with his fist. The sound of wildebeests was heard once more in the room.

"Pretty, isn't it?" said Gus sardonically. "Which are our congeners?" He pushed the buttons and turned the knobs, changing from the Serengeti sound to Quotion-in-translation repeatedly. "Which the human, and which the animal? Can you tell? Does it matter? Why split hairs?"

He was vibrant with indignation. With an effort, he calmed himself and went on.

"Their grandparents, only two generations ago, lost faith in speech and prohibited it. From that time on all communication was to be nonverbal. Encounter groups. Feelie groups. Moans and sighs; but no grammar. No meta-language. No contra-factual conditional. No possibility of a discovery process. No *intellect*. Very jolly, no doubt, but what conceivable use would those animals out there be for bringing civilization to another planet?"

Lester interrupted, laughing. "Now wait a minute, Gus. It's not that bad. They've only been like this for two generations. It's just cultural. They could learn speech back again."

"The Quotions kill anyone caught saying anything intelligible."

"Well," said Linus, "you're both right. Now it's just somatic. But eventually it will be genetic. The Baldwin effect. 'What we are we become.' "

"They *are* dumb," admitted Lester ruefully. "But why shouldn't they be? For five thousand years they've had everything done for them: food coming out of spigots, waste-chutes taking care of the waste; no problems to solve. Why shouldn't they be dumb? Absolutely no selective advantage to being otherwise. All the selection they've been subject to they've created themselves. A circular, destructive process. They're not the people who were put aboard in the beginning. They are literally incapable of taking care of themselves any place else."

"And what about us?" asked Sinjon, leaning forward. "Haven't we been just as much coddled as they? Why aren't we just as 'dumb' —as you call it—as they?"

"You have a good point, Sinjon," said Lester, "and we soon would be, if this voyage kept on much longer. But remember, the whole project was based on protecting the intelligence of the Argotes against that very sort of deterioration. Since the Immortals didn't reproduce, their intelligence was shielded from recombination and natural selection in an environment where welfare was completely taken care of. That protective system came to an end when we Argotes regained our sexuality. Another ten generations of the easy life, and we'd be not much better than the Quotions. Even if the Dyson hadn't been running down we should have headed back for Earth or pretty soon we wouldn't be able to solve even the problem of debarkation."

"Who can?" said Jeannie, fluttering her hands. "I can't. Nobody can now—except clever Linus here. How would we ever get off without him?"

"Remember the Emergencies we used to have when we were kids?" asked Gus. "Those shattering, grinding noises that we thought would never stop? They were programed into the ship by the Earth-people to keep us on our toes. Only by solving some complicated equations could the Argotes push the right buttons and stop the Emergency. Then the next Emergency was based on a new problem. They kept people on their toes. We'd still have them if Linus's father (who was *really* bright) hadn't found a general solution and put a stop to the Emergencies forever."

"What a paradox!" said Lester. "Because one of us was a super-genius and found the Final Solution, the rest of us are destined ultimately to become imbeciles, since intelligence is no longer needed."

"The story of civilization," muttered Rivers.

Sinjon looked at the Baron. "So it is admitted, then, that there is no *essential* difference between Argotes and Quotions. Then what's to stop us from taking a proportionate number of Quotions aboard?"

The Baron started, with a look of incredulity on his face. He hesitated a few moments before replying.

"I guess it would be futile to answer you in mathematical terms; and not necessary anyway, because there's a substantive issue that strictly limits our options. Linus: What if we decide to take some Quotions aboard? How can we do it?"

"We can't."

"Why not?"

"We're sealed off. When the Immortals discovered the Three Graces—and their own libidos—they investigated. They found the sprung door and realized it would have to be repaired. They weren't about to give up their newfound pleasure, and they had sense enough to realize they were playing with fire. Many more Quotions coming into the mountain would absolutely swamp posterity with stupidity. The connection between the two parts was originally designed to permit either Quotions or Argotes (or both) to furnish colonizers for the new world they were supposed to find. The only way they could guard against swamping was to seal off the Quotions for good, even though that prevented their ever being used as colonizers.

"I've looked at the seal. It's solid. We'd use so much energy trying to break it we might not have enough left to get off the ship."

Sinjon spoke, more to himself than to others; bitterly. "Elitists. Those God-forsaken elitists!"

The Baron spoke judicially. "There's room for difference of opinion here; but we can't undo what was done a hundred years ago. We've got to go on from this point, like it or not.

"We Argotes have only two options. We can get on the shuttle ship and head for Earth, or we can stay here. If we stay here we have enough energy left for another two months, and that's it. A cold death for everyone. On the other hand, if we Argotes take the shuttle, we can make it to Earth and the Quotions will have enough energy for about a week. If the shuttle does go, individuals can opt out and stay here if they want to." The Baron was looking at Sinjon through half-closed eyelids.

"I shall certainly opt out," said Sinjon. "I see my duty plainly. What a pity the rest of you cannot."

Sinjon wrapped himself in calmness like a cloak. "The death the wretched of our world must face shall be my death. Their last lingering moment shall be my moment. I shall be one with humanity."

Lester looked at him wonderingly; then surreptitiously at the Baron, whose eyes caught his and said *Go ahead.*

"There are also two options for our humble friends," said Lester. "*Our* options *for* them, since they are powerless to determine their own future.

"The first: we can do nothing. If it is possible 'to do nothing.' But I dare say this will appeal to some of you.

"The second: we can make it possible for them to step out of this world painlessly—painlessly because they won't know they're leaving."

Reaching into a vest pocket, Lester pulled out a key, which he held up thoughtfully for all to see.

"The original planners foresaw some such possibility, though they no doubt didn't believe it would happen. This key fits a lock downstairs. When I open it there's a button I can press. Pressing the button will release an odorless, tasteless, and utterly lethal gas that will instantly and painlessly kill all the inhabitants of the Plain of Quo.

I propose that we turn this key tonight, after they've all gone to sleep. It will save them a lingering and painful death. And since they will not even contemplate death, there is no sense whatever in which it can be said that they will suffer."

Sinjon stared at him, horror-struck. "Their blood will be on your head."

"No blood, my dear fellow. No blood at all. Just sleep, which becomes permanent."

"And there's no difference between sleep and death?"

"None except permanence. We die, and come to life, three hundred and sixty-five times each year. Finally there comes the year in which we come to life again only three hundred and sixty-four times. That is the year memorialized on our tombstone. It isn't death but the dying that hurts"—wagging the key—"and we have it in our power to erase the evil of dying. Shall we do so?"

There were faint murmurs of *Yes* matched by Sinjon's loud, carefully modulated *No*.

"We cannot take even a single innocent life. That's God's prerogative, not ours. If you will not stay here and share their death on the commons, as you should in all humanity, then you must leave them unscathed as you go down to Earth and seek to mount a rescue mission for them."

"I would remind you," said the Baron, "that there are a million of them who would have to be removed in a week's time—without any previous plans having been made."

"Also," added Linus, "we have no reason to think that Earth has such capabilities now. We've heard nothing from them; though they surely must see us by this time."

"No matter," replied Sinjon, "we still must try. Human dignity demands that we take any chance, no matter how remote, rather than assume the responsibility for snuffing out a single human life."

"And," snapped Rivers, "how much dignity is there in a lingering death for a million human beings?"

"The felicific calculus does not exist whereby one may legitimately balance the one against the other," replied Sinjon haughtily. "We cannot measure good against evil. They are incommensurable. We must do what is intrinsically right."

Rivers looked as if he might vomit. Ellen turned and whispered something to Gus, and the two suppressed laughs. No one cared to continue the debate.

"We've got a hard day ahead of us tomorrow," said the Baron, "and too much to think about tonight. I think everybody had better take a sleeping pill now so we can get some rest."

Linus looked up from his slide-rule. "How long will it take for the pills to have effect?"

"About half an hour."

"That ought to be about right." Linus got up and went to the control board. He waited there while the Baron passed out the pills and Gus came around with water.

Sinjon refused his pill. "I have better things to do," he snapped and walked off down a corridor.

When the pills had been swallowed Linus spoke. "I programed this maneuver two days ago. I think it's going to be rather pretty. When I push this button the third derivative becomes positive for a while and you will ultimately feel an acceleration of about one-tenth *g*, so hang on. Then we'll come to equilibrium in our final holding pattern. So keep your eyes open."

He pushed the button. It was deep twilight now, and the Quotions had gone to sleep. Only two small lanterns illuminated the deck. There was a tinkle of glass as some of the objects on the tables rolled together when the acceleration increased. Then Earth, blue and swirling with clouds, appeared at the horizon visible through the plastic dome. *Ohs* and *ahs* were intermingled with murmurings of "Home!" and "At last."

" 'Earth has not anything to show more fair,' " muttered Marcel; but the allusion escaped them.

Henrietta, practical as always, broke the spell. "So that's what we took five thousand years to return to. Looks pretty nice. Why did we go away in the first place? What made us think we'd find another place half as good?"

"Modesty," said Rivers. "A queer sort of modesty that was in fashion when the Immortals left Earth. In earlier times man thought he was living on the only world there was, around which the sun and all the rest of the universe revolved. Man was unique and the sole concern of his God.

"Then fashions changed some time after it was learned that the earth revolved around the sun, and that the universe was huge; and that there wasn't any up and down, hence no Heaven and no God. An attack of humility set in. No man was better than any other man, no moral standards any better than any other, no place better than any other place—*so let's keep moving, moving, moving!* (Certainly the nest we've just fouled doesn't smell so sweet.) Like gorillas:

make a new nest every night, crap all over everything, then move on. That was the frontier hero—who clung too long to life.

"Men began asking again whether Man was unique; and fashionable humility dictated the answer. It would be egotistical to suppose Man was unique, therefore he could not be, therefore there must be an infinity of other worlds, therefore his unconquerable spirit compelled him to go and conquer them—therefore the Voyage of the Spaceship *Beagle*."

"Magnificent logic," said Gus.

"*Convenient* logic," said Lester. "If man is not unique, he has no obligation to husband his resources. Humility justifies irresponsibility."

"What if the Argotes had found another world but one that already had people on it?"

"We would have killed them off, of course. The Exploratory Imperative would have compelled us to."

There was a long silence.

"Now we know we are unique," said Aline softly.

"Yes. And it cost us five thousand years," said Marcel. He spoke musingly. "Do you know, there was another ship called the *Beagle* in the nineteenth century, an ordinary sailing ship. An inconsequential little ship, except that a most remarkable young man spent nearly five years on board her, traveling around the world on a naval mission as an unpaid civilian scientist. His name was Charles Darwin. He was a biologist and a geologist, and as he looked at the world he realized that most learned men were wrong about man's place in the world, about his origin, and about the future-generating process. He discovered the mechanism of natural selection, a discovery that revolutionized the intellectual basis of human existence —and challenged its deepest mores. All this because he happened to make that voyage on the *Beagle*.

"There's nothing in the archives to tell us why the name *Beagle* was chosen for our own ship, but I have a suspicion that it was suggested by someone who realized the earth-shaking importance of the voyage of the earlier *Beagle* and hoped that the voyage of our spaceship would be of equal importance to the universe. Universe-shattering, one might say."

"What a foolish idea! Pure sympathetic magic. He who consciously sets out to make history cannot do so, precisely because he tries. If the theological concept of 'grace' is ever justified—and I am not entirely convinced that it is—but if it is, and if 'history' is understood not as the record but as the act, then we must say that history is a gift of grace."

Marcel stopped, blinking his eyes, looking expectantly at the others, waiting for comments; but the speaker had lost his audience.

Taking advantage of the lull, Rivers returned to his own musing. "The most learned men at the time of the take-off really believed that there must be millions of worlds as good as the earth. Well: it's still possible. But five thousand years of looking has not uncovered even one. Our electronic probes, so long as they still functioned, failed to reveal even a single planetary surface that was suitable for *our* kind of life—and who cares about any other? We examined over a hundred likely candidates. All washouts.

"Maybe there is, out there somewhere, another Earth. Maybe there is. . . . But we're heading home."

Pierre had wandered over to the edge of the deck, where he wrapped his arm around an upright while he looked with glistening eyes at Earth. "What blues," he murmured. "What blues!"

He turned slowly and faced the others as he talked, seemingly, to himself.

"We were sent out into the boundless universe, but were not happy until we rediscovered boundedness. Lacking a tradition of our own we have tried on the traditions of our ancestors, one after another. The time of Good Queen Anne, the Golden Age of Greece, the Gay Nineties, Shakespeare's Mermaid Tavern—all these we've play-acted and many more. Like Marie Antoinette playing shepherdess while the guillotine was being invented. Now we're coming home. A home that used to house the restaurant in the Seine at the Sign of the Frog— which men destroyed and replaced with mounds of coal and grimy factories. Sweet water with muck. In five millennia, I wonder, will they have learned anything? Is there now anywhere on Earth anything as fair as the Sign of the Frog?"

He looked at the placid Alphonsine as though hoping for an answer, but not expecting it. He thoughtfully rubbed the satin of her cheek with his hand, then turned and sat down beside Aline, slipping his arm through hers.

"Come on," said the Baron gruffly. "Off to sleep."

Daylight again. Piles of space suits were scattered around the porch; only the Baron had put his on, though not yet the helmet. Evidently he had been giving instructions on the new clothing. The rest of the Argotes, still in their nineteenth-century costumes, laughed as they puzzled over the unfamiliar garb.

"I know it's not pretty," said Linus, "but once the shuttle has cast off there's no gravity and it'd be dangerous to have a lot of finery to get tangled up in the machinery. We'll have to leave those clothes behind. When we get to Earth we'll have a lot to choose from, I don't doubt."

A scream rent the air, stopping everyone in his tracks.

"What in the world? . . ."

Jeannie came running, sobbing, onto the deck.

"Lester . . . he's been stabbed! He's dead!"

"Where?"

"In the little alcove off the control room. He must have been sleeping there. Someone stabbed him in his sleep. The knife is still stuck in his chest."

From the right, Sinjon walked slowly in. Quite calmly he took in the scene before speaking.

"I did it."

"You!"

Utter silence. After seconds that seemed ages Ellen broke the spell.

"A good man—he was a *good* man. And you—you son of a bitch —you who are no man at all, you have to kill this good man. . . ."

"A good man, possibly," Sinjon said in icy tones, "but not an innocent one. He was going to murder a million people. I killed Lester, and I destroyed the key. It was a fearful responsibility to take, killing a fellow man; but this is the only kind of killing that is morally excusable. To kill for the sake of the innocent. By killing one man I have saved a million. There was no other way."

"I see," said Rivers with venom, "so you do have a felicific calculus after all. To each his own."

Gus grabbed a lamp as a weapon and started toward Sinjon, but the Baron stopped him.

"It's no use, Gus. You can't bring Lester back to life. Don't risk hurting yourself; we'll need you on Earth. We've had a viper in our midst, but that's all past now: he's staying behind anyway."

"No, I'm not," said Sinjon. "I'm going with you now."

"But I thought—"

"All that is changed now. I must stand trial for what I've done. It is my moral obligation."

"Why the devil should you?" asked Rivers contemptuously. "We're not interested. You can just jolly well stay here and freeze with your dear friends out there. Do you think we want to ride in the same ship with a murderer? To what end? If there's no one on Earth when we get there, we'll kill you. If civilization is still going, we'll turn you over to the courts and they'll sentence you to death for this murder."

"No, they won't," said Sinjon imperturbably. "Fortunately they advanced in morality far beyond your abysmal level before we ever left Earth.

"In the nineteenth century a ship named the *William Brown* was wrecked. A life raft set out from it, overloaded with people. Some of them took the law into their own hands and killed the surplus. The safely loaded raft reached shore. The ringleaders were tried, found guilty of murder, and executed.

"The ringleaders offered as their defense the fact that *all* would have died if they had not taken it upon themselves to kill *some*. The court stipulated the facts but rightly said they were irrelevant. There is an absolute morality that binds all men at all times in all places. In the eyes of God it is better that all die than that some survive by murdering the innocent.

"We are on a life raft here. By killing a murderer-in-intention, I have prevented a massacre of the innocents. The law will find me guiltless. But I cannot, like a coward, stay here to share the Quotions' fate, much as I would like to. It is now my responsibility to stand trial before a jury of my peers."

After a long and absolute silence Rivers spoke in a low voice, a voice with a burred edge.

"You are incredible! Absolutely incredible. If you had not acted as you did, a million people would have died quickly and painlessly in their sleep. But because you killed one man, the same millions will now die slowly and painfully over many hours. How can you live with yourself?"

Sinjon looked at him scornfully. "Innocence must be cherished."

"Enough!" said the Baron slapping his mittened hands together. "Enough! Let's get going. Get into your clothes and down the hatch into the shuttle. When the last one is in, we're off. Linus and I will go down first; Gus, you come last."

The Baron set about putting his helmet on. At his side, Alphonsine roused herself from a trance and began to strip off her boating-party garments, one by one. As they dropped to the floor great tears streamed down her face. The Baron, completely dressed, helmet and all, suddenly became aware of her. He stopped in his tracks for a long, wondering look at her cornflower-blue eyes. Gently he lifted from her head the last remaining bit of apparel, the straw hat with a ribbon that matched her eyes; gravely he enclosed the yellow curls in a space helmet. Looking at the gleaming metal surface of the rim pressing into the creamy, resilient flesh of her shoulders, he shook his head like one thinking he knows not what; heaved a sigh, turned and headed down the stairwell, his great body off balance, his massive boots clumping heavily, catching in the spidery supports, his helmeted head tilted forward to try to see where his feet were going, his torso weaving clumsily around the corners as he went down, down, down toward the waiting shuttle ship—and to Earth.

Appendices
and Index

A. Notes and References

Most people who read a book like this have no desire to be bombarded with footnotes. A few, however, may occasionally wonder about the source of some of the less well-known ideas and facts. It is for this latter group that I include this section.

Many of the classic papers have been reprinted in my anthology, *Population, Evolution, and Birth Control*, 2nd edition (San Francisco: Freeman and Co., 1969). This fact is indicated by the abbreviation *PEBC*.

Center numbers refer to chapters.

1.

My first attempt to outline the crucial political problem of extended space travel was in "Interstellar Migration and the Population Problem," *Journal of Heredity*, 50:68–70; reprinted in PEBC. This paper was rejected for publication by *Science* even though (or because?) the editor was a good friend of mine. He told me that "everybody knew" the conclusions already. It has subsequently been reprinted six times (not including PEBC), so I think the conclusions must not have been as obvious as he thought.

I owe the naming of the spaceship to Beatrice Rosenfeld and Richard Lewis. I am chagrined: I should have thought of it myself, since Darwin is a hobby of mine. (See my *Nature and Man's Fate*, New York: Rinehart, 1959; paperback by Mentor.)

2.

An excellent collection of articles by many authors dealing with environmental problems is this: *Man and the Ecosphere*, Paul R. Ehrlich,

John P. Holdren, and Richard W. Holm, eds. (San Francisco: Freeman and Co., 1971).

Kenneth E. Boulding's essay "The Economics of the Coming Spaceship Earth" has been influential in getting professionals to accept the stance adopted in this book. First published in 1966, it has been frequently reprinted. See PEBC for a portion; and for the whole, Boulding's *Beyond Economics* (Ann Arbor: University of Michigan Press, 1968).

Fundamental limits to existence on a spaceship are set by natural resources, both renewable and nonrenewable. A committee of the National Academy of Sciences under the chairmanship of Preston Cloud evaluated these most carefully in *Resources and Man* (San Francisco: Freeman, 1969).

The results of transgressing the limits of the environment were first systematically described by George Perkins Marsh in his *Man and Nature*, first published in 1864; it was republished by the Belknap Press of the Harvard University Press in 1965. *Man's Impact on the Global Environment* (Cambridge, Mass.: MIT Press, 1970) gives the conclusions of a study group evaluating the dangers of present and projected pollution of the environment. See also Wesley Marx, *Man and His Environment: Waste* (New York: Harper & Row, 1971).

3.

LaMont C. Cole's article, "The Ecosphere," *Scientific American*, April 1958, gives a good orientation. (The term "ecosphere" is, in fact, Cole's coinage.) This article is reprinted in Ehrlich, Holdren, and Holm, cited under #2.

4.

George M. Woodwell, "Toxic Substances and Ecological Cycles," *Scientific American*, March 1967. Reprinted in Ehrlich, Holdren, and Holm, cited under #2.

Report of the Secretary's Commission on Pesticides and Their Relationship to Environmental Health, Parts I and II (Washington, D.C.: U.S. Dept. of Health, Education and Welfare, 1969).

5.

I have borrowed the image of the "hedgehog" from *The Hedgehog and the Fox*, Isaiah Berlin (London: Weidenfeld and Nicolson, 1953).

The book that did most to get the ecological idea out to the general public was, of course, *Silent Spring*, by Rachel Carson; first published in 1962, now available in paperback by Fawcett World. Miss Carson's position was strongly supported by Robert L. Rudd in his *Pesticides and the Living Landscape* (Madison, Wis.: University of Wisconsin Press, 1966).

The essential unsoundness of the chemical method of pest control is suggested by the fact that over 500 different compounds are used in some 56,000 different formulations (*Nuclear Information,* May 1964, p. 3). A systematic approach to pest control, alternative to the purely chemical methods, is described in *Biological Control,* by C. B. Huffaker, ed. (New York: Plenum Press, 1971).

The lines by Francis Thompson (1859–1907) are from his poem "The Mistress of Vision."

6.

The quotation from Oscar Wilde (1854–1900) is from his essay "The Soul of Man Under Socialism," 1891, reprinted in Vol. X of *The Complete Works of Oscar Wilde* (Garden City, N.Y.: Doubleday, Page, 1923).

A good discussion of the application of the systems approach to ethics may be found in *Situation Ethics,* by Joseph Fletcher (Philadelphia: Westminster Press, 1966). An illuminating example of this approach to environmental problems is found in "The Economist's Approach to Pollution and Its Control," by Robert M. Solow, *Science,* 173:498–503, 1971. See also *Patient Earth,* by John Harte and Robert H. Socolow (New York: Holt, Rinehart, and Winston, 1971).

A collection of articles showing the evils that can result from the Newtonian distortion of Darwinian urban problems are to be found in Part III of *Science, Conflict, and Society,* Garrett Hardin, ed. (San Francisco: Freeman, 1969). The great classic in the field of urbanology is *The Death and Life of Great American Cities,* by Jane Jacobs (New York: Random House, 1961).

Jay W. Forrester's *World Dynamics* (Cambridge, Mass.: Wright-Allen Press, 1971) is a good introduction to the systems approach to large problems.

I am indebted to Herman E. Daly for the etymological analysis of "proletariat" which is given in his stimulating article "A Marxian-Malthusian View of Poverty and Development," *Population Studies,* 25:25–37, 1971.

7.

The account of the death of Charles II is taken from p. 33 of *Early Medieval Medicine with Special Reference to France and Chartres,* by Loren C. MacKinney (Baltimore: Johns Hopkins Press, 1937).

The Oscar Wilde citation is given under #6.

The story of thalidomide, the F.D.A., and the drug industry is recounted in "The Thalidomide Syndrome," by Helen B. Taussig, *Scientific*

American, August 1962; and reprinted in *39 Steps to Biology,* Garrett Hardin, ed. (San Francisco: Freeman, 1968).

A lawyer's approach to the difficulties of weaning the law away from its Newtonian vision is found in *Defending the Environment,* by Joseph L. Sax (New York: Knopf, 1971). Also excellent is Earl Finbar Murphy, *Man and His Environment: Law* (New York: Harper & Row, 1971).

8.

The story of the results of the Kariba Dam is from an article of this title by Thayer Scudder, part of a valuable supplement to *Natural History,* 78(2):41–72, 1969, entitled "The Unforeseen International Ecologic Boomerang." Also valuable is a special issue on ecology of *BioScience,* July 1964. In this, Paul B. Sears first spoke of ecology as "a subversive subject," which it certainly is: it subverts the finely honed word magic perfected over the last two centuries of mistreatment of the environment.

9.

Ezra J. Mishan of the London School of Economics has probably had more effect than anyone else in steering economists back onto the path of morality. See his *The Costs of Economic Growth* (New York: Praeger, 1967). Also, *Growth: The Price We Pay* (London: Staples Press, 1969).

John M. Culbertson of the University of Wisconsin has made a fine synthesis in his *Economic Development: An Ecological Approach* (New York: Knopf, 1971). Culbertson shows how the do-goodism of foreign aid can be every bit as destructive of human values as the profit motive of local free enterprise.

The lovely euphemism for cheating was recorded by C. G. Hecht and A. J. Klein, *ETC.,* **27**:383, 1970.

10.

The historical analysis of the internalization of costs was first given in my essay "Not Peace, but Ecology," published in *Diversity and Stability in Ecological Systems* (Upton, N.Y.: Brookhaven National Laboratory, 1969).

Barry Commoner and Paul Ehrlich have had a running debate on the importance of population growth in producing pollution. A minimizing of this role characterizes a paper by Barry Commoner, Michael Corr, and Paul J. Stamler, "The Causes of Pollution," *Environment,* 13(3):2–19, 1971. Ehrlich's criticism of this argument is to be found in Paul R. Ehrlich and John P. Holdren, "Impact of Population Growth," *Science,* **171**:1212–1217, 1971.

One way to internalize pollution costs, and to discourage the pollution itself, is to tax it at a high enough rate. The details of such a scheme have been worked out by J. H. Dales, *Pollution, Property & Prices* (Toronto: University of Toronto Press, 1970).

Dissonance resolution is discussed in Leon Festinger, "Cognitive Dissonance," *Scientific American*, October 1962. This has been reprinted in *Science, Conflict, and Society*, Garrett Hardin, ed. (San Francisco: Freeman, 1969).

11.

Nothing of this sort can be written without a deep debt to George Orwell, particularly his *Animal Farm* and *Nineteen Eighty-Four*. For a scholarly source one might read Herbert Marcuse's essay "Repressive Tolerance," in *A Critique of Pure Tolerance*, by R. P. Wolff, B. Moore, Jr., and H. Marcuse (Boston: Beacon Press, 1965). The scholar is his own caricature.

The "Zwingli-Dyson Pack" has its origin in a suggestion by Freeman J. Dyson, "Interstellar Transport," *Physics Today*, 21:41–45, 1968. For dramatic reasons I modified the nuclear machinery somewhat from Dyson's specifications; hence the addition of the meaningless name, "Zwingli."

12.

P. W. Bridgman's remark on responsibility is to be found in his *Reflections of a Physicist* (New York: Philosophical Library, 1950). There is a fine unity in this physicist's writings. The most stimulating of them is his little-known *The Intelligent Individual and Society* (New York: Macmillan, 1938). It is perhaps too rational to be widely accepted.

The passage from Danilo Dolci is from pp. 95–96 of his *Report from Palermo* (New York: Orion Press, 1959). His reportage is in the fine tradition of Oscar Lewis, though not so impressive. It is deficient in this remarkable way: that not once does he show the slightest suspicion that large families might have something to do with poverty. In this respect his ignorance has matched or exceeded that of the people he has labored to help for two decades.

The quotation from Charles Frankel is from p. 203 of *The Case for Modern Man* (New York: Harper, 1955).

13.

Lloyd's lectures, difficult to find in the original, have fortunately been republished: *Lectures on Population, Value, Poor-Laws and Rent*, republished in New York by Augustus M. Kelley, 1968. The most significant passage is reprinted in PEBC.

The analysis of this chapter is essentially that of my 1968 essay, reprinted in the following section of the Appendix; but here clarified by the matrix first published in *Population, Environment, and People*, Noel Hinrichs, ed. (New York: McGraw-Hill, 1971).

The quotation from A. N. Whitehead comes from p. 17 of his *Science and the Modern World* (New York: Mentor, 1948). These lectures, originally published in 1925, are probably the wisest ever given as part of an endowed lecture series.

14.

The quotation from the Ehrlichs is from p. 107 of Paul R. Ehrlich and Anne H. Ehrlich, *Population, Resources, Environment* (San Francisco: Freeman, 1970).

The whaling tragedy is told in Scott McVay, "The Last of the Great Whales," *Scientific American*, August 1966; reprinted in *39 Steps to Biology*, Garrett Hardin, ed. (San Francisco: Freeman, 1968).

The following two books are good presentations of economists' approach to pollution control: Allen V. Kneese, Robert V. Ayres, and Ralph C. d'Arge, *Economics and the Environment* (Baltimore: Johns Hopkins Press, 1970); J. H. Dales, *Pollution, Property & Prices,* (Toronto: University of Toronto Press, 1970).

An important modification of the theory of the commons, putting it on a mathematical basis, is found in Daniel Fife's essay "Killing the Goose," *Environment*, 13(3):20–27, 1971.

15.

The idea of the double bind as a means of egotistically controlling others while hiding the instrument of control, was first analyzed in a classic paper by Gregory Bateson, D. D. Jackson, J. Haley, and J. Weakland, "Toward a Theory of Schizophrenia," *Behavioral Science*, 1:251–264, 1956. As with all great ideas, its roots extend backward in time. In Chapter 25 of Nietzsche's *Thus Spake Zarathustra* there is the following statement: "Beggars, however, one should entirely do away with! Verily, it annoyeth one to give unto them, and it annoyeth one not to give unto them." The Moslem religion emphasizes the seeking of salvation through alms-giving. One wonders: What is the Moslem reaction to Nietzsche, to the Bateson paper, to Western psychoanalysis, and to Western law? Would the answers to these questions, if known, throw light on the comparative difficulties of protecting the environment in Moslem and Christian countries?

The quotation from Paul Goodman is from the *New York Review of Books*, 10(8):22, May 23, 1968.

16.

The *quis custodiet* problem was discussed in my original essay, but Beryl L. Crowe convinced me that I had grossly underestimated its difficulty. See his perceptive essay, "The Tragedy of the Commons Revisited," *Science*, **166**:1103–1107, 1969.

If I differ at all from Crowe, I think it is in my optimism. By temperament I feel that if a problem can be clearly defined it can be solved in some sense that will permit us to regain our freedom as we perceive the necessities. The pessimist who shows (as he thinks) how absolutely insoluble the problem is, unwittingly furnishes the foundation stones needed by those of a different temperament to begin their constructive work.

The ambitious investigator's best guide is, in my opinion, John R. Platt's "Strong Inference," *Science*, **146**:347–352, 1964.

17.

In preparing this chapter I have cannibalized three previous works of mine:

1. "The Semantics of Space," *ETC.*, **23**:167–171, 1966.
2. "To Trouble a Star: The Cost of Intervention in Nature," *Science and Public Affairs*, **26**(1):17–20, 1970.
3. A lecture of nearly the same title given in 1971 at Radford College under the auspices of the University Center of Roanoke, Virginia.

The basic source on the SST is a book assembled by the physicist William A. Shurcliff, who led the fight against it: *S/S/T and Sonic Boom Handbook* (New York: Ballantine, 1970). For the data on upper atmospheric effects see Harold Johnston, "'Reduction of Stratospheric Ozone by Nitrogen Oxide Catalysts from Supersonic Transport Exhaust," *Science*, **173**:517–522, 1971.

J. B. Bury's *The Idea of Progress* (New York: Macmillan, 1932) is the classic account of the origins of this idea. Selections from the classical readings that led to this idea are gathered together in Frederick J. Teggart, *The Idea of Progress: A Collection of Readings* (Berkeley: University of California Press, 1949).

19.

The mathematics is that of the "competitive exclusion principle," an idea that goes back at least to Darwin. It was first given its present name in my *Nature and Man's Fate* (New York: Rinehart, 1959). The intellectual history is given in "The Competitive Exclusion Principle," *Science*, **131**:1292–1297, 1960. I discussed its significance for sociology in two further papers:

1. "The Cybernetics of Competition: A Biologist's View of Society," *Perspectives in Biology and Medicine,* 7:58–84, 1963.

2. "Population, Biology, and the Law," *Journal of Urban Law,* 48:563–578, 1971.

To the best of my knowledge no sociologist has ever discussed the principle, even to refute it. Evidently it is under a total taboo.

20.

Edward S. Deevey, Jr., has given a very thoughtful discussion of population growth in his article "The Human Population," *Scientific American,* September 1960. This has been reprinted in *39 Steps to Biology,* Garrett Hardin, ed. (San Francisco: Freeman, 1968).

Quietists who trust that population problems will spontaneously iron themselves out as the poor countries go through a "demographic transition" like Europe's should read Kingsley Davis's "Population," *Scientific American,* September 1963; also reprinted in *Science, Conflict, and Society,* Garrett Hardin, ed. (San Francisco: Freeman, 1969).

Economists are now beginning to consider seriously the problems of living in a no-growth world. Herman E. Daly has written a stimulating essay on this subject, "Toward a Stationary-State Economy," in John Harte and Robert H. Socolow, *Patient Earth* (New York: Holt, Rinehart, and Winston, 1971).

21.

The quotation from Linnaeus is taken from p. 118 of K. Hagberg, *Carl Linnaeus* (New York: Dutton, 1953). The documentation on prostitution in Rome will be found on pp. 362–63 of John T. Noonan, Jr., *Contraception* (Cambridge, Mass.: Harvard University Press, 1965). The "heredity" of prolificness is discussed in an unpublished master's thesis, University of Maryland, 1969: F. Godley, "Relationship of Size of Family of Origin to the Fertility of Contemporary American Women." The role of infanticide in family planning in Europe is revealed in William L. Langer, "Europe's Initial Population Explosion," *American Historical Review,* 69: 1–17, 1963. The passage quoted has been slightly modified by Professor Langer to make it correspond with his latest findings. Part of this is reprinted in PEBC. For a general discussion of techniques and ethical questions see my *Birth Control* (New York: Pegasus, 1970).

22.

Several of my articles have been cannibalized to produce this chapter, principally the following:

1. "Parenthood: Right or Privilege?" *Science,* 169:427, 1970.

2. "Choices of Parenthood," *Science,* **170**:259–262, 1970.

3. "Abortion—or Compulsory Pregnancy?" *Journal of Marriage and the Family,* **30**:246–251, 1968. (Also in PEBC.)

4. "Multiple Paths to Population Control," *Family Planning Perspectives,* **2**(3):24–26, 1970.

5. "Education in an Overpopulated World," *The Science Teacher,* **38** (5):20–23, 1971.

The classic study of the cost of unwanted children is: Hans Forssman and Inga Thuwe, "One Hundred and Twenty Children Born After Application for Therapeutic Abortion Refused," *Acta Psychiatrica Scandinavica,* **42**:71–88, 1966. This has been reprinted in *Abortion and the Unwanted Child,* Carl Reiterman, ed. (New York: Springer, 1971).

For a thorough survey of population-control possibilities read the following:

1. Bernard Berelson, "Beyond Family Planning," *Science,* **163**:533–543, 1969.

2. Lenni W. Kangas, "Integrated Incentives for Fertility Control," *Science,* **169**:1278–1283, 1970.

3. Edward Pohlman, *Incentives and Compensations in Birth Planning* (Chapel Hill: University of North Carolina Press, 1971).

The limits of birth control technology are discussed in Carl Djerassi, "Birth Control after 1984," *Science,* **169**:941–951, 1970.

Kenneth Boulding's proposal to allocate rights to reproduction by using the market mechanism is taken from page 135 of his *The Meaning of the 20th Century* (New York: Harper & Row, 1964).

23.

Shelley's lines are from *Epipsychidion,* written in 1821, when he was twenty-nine years old. The quotation from Robert Graves is from the *Saturday Review,* December 7, 1963. I have taken the "facts" on Teiresias from Graves's *The Greek Myths* (Baltimore: Penguin Books, 1955).

24.

E. J. Mishan's stimulating essay, "On Making the Future Safe for Mankind," *Public Interest,* **24**:33–61, 1971, is the source of the quotation on the automobile.

25.

The sonnet was first published in *Perspectives in Biology and Medicine,* **9**:225, 1966.

B. The Original Essay

The argument was first presented as a presidential address before the meeting of the Pacific Division of the American Association for the Advancement of Science, at Utah State University, in Logan on June 25, 1968. It was completely ignored by the press. The manuscript was subsequently revised once more and published in *Science*, Volume 162, pages 1243–1248, December 13, 1968. Here reprinted by permission of the publisher. © 1968, by the American Association for the Advancement of Science.

The Tragedy of the Commons

*The population problem has no technical solution;
it requires a fundamental extension in morality.*

GARRETT HARDIN

At the end of a thoughtful article on the future of nuclear war, Wiesner and York (*1*) concluded that: "Both sides in the arms race are . . . confronted by the dilemma of steadily increasing military power and steadily decreasing national security. *It is our considered professional judgment that this dilemma has no technical solution.* If the great powers continue to look for solutions in the area of science and technology only, the result will be to worsen the situation."

I would like to focus your attention not on the subject of the article (national security in a nuclear world) but on the kind of conclusion they reached, namely that there is no technical solution to the problem. An implicit and almost universal assumption of discussions published in professional and semipopular scientific journals is that the problem under discussion has a technical solution. A technical solution may be defined as one that requires a change only in the techniques of the natural sciences, demanding little or nothing in the way of change in human values or ideas of morality.

In our day (though not in earlier times) technical solutions are always welcome. Because of previous failures in prophecy, it takes courage to assert that a desired technical solution is not possible. Wiesner and York exhibited this courage; publishing in a science journal, they insisted that the solution to the problem was not to be found in the natural sciences. They cautiously qualified their statement with the phrase, "It is our considered professional judgment. . . ." Whether they were right or not is not the concern of the present article. Rather, the concern here is with the important concept of a class of human problems which can be called "no technical solution problems," and more specifically, with the identification and discussion of one of these.

It is easy to show that the class is not a null class. Recall the game of tick-tack-toe. Consider the problem, "How can I win the game of tick-tack-toe?" It is well known that I cannot, if I assume (in keeping with the conventions of game theory) that my opponent understands the game perfectly. Put another way, there is no "technical solution" to the problem. I can win only by giving a radical meaning to the word "win." I can hit my opponent over the head; or I can falsify the records. Every way in which I "win" involves, in some sense, an abandonment of the game, as we intuitively understand it. (I can also, of course, openly abandon the game—refuse to play it. This is what most adults do.)

The class of "no technical solution problems" has members. My thesis is that the "population problem," as conventionally conceived, is a member of this class. How it is conventionally conceived needs some comment. It is fair to say that most people who anguish over the population problem are trying to find a way to avoid the evils of overpopulation without relinquishing any of the privileges they now enjoy. They think that farming the seas or developing new strains of wheat will solve the problem— technologically. I try to show here that the solution they seek cannot be found. The population problem cannot be solved in a technical way, any more than can the problem of winning the game of tick-tack-toe.

What Shall We Maximize?

Population, as Malthus said, naturally tends to grow "geometrically," or, as we would now say, exponentially. In a finite world this means that the per-capita share of the world's goods must decrease. Is ours a finite world?

A fair defense can be put forward for the view that the world is infinite; or that we do not know that it is not. But, in terms of the practical problems that we must face in the next few generations with the foreseeable technology, it is clear that we will greatly increase human misery if we do not, during the immediate future, assume that the world available to the terrestrial human population is finite. "Space" is no escape (2).

A finite world can support only a finite population; therefore, population growth must eventually equal zero. (The case of perpetual wide fluctuations above and below zero is a trivial variant that need not be discussed.) When this condition is met, what will be the situation of mankind? Specifically, can Bentham's goal of "the greatest good for the greatest number" be realized?

No—for two reasons, each sufficient by itself. The first is a theoretical one. It is not mathematically possible to maximize for two (or more) variables at the same time. This was clearly stated by von Neumann and Morgenstern (3), but the principle is implicit in the theory of partial differential equations, dating back at least to D'Alembert (1717–1783).

The second reason springs directly from biological facts. To live, any organism must have a source of energy (for example, food). This energy is utilized for two purposes: mere maintenance and work. For man, maintenance of life requires about 1600 kilocalories a day ("maintenance calories"). Anything that he does over and above merely staying alive will be defined as work, and is supported by "work calories" which he takes in. Work calories are used not only for what we call work in common speech; they are also required for all forms of enjoyment, from swimming and automobile racing to playing music and writing poetry. If our goal is to maximize population it is obvious what we must do: We must make the work calories per person approach as close to zero as possible. No gourmet meals, no vacations, no sports, no music, no literature, no art. . . . I think that everyone will grant, without argument or proof, that maximizing population does not maximize goods. Bentham's goal is impossible.

In reaching this conclusion I have made the usual assumption that it is the acquisition of energy that is the problem. The appearance of atomic energy has led some to question this assumption. However, given an infinite source of energy, population growth still produces an inescapable problem. The problem of the acquisition of energy is replaced by the problem of its dissipation, as J. H. Fremlin has so wittily shown (4). The arithmetic signs in the analysis are, as it were, reversed; but Bentham's goal is unobtainable.

The optimum population is, then, less than the maximum. The difficulty of defining the optimum is enormous; so far as I know, no one has seriously tackled this problem. Reaching an acceptable and stable solution will surely require more than one generation of hard analytical work— and much persuasion.

We want the maximum good per person; but what is good? To one person it is wilderness, to another it is ski lodges for thousands. To one it is estuaries to nourish ducks for hunters to shoot; to another it is factory land. Comparing one good with another is, we usually say, impossible because goods are incommensurable. Incommensurables cannot be compared.

Theoretically this may be true; but in real life incommensurables *are* commensurable. Only a criterion of judgment and a system of weighting are needed. In nature the criterion is survival. Is it better for a species to be small and hideable, or large and powerful? Natural selection commensurates the incommensurables. The compromise achieved depends on a natural weighting of the values of the variables.

Man must imitate this process. There is no doubt that in fact he already does, but unconsciously. It is when the hidden decisions are made explicit that the arguments begin. The problem for the years ahead is to work out an acceptable theory of weighting. Synergistic effects, nonlinear variation, and difficulties in discounting the future make the intellectual problem difficult, but not (in principle) insoluble.

Has any cultural group solved this practical problem at the present time, even on an intuitive level? One simple fact proves that none has: there is no prosperous population in the world today that has, and has had for some time, a growth rate of zero. Any people that has intuitively identified its optimum point will soon reach it, after which its growth rate becomes and remains zero.

Of course, a positive growth rate might be taken as evidence that a population is below its optimum. However, by any reasonable standards, the most rapidly growing populations on earth today are (in general) the most miserable. This association (which need not be invariable) casts doubt on the optimistic assumption that the positive growth rate of a population is evidence that it has yet to reach its optimum.

We can make little progress in working toward optimum population size until we explicitly exorcise the spirit of Adam Smith in the field of practical demography. In economic affairs, *The Wealth of Nations* (1776) popularized the "invisible hand," the idea that an individual who "intends only his own gain," is, as it were, "led by an invisible hand to promote . . . the public interest" (5). Adam Smith did not assert that this was invariably true, and perhaps neither did any of his followers. But he contributed to a dominant tendency of thought that has ever since interfered with positive action based on rational analysis, namely, the tendency to assume that decisions reached individually will, in fact, be the best decisions for an entire society. If this assumption is correct it justifies the continuance of our present policy of *laissez-faire* in reproduction. If it is correct we can assume that men will control their individual fecundity so as to produce the optimum population. If the assumption is not correct, we need to re-examine our individual freedoms to see which ones are defensible.

Tragedy of Freedom in a Commons

The rebuttal to the invisible hand in population control is to be found in a scenario first sketched in a little-known pamphlet (6) in 1833 by a mathematical amateur named William Forster Lloyd (1794–1852). We may well call it "the tragedy of the commons," using the word "tragedy" as the philosopher Whitehead used it (7): "The essence of dramatic tragedy is not unhappiness. It resides in the solemnity of the remorseless working of things." He then goes on to say, "This inevitableness of destiny can only be illustrated in terms of human life by incidents which in fact involve unhappiness. For it is only by them that the futility of escape can be made evident in the drama."

The tragedy of the commons develops in this way. Picture a pasture open to all. It is to be expected that each herdsman will try to keep as many cattle as possible on the commons. Such an arrangement may work reasonably satisfactorily for centuries because tribal wars, poaching, and disease keep the numbers of both man and beast well below the carrying capacity of the land. Finally, however, comes the day of reckoning, that is, the day when the long-desired goal of social stability becomes a reality. At this point, the inherent logic of the commons remorselessly generates tragedy.

As a rational being, each herdsman seeks to maximize his gain. Explicitly or implicitly, more or less consciously, he asks, "What is the utility *to me* of adding one more animal to my herd?" This utility has one negative and one positive component.

1) The positive component is a function of the increment of one animal. Since the herdsman receives all the proceeds from the sale of the additional animal, the positive utility is nearly +1.

2) The negative component is a function of the additional overgrazing created by one more animal. Since, however, the effects of overgrazing are shared by all the herdsmen, the negative utility for any particular decision-making herdsman is only a fraction of −1.

Adding together the component partial utilities, the rational herdsman concludes that the only sensible course for him to pursue is to add another animal to his herd. And another. . . . But this is the conclusion reached by each and every rational herdsman sharing a commons. Therein is the tragedy. Each man is locked into a system that compels him to increase his herd without limit—in a world that is limited. Ruin is the destination toward which all men rush, each pursuing his own best interest in a society that believes in the freedom of the commons. Freedom in a commons brings ruin to all.

Some would say that this is a platitude. Would that it were! In a sense, it was learned thousands of years ago, but natural selection favors the forces of psychological denial (8). The individual benefits as an individual from his ability to deny the truth even though society as a whole, of which he is a part, suffers. Education can counteract the natural tendency to do the wrong thing, but the inexorable succession of generations requires that the basis for this knowledge be constantly refreshed.

A simple incident that occurred a few years ago in Leominster, Massachusetts, shows how perishable the knowledge is. During the Christmas shopping season the parking meters downtown were covered with plastic bags that bore tags reading: "Do not open until after Christmas. Free parking courtesy of the mayor and city council." In other words, facing the prospect of an increased demand for already scarce space, the city fathers reinstituted the system of the commons. (Cynically, we suspect that they gained more votes than they lost by this retrogressive act.)

In an approximate way, the logic of the commons has been understood for a long time, perhaps since the discovery of agriculture or the invention of private property in real estate. But it is understood mostly only in special cases which are not sufficiently generalized. Even at this late date, cattlemen leasing national land on the Western ranges demonstrate no more than an ambivalent understanding, in constantly pressuring federal authorities to increase the head count to the point where overgrazing produces erosion and weed-dominance. Likewise, the oceans of the world continue to suffer from the survival of the philosophy of the commons. Maritime nations still respond automatically to the shibboleth of the "freedom of the seas." Professing to believe in the "inexhaustible resources of the oceans," they bring species after species of fish and whales closer to extinction (9).

The National Parks present another instance of the working out of the tragedy of the commons. At present, they are open to all, without limit. The parks themselves are limited in extent—there is only one Yosemite Valley—whereas population seems to grow without limit. The values that visitors seek in the parks are steadily eroded. Plainly, we must soon cease to treat the parks as commons or they will be of no value to anyone.

What shall we do? We have several options. We might sell them off as private property. We might keep them as public property, but allocate the right to enter them. The allocation might be on the basis of wealth, by the use of an auction system. It might be on the basis of merit, as defined by some agreed-upon standards. It might be by lottery. Or it might be on a first-come, first-served basis, administered to long queues. These, I think, are all objectionable. But we must choose—or acquiesce in the destruction of the commons that we call our National Parks.

Pollution

In a reverse way, the tragedy of the commons reappears in problems of pollution. Here it is not a question of taking something out of the commons, but of putting something in—sewage, or chemical, radioactive, and heat wastes into water; noxious and dangerous fumes into the air; and distracting and unpleasant advertising signs into the line of sight. The calculations of utility are much the same as before. The rational man finds that his share of the cost of the wastes he discharges into the commons is less than the cost of purifying his wastes before releasing them. Since this is true for everyone, we are locked into a system of "fouling our own nest," so long as we behave only as independent, rational, free-enterprisers.

The tragedy of the commons as a food basket is averted by private property, or something formally like it. But the air and waters surrounding us cannot readily be fenced, and so the tragedy of the commons as a cesspool must be prevented by different means, by coercive laws or taxing devices that make it cheaper for the polluter to treat his pollutants than to discharge them untreated. We have not progressed as far with the solution of this problem as we have with the first. Indeed, our particular concept of private property, which deters us from exhausting the positive resources of the earth, favors pollution. The owner of a factory on the bank of a stream—whose property extends to the middle of the stream—often has difficulty seeing why it is not his natural right to muddy the waters flowing past his door. The law, always behind the times, requires elaborate stitching and fitting to adapt it to this newly perceived aspect of the commons.

The pollution problem is a consequence of population. It did not much matter how a lonely American frontiersman disposed of his waste. "Flowing water purifies itself every ten miles," my grandfather used to say, and the myth was near enough to the truth when he was a boy, for there were not too many people. But as population became denser, the natural chemical and biological recycling processes became overloaded, calling for a redefinition of property rights.

How to Legislate Temperance?

Analysis of the pollution problem as a function of population density uncovers a not generally recognized principle of morality, namely: *the morality of an act is a function of the state of the system at the time it is performed* (10). Using the commons as a cesspool does not harm the general public under frontier conditions, because there is no public; the same behavior in a metropolis is unbearable. A hundred and fifty years ago a plainsman could kill an American bison, cut out only the tongue for his dinner, and discard the rest of the animal. He was not in any important sense being wasteful. Today, with only a few thousand bison left, we would be appalled at such behavior.

In passing, it is worth noting that the morality of an act cannot be determined from a photograph. One does not know whether a man killing an elephant or setting fire to the grassland is harming others until one knows the total system in which his act appears. "One picture is worth a thousand words," said an ancient Chinese; but it may take ten thousand words to validate it. It is as tempting to ecologists as it is to reformers in general to try to persuade others by way of the photographic shortcut. But the essence of an argument cannot be photographed: it must be presented rationally—in words.

That morality is system-sensitive escaped the attention of most codifiers of ethics in the past. "Thou shalt not . . ." is the form of traditional ethical directives which make no allowance for particular circumstances. The laws of our society follow the pattern of ancient ethics, and therefore are poorly suited to governing a complex, crowded, changeable world. Our epicyclic solution is to augment statutory law with administrative law. Since it is practically impossible to spell out all the conditions under which it is safe to burn trash in the back yard or to run an automobile without smog-control, by law we delegate the details to bureaus. The result is administrative law, which is rightly feared for an ancient reason —*Quis custodiet ipsos custodes?*—"Who shall watch the watchers themselves?" John Adams said that we must have "a government of laws and not men." Bureau administrators, trying to evaluate the morality of acts in the total system, are singularly liable to corruption, producing a government by men, not laws.

Prohibition is easy to legislate (though not necessarily to enforce); but how do we legislate temperance? Experience indicates that it can be accomplished best through the mediation of administrative law. We limit possibilities unnecessarily if we suppose that the sentiment of *Quis custodiet* denies us the use of administrative law. We should rather retain the phrase as a perpetual reminder of fearful dangers we cannot avoid. The great challenge facing us now is to invent the corrective feedbacks that are needed to keep custodians honest. We must find ways to legitimate the needed authority of both the custodians and the corrective feedbacks.

Freedom to Breed Is Intolerable

The tragedy of the commons is involved in population problems in another way. In a world governed solely by the principle of "dog eat dog" —if indeed there ever was such a world—how many children a family had would not be a matter of public concern. Parents who bred too exuberantly would leave fewer descendants, not more, because they would be unable to care adequately for their children. David Lack and others have found that such a negative feedback demonstrably controls the fecundity of birds (*11*). But men are not birds, and have not acted like them for millenniums, at least.

If each human family were dependent only on its own resources; *if* the children of improvident parents starved to death; *if*, thus, overbreeding brought its own "punishment" to the germ line—*then* there would be no public interest in controlling the breeding of families. But our society is confronted with another aspect of the tragedy of the commons.

In a welfare state, how shall we deal with the family, the religion, the race, or the class (or indeed any distinguishable and cohesive group) that adopts overbreeding as a policy to secure its own aggrandizement (13)? To couple the concept of freedom to breed with the belief that everyone born has an equal right to the commons is to lock the world into a tragic course of action.

Unfortunately this is just the course of action that is being pursued by the United Nations. In late 1967, some thirty nations agreed to the following (14):

"The Universal Declaration of Human Rights describes the family as the natural and fundamental unit of society. It follows that any choice and decision with regard to the size of the family must irrevocably rest with the family itself, and cannot be made by anyone else."

It is painful to have to deny categorically the validity of this right; denying it, one feels as uncomfortable as a resident of Salem, Massachusetts, who denied the reality of witches in the seventeenth century. At the present time, in liberal quarters, something like a taboo acts to inhibit criticism of the United Nations. There is a feeling that the United Nations is "our last and best hope," that we shouldn't find fault with it; we shouldn't play into the hands of the archconservatives. However, let us not forget what Robert Louis Stevenson said: "The truth that is suppressed by friends is the readiest weapon of the enemy." If we love the truth we must openly deny the validity of the Universal Declaration of Human Rights, even though it is promoted by the United Nations. We should also join with Kingsley Davis (15) in attempting to get Planned Parenthood–World Population to see the error of its ways in embracing the same tragic ideal.

Conscience Is Self-Eliminating

It is a mistake to think that we can control the breeding of mankind in the long run by an appeal to conscience. Charles Galton Darwin made this point when he spoke on the centennial of the publication of his grandfather's great book. The argument is straightforward and Darwinian.

People vary. Confronted with appeals to limit breeding, some people will undoubtedly respond to the plea more than others. Those who have more children will produce a larger fraction of the next generation than those with more susceptible consciences. The differences will be accentuated, generation by generation.

In C. G. Darwin's words: "It may well be that it would take hundreds of generations for the progenitive instinct to develop in this way, but if it should do so, nature would have taken her revenge, and the variety *Homo contracipiens* would become extinct and would be replaced by the variety *Homo progenitivus*" (*16*).

The argument assumes that conscience or the desire for children (no matter which) is hereditary—but hereditary only in the most general formal sense. The result will be the same whether the attitude is transmitted through germ cells, or exosomatically, to use A. J. Lotka's term. (If one denies the latter possibility as well as the former, then what's the point of education?) The argument has here been stated in the context of the population problem, but it applies equally well to any instance in which society appeals to an individual exploiting a commons to restrain himself for the general good—by means of his conscience. To make such an appeal is to set up a selective system that works toward the elimination of conscience from the race.

Pathogenic Effects of Conscience

The long-term disadvantage of an appeal to conscience should be enough to condemn it; but it has serious short-term disadvantages as well. If we ask a man who is exploiting a commons to desist "in the name of conscience," what are we saying to him? What does he hear?—not only at the moment but also in the wee small hours of the night when, half asleep, he remembers not merely the words we used but also the non-verbal communication cues we gave him unawares? Sooner or later, consciously or subconsciously, he senses that he has received two communications, and that they are contradictory: (i) (intended communication) "If you don't do as we ask, we will openly condemn you for not acting like a responsible citizen"; (ii) (the unintended communication) "If you *do* behave as we ask, we will secretly condemn you for a simpleton who can be shamed into standing aside while the rest of us exploit the commons."

Everyman then is caught in what Bateson has called a "double bind." Bateson and his co-workers have made a plausible case for viewing the double bind as an important causative factor in the genesis of schizophrenia (*17*). The double bind may not always be so damaging, but it always endangers the mental health of anyone to whom it is applied. "A bad conscience," said Nietzsche, "is a kind of illness."

To conjure up a conscience in others is tempting to anyone who wishes to extend his control beyond the legal limits. Leaders at the highest level succumb to this temptation. Has any President during the past generation failed to call on labor unions to moderate voluntarily their demands for higher wages, or to steel companies to honor voluntary guidelines on prices? I can recall none. The rhetoric used on such occasions is designed to produce feelings of guilt in noncooperators.

For centuries it was assumed without proof that guilt was a valuable, perhaps even an indispensable, ingredient of the civilized life. Now, in this post-Freudian world, we doubt it.

Paul Goodman speaks from the modern point of view when he says: "No good has ever come from feeling guilty, neither intelligence, policy, nor compassion. The guilty do not pay attention to the object but only to themselves, and not even to their own interests, which might make sense, but to their anxieties" (18).

One does not have to be a professional psychiatrist to see the consequences of anxiety. We in the Western world are just emerging from a dreadful two-centuries-long Dark Ages of Eros that was sustained partly by prohibition laws, but perhaps more effectively by the anxiety-generating mechanisms of education. Alex Comfort has told the story well in The Anxiety Makers (19); it is not a pretty one.

Since proof is difficult, we may even concede that the results of anxiety may sometimes, from certain points of view, be desirable. The larger question we should ask is whether, as a matter of policy, we should ever encourage the use of a technique the tendency (if not the intention) of which is psychologically pathogenic. We hear much talk these days of responsible parenthood; the coupled words are incorporated into the titles of some organizations devoted to birth control. Some people have proposed massive propaganda campaigns to instill responsibility into the nation's (or the world's) breeders. But what is the meaning of the word responsibility in this context? Is it not merely a synonymn for the word conscience? When we use the word responsibility in the absence of substantial sanctions are we not trying to browbeat a free man in a commons into acting against his own interest? Responsibility is a verbal counterfeit for a substantial *quid pro quo*. It is an attempt to get something for nothing.

If the word responsibility is to be used at all, I suggest that it be in the sense Charles Frankel uses it (20). "Responsibility," says this philosopher, "is the product of definite social arrangements." Notice that Frankel calls for social arrangements—not propaganda.

Mutual Coercion Mutually Agreed Upon

The social arrangements that produce responsibility are arrangements that create coercion, of some sort. Consider bank-robbing. The man who takes money from a bank acts as if the bank were a commons. How do we prevent such action? Certainly not by trying to control his behavior solely by a verbal appeal to his sense of responsibility. Rather than rely on propaganda we follow Frankel's lead and insist that a bank is not a commons; we seek the definite social arrangements that will keep it from becoming a commons. That we thereby infringe on the freedom of would-be robbers we neither deny nor regret.

The morality of bank-robbing is particularly easy to understand because we accept complete prohibition of this activity. We are willing to say "Thou shalt not rob banks," without providing for exceptions. But temperance also can be created by coercion. Taxing is a good coercive device. To keep downtown shoppers temperate in their use of parking space we introduce parking meters for short periods, and traffic fines for longer ones. We need not actually forbid a citizen to park as long as he wants to; we need merely make it increasingly expensive for him to do so. Not prohibition, but carefully biased options are what we offer him. A Madison Avenue man might call this persuasion; I prefer the greater candor of the word coercion.

Coercion is a dirty word to most liberals now, but it need not forever be so. As with the four-letter words, its dirtiness can be cleansed away by exposure to the light, by saying it over and over without apology or embarrassment. To many, the word coercion implies arbitrary decisions of distant and irresponsible bureaucrats; but this is not a necessary part of its meaning. The only kind of coercion I recommend is mutual coercion, mutually agreed upon by the majority of the people affected.

To say that we mutually agree to coercion is not to say that we are required to enjoy it, or even to pretend we enjoy it. Who enjoys taxes? We all grumble about them. But we accept compulsory taxes because we recognize that voluntary taxes would favor the conscienceless. We institute and (grumblingly) support taxes and other coercive devices to escape the horror of the commons.

An alternative to the commons need not be perfectly just to be preferable. With real estate and other material goods, the alternative we have chosen is the institution of private property coupled with legal inheritance. Is this system perfectly just? As a genetically trained biologist I deny that it is. It seems to me that, if there are to be differences in individual inheritance, legal possession should be perfectly correlated with biological inheritance—that those who are biologically more fit to be the custodians of property and power should legally inherit more. But genetic recombination continually makes a mockery of the doctrine of "like father, like son" implicit in our laws of legal inheritance. An idiot can inherit millions, and a trust fund can keep his estate intact. We must admit that our legal system of private property plus inheritance is unjust —but we put up with it because we are not convinced, at the moment, that anyone has invented a better system. The alternative of the commons is too horrifying to contemplate. Injustice is preferable to total ruin.

It is one of the peculiarities of the warfare between reform and the status quo that it is thoughtlessly governed by a double standard. Whenever a reform measure is proposed it is often defeated when its opponents triumphantly discover a flaw in it. As Kingsley Davis has pointed out (21), worshipers of the status quo sometimes imply that no reform is possible without unanimous agreement, an implication contrary to historical fact. As nearly as I can make out, automatic rejection of proposed reforms is based on one of two unconscious assumptions: (i) that the status quo is perfect; or (ii) that the choice we face is between reform and no action; if the proposed reform is imperfect, we presumably should take no action at all, while we wait for a perfect proposal.

But we can never do nothing. That which we have done for thousands of years is also action. It also produces evils. Once we are aware that the status quo is action, we can then compare its discoverable advantages and disadvantages with the predicted advantages and disadvantages of the proposed reform, discounting as best we can for our lack of experience. On the basis of such a comparison, we can make a rational decision which will not involve the unworkable assumption that only perfect systems are tolerable.

Recognition of Necessity

Perhaps the simplest summary of this analysis of man's population problems is this: the commons, if justifiable at all, is justfiable only under conditions of low-population density. As the human population has increased, the commons has had to be abandoned in one aspect after another.

First we abandoned the commons in food gathering, enclosing farm land and restricting pastures and hunting and fishing areas. These restrictions are still not complete throughout the world.

Somewhat later we saw that the commons as a place for waste disposal would also have to be abandoned. Restrictions on the disposal of domestic sewage are widely accepted in the Western world; we are still struggling to close the commons to pollution by automobiles, factories, insecticide sprayers, fertilizing operations, and atomic energy installations.

In a still more embryonic state is our recognition of the evils of the commons in matters of pleasure. There is almost no restriction on the propagation of sound waves in the public medium. The shopping public is assaulted with mindless music, without its consent. Our government is paying out billions of dollars to create a supersonic transport which will disturb 50,000 people for every one person who is whisked from coast to coast 3 hours faster. Advertisers muddy the airwaves of radio and television and pollute the view of travelers. We are a long way from outlawing the commons in matters of pleasure. Is this because our Puritan inheritance makes us view pleasure as something of a sin, and pain (that is, the pollution of advertising) as the sign of virtue?

Every new enclosure of the commons involves the infringement of somebody's personal liberty. Infringements made in the distant past are accepted because no contemporary complains of a loss. It is the newly proposed infringements that we vigorously oppose; cries of "rights" and "freedom" fill the air. But what does "freedom" mean? When men mutually agreed to pass laws against robbing, mankind became more free, not less so. Individuals locked into the logic of the commons are free only to bring on universal ruin; once they see the necessity of mutual coercion, they become free to pursue other goals. I believe it was Hegel who said, "Freedom is the recognition of necessity."

The most important aspect of necessity that we must now recognize, is the necessity of abandoning the commons in breeding. No technical solution can rescue us from the misery of overpopulation. Freedom to breed will bring ruin to all. At the moment, to avoid hard decisions many of us are tempted to propagandize for conscience and responsible parenthood. The temptation must be resisted, because an appeal to independently acting consciences selects for the disappearance of all conscience in the long run, and an increase in anxiety in the short.

The only way we can preserve and nurture other and more precious freedoms is by relinquishing the freedom to breed, and that very soon. "Freedom is the recognition of necessity"—and it is the role of education to reveal to all the necessity of abandoning the freedom to breed. Only so, can we put an end to this aspect of the tragedy of the commons.

References

1. J. B. Wiesner and H. F. York, *Sci. Amer.* 211 (No. 4), 27 (1964).
2. G. Hardin, *J. Hered.* 50, 68 (1959); S. von Hoernor, *Science* 137, 18 (1962).
3. J. von Neumann and O. Morgenstern, *Theory of Games and Economic Behavior* (Princeton Univ. Press, Princeton, N.J., 1947), p. 11.
4. J. H. Fremlin, *New Sci.*, No. 415 (1964), p. 285.
5. A. Smith, *The Wealth of Nations* (Modern Library, New York, 1937), p. 423.
6. W. F. Lloyd, *Two Lectures on the Checks to Population* (Oxford Univ. Press, Oxford, England, 1833), reprinted (in part) in *Population, Evolution, and Birth Control*, G. Hardin, Ed. (Freeman, San Francisco, 1964), p. 37.
7. A. N. Whitehead, *Science and the Modern World* (Mentor, New York, 1948), p. 17.
8. G. Hardin, Ed., *Population, Evolution, and Birth Control* (Freeman, San Francisco, 1964), p. 56.
9. S. McVay, *Sci. Amer.* 216 (No. 8), 13 (1966).
10. J. Fletcher, *Situation Ethics* (Westminster, Philadelphia, 1966).
11. D. Lack, *The Natural Regulation of Animal Numbers* (Clarendon Press, Oxford, 1954).
12. H. Girvetz, *From Wealth to Welfare* (Stanford Univ. Press, Stanford, Calif., 1950).
13. G. Hardin, *Perspec. Biol. Med.* 6, 366 (1963).

14. U Thant, *Int. Planned Parenthood News,* No. 168 (February 1968), p. 3.
15. K. Davis, *Science* 158, 730 (1967).
16. S. Tax, Ed., *Evolution after Darwin* (Univ. of Chicago Press, Chicago, 1960), vol. 2, p. 469.
17. G. Bateson, D. D. Jackson, J. Haley, J. Weakland, *Behav. Sci.* 1, 251 (1956).
18. P. Goodman, *New York Rev. Books* 10(8), 22, (23 May 1968).
19. A. Comfort, *The Anxiety Makers* (Nelson, London, 1967).
20. C. Frankel, *The Case for Modern Man* (Harper, New York, 1955), p. 203.
21. J. D. Roslansky, *Genetics and the Future of Man* (Appleton-Century-Crofts, New York, 1966), p. 177.

Index

Abortion, 106, 107 and *n.*, 181 and *n.*, 193, 194; costs of, and alternative to, 106, 106 (table); elective, 105–106, 193; illegal, 107*n.*, 181; legalization of, 107, 181

Absolutist ethics, 134, 257

Accidents, rationalization of, 82

Adams, John, 257

Administrative law, 134, 135, 139, 140, 257

Advertising, 262; and fictitious demand, 152

Aerospace industry, 142

Agriculture, beginnings of, 170

Alembert, d', Jean le Rond, 252

Algae: in food chain, 34, 63; and phosphates, 63

Anxiety Makers, The (Comfort), 260

Aquinas, Saint Thomas, 85

Arge, d', Ralph C., 246

Aristophanes, 207

Aristotle, 38, 83, 84

Army Corps of Engineers, 62, 123

Astronomy, 44

Aswan Dam, ecological consequences of, 40

Atmosphere: nitrous oxides discharged into, 144; ultraviolet filter of, 145

Atomic-power program, question of safety of, 32

Automation, 105

Automobile, social destruction caused by, 213–14

Ayres, Robert V., 246

Babylon, 23

Bateson, Gregory, 131, 246, 259

Beauvoir, de, Simone, 180

Bentham, Jeremy, 252

Berelson, Bernard, 249

Berlin, Isaiah, 38, 242; quoted, 38

Bernard, Claude, 48

Bikini nuclear test, 31

Biological magnification, 31, 32, 32 (table), 37; food-chain, 32, 33, 33 (table), 34, 35, 36; idiosyncratic, 32–33

Biology, outlook in, contrasted with physicists', 45–46

Birds: and DDT, 33, 33 (table), 34; distribution of mercury in feathers of, 27–28

Birth control, 180, 181n., 193, 194, 195, 196 (table), 249; distinguished from population control, 194, 195, 196 (table), 197; rhythm method of, 195
Black Plague, 172
Blake, William, 18, 48
Boone, Daniel, 87
Bosch, Hieronymus, 14
Boswell, James, quoted, 80
Boulding, Kenneth, 76, 200, 242, 249; quoted, 200–201
Bridgman, Percy W., 101, 102, 245
British Columbia, University of, 55–56
Bronze industry, 77, 78
Bureaucracy, 137, 138, 140
Burnham, James, 142
Bury, J. B., 247
Byzantium, 93

Cadmium, as pollutant, 64
California, University of, 55
Cancer, thyroid, 33
Cantlon, John, 9
Carbon cycle, 25
Carbon dioxide, 19, 25, 26
Carbon monoxide, 19, 25, 26
Carlyle, Thomas, 109
Carnegie, Andrew, 111
Carrying capacity, concept of, 113–114, 114 (table)
Carson, Rachel, 42, 66–67, 242; quoted, 42–43
Celibacy, as population control, 179
Charles II, medical treatment of, 57, 58, 243
Chromium, as pollutant, 23, 24
Churchill, Winston, 45n.
Coast Guard, U.S., 138, 139
Cobalt, 33
Coercion: vs. conscience, 128, 129, 130, 132, 186–87; freedom reconciled with, 128–32; mutual, 260–62, 263
Coitus interruptus, 180
Cole, LaMont C., 8, 179, 242
Comfort, Alex, 260
Commoner, Barry, 8, 244
Commons system, 110 (table), 111, 114 (table), 115–16, 117–18, 119, 128, 184 (table), 246; decision-making in, 116–17, 118, 136 (table); and information, treatment of, 135–36; pollution problems created by, 124; population control impossible in, 187, 189; and quis custodiet problem, 136 (table); tragedy of, 118, 121, 188, 250–63; and welfare state, 187, 188, 189
Communism, 69, 143
Community Chest, 186
Competitive exclusion principle, 160, 185, 247–48
Concentration, biological, see Biological magnification
Condorcet, Marquis de, 141, 214, 215
Conscience: vs. coercion, 128, 129, 130, 132, 186–87; pathogenic effects of, 259–60; self-elimination of, 258–59
Conservation of matter and energy, 23
Conservatives, economic, 142, 143
Contraception, 180, 181n.; see also Birth control
Corfam, 150, 151
Corr, Michael, 244
Cotton-picking machine, social effects of, 213
Counterintuitive solutions, 50
Cowles, Ray, 8
Crime, problem of, 53, 56
Crowe, Beryl L., 247
Culbertson, John M., 244

Cultural heredity, 93, 94
Cultural revolutions, 170
Cyanides, recycling of, 19

Dales, J. H., 245, 246
Daly, Herman E., 243, 248
Darwin, Charles, 39, 42, 46, 233, 247; quoted, 39
Darwin, Charles Galton, 188, 258
David, Edward E., 150
Davis, Kingsley, 248, 258, 261
DDT, 7, 33, 36, 45, 67; in birds, 33, 33 (table), 34; in pickerel, 33 (table), 34; in plankton, 33 (table); in shrimp, 33 (table), 34
Declaration of Human Rights, Universal, 187, 258
Deevey, Edward S., Jr., 9, 168, 248
Delinquency, juvenile, 53, 54
Deoxyribonucleic acid (DNA), 93, 94, 188
Depression, economic (1930s), 4
Detergents, 62–63, 65
Development, as misused term, 69–70
Diatoms, in food chain, 34
Dilution of pollutants, 19, 24; failure of, 19–20, 29–37
Disease, industrial, internalization of costs of, 82
Displacement of pollutants, 18–19; failure of, 19, 20
Disraeli, Benjamin, 181, 183
Dissonance resolution, 83, 84, 245
Djerassi, Carl, 202, 249
DNA (deoxyribonucleic acid), 93, 94, 188
Dolci, Danilo, 101, 245
Double bind (Bateson), 131, 246, 259
Douglas, William O., 42
Du Pont Corp., 150, 151
Dyson, Freeman J., 245

Ecological Tithe, Rule of, 34, 109
Ecology, 7, 8, 9, 40, 42, 48, 64, 73, 242, 244
Economics, 73, 74, 76
Egypt, Aswan Dam in, 40–41
Ehrlich, Anne H., 246; quoted, 119–20
Ehrlich, Paul R., 7, 8, 241, 242, 244, 246; quoted, 119–20
Einstein, Albert, 23
Elemental pollution, 25, 26–28
Enclosure acts, British, 116
Energy and matter, conservation of, 23
Engineers, Army Corps of, 62, 123
Environmental Policy Act (1969), 61
Environmental Protection Agency (EPA), 62, 71
Environmental utilization, political systems of; see Political systems of environmental utilization
Enzymes, 63, 64; in detergents, allergic reactions to, 63, 64; inactivated by mercury, 26
Erie, Lake, pollution of, 124
Ethics: absolutist, 134, 257; professional codes of, 108; situation, 134
Ethyl, as pollutant, 30
Eutrophication, 63
Evils, Newtonian and Darwinian responses to, 54 (table), 55
Exclusion principle, competitive, 160, 185, 247–48
External costs, 74–75, 77; internalization of, 78, 79, 80, 81, 81 (table), 82, 83, 85, 87, 244

FAA (Federal Aviation Administration), 137, 145
Family population control, 178, 179, 180, 181, 183, 187, 248
Famine, as population control, 178
Fatalism, 213

FDA (Food and Drug Administration), 60, 137

Federal Aviation Administration (FAA), 137, 145

Federal Trade Commission (FTC), 137

Fermat, de, Pierre, 82

Festinger, Leon, 245

Fife, Daniel, 125, 246

Fish, mercury in, 27, 28, 36

Fisheries, oceanic, 119, 120, 122, 255

Fletcher, Joseph, 181n., 243

Food, Drug and Cosmetics Act, Kefauver–Harris amendments to, 59–60

Food and Drug Administration (FDA), 60, 137

Food chain, 34, 35, 37

Forest Service, U.S., 42

Forrester, Jay M., 55, 243

Forssman, Hans, 249

Foundling hospitals, nineteenth-century, 182

Fourteenth Amendment, 85

France, 182; illegal abortion in, 181

Frankel, Charles, 102, 105, 106, 107, 149, 245, 260

Free enterprise; *see* Private enterprise

Freedom: as recognition of necessity, 262–63; reconciled with coercion, 128–32; tragedy of, in commons, 254–55

Fremlin, J. H., 252

Freud, Sigmund, 18

Friedan, Betty, 180

Friedman, Milton, 74

FTC (Federal Trade Commission), 137

Fuller, Margaret, 109, 110, 132

General Motors Corp., 23, 24, 138

Genetics, 93

George, J. David, 30

Godley, F., 248

Goethe, Johann Wolfgang von, 38, 94

Goldman, Marshall, 124

Goodman, Paul, 131, 246, 260

Graves, Robert, 210, 211, 249

Greece, ancient, 22, 152, 209

Guilt feeling, question of value of, 260

Hagberg, K., 248

Haley, J., 246

Handler, Philip, 8

Hard detergents, 63

Hardin, Garrett, 9, 243, 244, 245, 246, 248, 250–63

Harte, John, 243, 248

Hecht, C. G., 244

Hegel, Georg, 132, 263

Heller, Walter, 131

Henderson, L. J., 57, 58

Herbert, George, 43

Heredity: cultural, 93, 94; genetic, 93, 94, 188

Hinrichs, Noel, 246

History of European Morals (Lecky), 180

Holdren, John P., 242, 244

Holling, C. S., 55

Holm, Richard W., 242

Housing Act (1949), 51, 52

Hudson River, pollution of, 23, 124

Huffaker, C. B., 243

ICC (Interstate Commerce Commission), 137

Illegitimacy rates, eighteenth-century, 182

Impotence principles (Whittaker), 132, 141–42

India, population growth in, 194, 197

Industrial disease, internalization of costs of, 82

Industrial-scientific revolution, 18, 170

Infanticide, as population control, 181, 182, 183, 248

Information, 135, 152; sabotage of, 135, 136 (table), 137, 184 (table)

Insurance, and rationalization of accidents, 82

Internalization of costs, 78, 79, 80, 81 (table), 82, 83, 85, 87, 244

International Whaling Commission, 121

Interstate Commerce Commission (ICC), 137

Iodine, 33; radioactive, 33

Italy, 183; illegal abortion in, 181

Jackson, D. D., 246

Jacobs, Jane, 243

Japan, 31; whaling by, 121

Jellyfish, titanium concentrated by, 33

John Birch society, 112

Johnston, Harold, 144, 247

Juvenile delinquency, 53, 54

Kangas, Lenni W., 249

Kapp, William, 76

Kariba Dam, 68, 244

Kefauver–Harris amendments, to Food, Drug and Cosmetics Act, 59–60

Kennedy, John F., 6

Klein, A. J., 244

Kneese, Allen V., 76, 246

Lack, David, 257

Langer, William L., 181, 248; quoted, 181–82

Language, coercive, 66, 67, 102, 143

Law, administrative, 134, 135, 139, 140, 257

Lead, as pollutant, 29, 30, 31

League of Nations, 122

Lecky, W. E. H., quoted, 180

Lewis, Oscar, 245

Lewis, Richard, 241

Linnaeus, Carl, 177, 183, 248

Lloyd, William F., 116, 225, 245, 254; quoted, 224

Loren, Sophia, quoted, 53

Los Angeles, 17

Lotka, A. J., 259

Lumbering industry, 125–26

Lysistrata (Aristophanes), 207

MacKinney, Loren C., 243

McVay, Scott, 246

Magnification, biological; *see* Biological magnification

Malthus, Thomas R., 172, 225, 251; quoted, 224

Marcuse, Herbert, 245

Marriage, 178, 197, 208; delayed, as population control, 179, 180

"Mars, man from," and objectivity, 72–73, 74, 112, 141

Marsh, George Perkins, 242

Marx, Karl, 55, 69, 143

Marx, Wesley, 242

Massachusetts Institute of Technology, 55

Matter-accounting, necessity of, 23, 24, 28

Matter and energy, conservation of, 23

Meadows, Dennis L., 55

Mercury: as pollutant, 26, 27, 28, 36, 64; sequestration of, 26, 27, 28; uses of, 27

Mill, John Stuart, 225; quoted, 224–25

Millett, Kate, 180

Milton, John, 8

Mishan, Ezra J., 76, 244, 249; quoted, 213–14

Mitchell, John N., 23, 24

Molecular pollution, 25–26

Monogamy, 207, 208, 211
Monopoly, regulated, 112, 113, 124
Montesquieu, Baron de, quoted, 171
Moore, B., 245
Morgenstern, O., 252
Muller, Herbert J., 45n.
Murphy, Earl Finbar, 244
My Wilderness: East of Katahdin (Douglas), 42

Nader, Ralph, 8–9, 139
Napoleon, 180, 182
National Environmental Policy Act (1969), 61
National Industrial Pollution Control Council, 61n.
National Parks, and tragedy of commons, 255
National Science Foundation, 5
National security, and control of information, 136, 137
Natural selection, 42, 233, 253, 254
Neumann, von, J., 252
New York City, 17
New York Review of Books, 203
Newton, Isaac, 41, 43, 44, 48, 171
Nietzsche, Friedrich, 38, 131, 246, 259
Niobium, 33
Nitrilotriacetate (NTA), 64
Nitrous oxides, discharged into atmosphere, 144
Nixon, Richard M., 61n., 131, 144
Noonan, John T., Jr., 248
NTA (nitrilotriacetate), 64
Nuclear-power program, question of safety of, 32

Objectivity, and euphemisms, 75
Ocean: as commons, 119; and fishing industry, 119, 120, 122, 255; lead compounds in, 29–30, 31; mercury in, 28, 36
Oedipus process, 94
Oil spills, 138, 139
Operations research, 48
Orians, Gordon, 8
Origin of Species (Darwin), 39, 42, 188
Orwell, George, 245
Ozone, 145

Parenthood, planned, 197, 258
Parks, National, and tragedy of commons, 255
Pascal, Blaise, 38, 82
Persian Letters (Montesquieu), 171
Peru, fisheries of, 120
Pesticides, 242–43; as coercive term, 67
Pfeiffer, E., 8
Philanthropy, 111, 183, 184 (table), 185–86; competitive exclusion principle in, 185
Philoprogenitiveness, 188, 200, 201
Phosphates, in soft detergents, 63, 64, 65
Photosynthesis, 31
Physics, 43; "inverse-square" phenomena in, 44, 45; outlook in, contrasted with biologists', 45–46
Picard, Jean, 29
Pickerel, DDT in, 33 (table), 34
Plankton, 30; DDT in, 33 (table)
Plastics, 86
Platt, John R., 247
Pohlman, Edward, 249
Political systems of environmental utilization, 110, 110 (table), 111–18, 184 (table); properties of, 114 (table); and quis custodiet problem, 136 (table)
Pollution, 18–21, 242, 244, 255–256; air, 122, 123, 256; control of, 71, 72, 82, 86, 87, 123, 130,

246; elemental, 25, 26–28; as function of population density, 256; molecular, 25–26; in Russia, 124; water, 122, 123, 256
Polyandry, 208, 210, 211, 212
Polychlorinated biphenyls, 86
Polygamy, 207, 208
Polygyny, 208, 211
Population, Resources, Environment (P. and A. Ehrlich), 119
Population control, 190–204, 205, 206; birth control distinguished from, 194, 195, 196, (table), 197; celibacy as, 179; coercive phase of, 193, 199–204, 205; delayed marriage as, 179, 180; educational phase of, 193, 197–98; family, 178, 179, 180, 181, 183, 187, 248; famine as, 178; impossible in commons systems, 187, 251; infanticide as, 181, 182, 183, 248; prostitution as, 179, 180; and sex determination, 206–207; and sterilization, 192; systems analysis of, 196 (table); and technology, 202–203, 205; voluntary phase of, 193–97, 199; women's responsibility for, 191
Population density: and internalization of external costs, 87; pollution as function of, 256; role of, in technological innovation, 65
Population growth, world; see World population growth
Poverty, problem of, 49, 50, 51, 52, 53, 55, 56, 186, 245
Private enterprise, 110, 110 (table), 112, 114, 114 (table), 125, 184 (table); decision-making in, 114, 126, 135, 136 (table); and quis custodiet problem, 136 (table)
Private property, in real estate, 78, 126, 256, 261
Probability theory, 82

Problems without technical solution, 250–51
Progress: origins of idea of, 141, 214, 247; as religion, 141, 142, 143, 144
"Prosperity," pollution increased by, 20
Prostitution, 179, 180, 248
Protozoa, in food chain, 34
Psychoanalysis, 246
"Pyramid problem," 4
Pythagoreans, 22, 23

Quis custodiet problem, 135–40, 152, 247, 257

Radioactivity, 23, 31, 32
Real estate, private property in, 78, 126, 256, 261
Recycling, 19, 65; failure of, 19
Reforestation, 125
Refuse Act (1899), 61, 123
Reiterman, Carl, 249
Renan, Ernest, 72
Research and development, 64, 151, 152
Responses to evil, Newtonian and Darwinian, 54 (table), 55
Responsibility: contrived, 103, 104, 107, 115, 136, 149; criterion of (Frankel), 103, 105, 106, 107, 149, 260; cybernetic concept of, 102; family rights separated from, and population control, 187, 189; intrinsic, 103, 104, 107, 114 (table), 115, 135, 136 (table), 184 (table); "jawbone," 104, 186, 203; and quis custodiet problem, 135
Reuss, Henry, 61
Robinson, Robert, 29, 30 and n., 31; quoted, 29–30
Rogers, Will, 147
Rosenfeld, Beatrice, 241
Rudd, Robert L., 242

Russia: environmental pollution in, 124; mixed economy in, 112; whaling by, 121

Sanger, Margaret, 178
Sartre, Jean-Paul, 209
Sax, Joseph L., 244
Schistosomiasis, 40–41
Schizophrenia, and double bind, 131, 259
Science, and principle of "guilty until proven innocent," 59
Scudder, Thayer, 244
Sea squirts, idiosyncratic concentration by, 32–33
Sears, Paul B., 244
Seeds, mercury-treated, 28
Sequestration of pollutants, 25, 26, 27, 28
SET (Supporting Ethical Theory), 83, 84, 85
Sewage disposal, 130, 262
Sex determination, and population control, 206–207
Shaw, George Bernard, 108
Shelley, Percy Bysshe, 18, 249; quoted, 207–208
Shrimp, DDT in, 33 (table), 34
Shurcliff, William A., 247
Side-effect, defined, 68
Silent Spring (Carson), 42, 66
Simrad Echo, 119, 120
Situation ethics, 134
Sketch for a Historical Picture of the Progress of the Human Mind (Condorcet), 141, 214
Slavery, institution of, 79, 80, 103
Smith, Adam, 253; quoted, 176
Socialism, 110 (table), 111, 112, 114 (table), 115, 121, 184 (table), 186; decision-making in, 115, 136, 136 (table); management of information in, 136; and quis custodiet problem, 136 (table)

Socolow, Robert H., 243, 248
Soft detergents, 63
Solow, Robert M., 243
Sonic boom, 145–46, 148, 149
Space program, 5, 17, 241
Spencer, Herbert, 112
SST (supersonic transport plane), 141, 142, 144, 145, 149, 150, 152, 213, 247; cost-benefit analysis of, 147–48; and sonic boom, 145–46, 148, 149
Stamler, Paul J., 244
Steady-state economy, 176
Stereotypes, personality, 84
Sterilization, and population control, 192
Stevenson, Adlai, quoted, 17
Stevenson, Robert Louis, 258
Strontium, 33; radioactive, 33, 36
Sulfur dioxide, 72
Sulfuric acid, converted to sulfates, 19
Supersonic transport plane; see SST
Supporting Ethical Theory (SET), 83, 84, 85
Sweden, abortion law in, 193
Swordfish, mercury in, 28, 36
Sybil (Disraeli), 181
Sylva, de, Don, 5
Systems analysis, 48, 55, 56; of population growth, 196 (table)

Taussig, Helen B., 243
Technological imperative, dogma of, 141, 142, 146, 149, 213
Technology, 142, 152, 212; limits of, 151; and population control, 202–203, 205
Teggart, Frederick J., 247
Telephone system, 112, 113
Tetrahymena, cobalt concentrated by, 33
Thalidomide, 59, 243
Thompson, Francis, 43, 44, 243

Thuwe, Inga, 249
Thyroid, cancer of, 33
Titanium, 33
Tool-making revolution, 170
"Tragedy of the Commons, The" (Hardin), 250–63
Trophic levels, 34, 35, 36
Tuna, 34, 36
Tunicates, idiosyncratic concentration by, 32–33
Two Lectures on the Checks to Population (Lloyd), 116

Ultraviolet filter of atmosphere, 145
Union Carbide Corp., 71
Union Oil Co., 138
United Nations, 122, 187, 258
United States Steel Corp., 71
Universal Declaration of Human Rights, 187, 258
Urban problem, 55, 213
Uses of the Past, The (Muller), 45n.

Vanadium, 32
Venice, 16–17
Vietnam, 144

Wage-price freeze, 131
War, nuclear, 250
Waterfleas, in food chain, 34
Watt, Kenneth E. F., 55
Weakland, J., 246
Wealth of Nations (Smith), 176, 253
Weather control, dangers of, 46

Web of life, 46, 47, 62, 64, 65, 67
Welfare state, 187, 188, 194, 258
Whaling Commission, International, 121
Whitehead, Alfred North, 118, 132, 142, 246, 254
Whittaker, Edmund, 132, 142
Wiesner, J. B., 250, 251
Wilde, Oscar, 49, 243; quoted, 58
Wiley, George A., quoted, 49
Wolff, R. P., 245
Women's Liberation Movement, 207, 210
Woodwell, George M., 242
World population growth, 168, 170, 171, 173, 175, 248; control of, 174; fluctuations in, 171; hypothetical future of, 172, 172 (table); laissez-faire attitude toward, 174; present-day, 169, 173; systems analysis of, 196 (table); in times past, 169, 169 (table), 170; zero, 170, 195, 196 (table), 197, 210, 212, 252; see also "Tragedy of the Commons, The" (Hardin)
World War II, 4, 26

Yannacone, Victor, 9
York, H. F., 250, 251

Zambezi River, side-effects of damming of, 68
ZPG (Zero Population Growth), 170, 195, 196 (table), 197, 210, 212, 252